T0355025

Big American PROBLEMS

Looking Left and Right for a Biblical Perspective

Sam Wittke

WESTBOW
PRESS®
A DIVISION OF THOMAS NELSON
& ZONDERVAN

Copyright © 2022 Sam Wittke.

All rights reserved. No part of this book may be used or reproduced by any means, graphic, electronic, or mechanical, including photocopying, recording, taping or by any information storage retrieval system without the written permission of the author except in the case of brief quotations embodied in critical articles and reviews.

This book is a work of non-fiction. Unless otherwise noted, the author and the publisher make no explicit guarantees as to the accuracy of the information contained in this book and in some cases, names of people and places have been altered to protect their privacy.

WestBow Press books may be ordered through booksellers or by contacting:

WestBow Press
A Division of Thomas Nelson & Zondervan
1663 Liberty Drive
Bloomington, IN 47403
www.westbowpress.com
844-714-3454

Because of the dynamic nature of the Internet, any web addresses or links contained in this book may have changed since publication and may no longer be valid. The views expressed in this work are solely those of the author and do not necessarily reflect the views of the publisher, and the publisher hereby disclaims any responsibility for them.

Any people depicted in stock imagery provided by Getty Images are models, and such images are being used for illustrative purposes only. Certain stock imagery © Getty Images.

Scriptures taken from the Holy Bible, New International Version®, NIV®. Copyright © 1973, 1978, 1984, 2011 by Biblica, Inc.™ Used by permission of Zondervan. All rights reserved worldwide. www.zondervan.com The "NIV" and "New International Version" are trademarks registered in the United States Patent and Trademark Office by Biblica, Inc.®

ISBN: 978-1-6642-5561-6 (sc)
ISBN: 978-1-6642-5560-9 (e)

Print information available on the last page.

WestBow Press rev. date: 01/21/2022

Preface

Christians should hide from the issues of the real world and bury their political opinions deep down. They do not belong in politics. They should try and blend more seamlessly with the culture around them. Conservatives in the United States of America also have sinned by taking a definitive political stance on certain single issues. They are missing the bigger picture. This is a disservice to God. All of them, when they become active in voicing their political opinion, are committing political idolatry.

The United States of America is a repulsive lie, and its Christian underpinnings are harmful to the modern mind, insensitive to the modern man, and distasteful to the modern tongue. Christians who promote religious ideals in the public square and love their country are caught up in "the big lie." The reunification of church and state is drawing dangerously near. As we continue committing violence and atrocities around the world in the name of God's American kingdom, we follow in the footsteps of crusaders, witch hunters and inquisitionists. We maintain a pattern of American tyranny and blind religiosity.

This is the way culture sees the church today. It is even the way much of the church has been taught to see itself. The church is torn between left and right, between progressive and conservative, both theologically and politically. Neutrality is proving to be a dangerous mess for any congregation trying to balance on the fence, and churches who claim middle ground in order to please both sides often end up offending both sides, eventually taking one side or another without knowing it. Many churches have integrated ideologies, teachings and positions antithetical to Christianity into theology in order to make life easier on themselves, to be more politically correct, to seem more tolerant and fair. Many have brought things like Marxism, Gnosticism, and new age teachings into church without even knowing it. Sometimes these imports are masked in various popular terms in order to fool church members who aren't familiar with their teachings. The shift toward a fairer, tolerant, and more politically correct attitude among churchgoers has historically resulted in unfairness and intolerance to certain congregants who object to that attitude. It also has resulted in church naivety and complacency concerning the straightforward moral issues of our times. In other words, the frantic search for more feeling and the quest for social enlightenment seem to be dumbing us down immensely.

The benefit of adopting this mindset, at least in part, is that churches are granted temporary asylum from a culture that is growing increasingly hostile toward Christianity, while having a convenient theology which has broken free from the shackles of its narrower minded predecessor.

Apparently, Christian conservatives don't know what they're actually reading when they read the Bible. If only *they* could stick closer to scripture, they would see. All it takes is a culturally acclimated Christian to understand how to better interpret the Bible as it pertains to 21st century problems. As long as the Bible is made progressive and bends its knee to the will of the world, it can be approved.

America is not a myth and neither is its Christian foundation. It is not an abstraction. Its success is not a figment of our imaginations. Neither is its founding philosophy a myth—a philosophy largely based on the tragic vision of humanity. Its Judeo Christian values and tragic vision both helped it flourish immensely. It's where we've deviated from those values historically that we've run into trouble.

~

Christian conservatives are not as confused as the left makes them out to be. We recognize the difference between the Kingdom of God and the kingdoms of this world, *including America*. We think it may be our accusers who are guiltier of entangling the religion of leftism with the state. Forgetting that our nation's birth, survival, prosperity and longevity all happened as a result of God's immediate sovereignty has encouraged church timidity when facing the issues of our times. The secular age sees these factors as disconnected from one another and the "one nation under God" motto to be an oversimplified myth. If this is a myth, so are national sovereignty and American exceptionalism. Such deconstruction leads to a philosophical and social disintegration of the individual, communal and national soul and body. This disintegration corresponds to a post-modern epoch, the fragmentation of the self.

This book hopes to show that this epoch is not quite as new as it may seem. To the degree that the church adopts chaotic interpretations about reality and America's place in it, the church plays into an ancient systemic pattern that has led to the downfall of many other nations. In short, I am sure that some of what progressive Christianity says may have some bearing on reality and may be worth exploring. It's the parts that aren't true and that are heretical and damaging to the church and outsiders which we will concern ourselves with in the following pages. Christians do not have some sort of moral obligation to remain politically or culturally neutral as culture and politics become more hostile towards them. They do however have an obligation to tell the truth, even if it hurts.

It is more difficult to expose myths than to write them at an unprecedented rate. Exposing myths becomes exponentially harder when they are masterfully crafted to align with our passions, fulfill the desires of our flesh, and camouflage with the truth. It is more difficult to build a house than to tear one down. A "Christian nation" may be an impossibility. A nation doesn't constitute all of Christianity as long as Christ transcends the nation. And Christianity doesn't constitute all of a nation as long as sinful humans create the nation. Dismissing America's Christian underpinnings does nothing to clarify our manifold predicament.

Holding up a caricature of Christian conservatives to the world as proof of the myth of American Christianity only quickens our social collapse. If the caricature isn't true and isn't a real person, the myth busters become the mythologists. They caricature themselves. The new myth they've written for this era has become convincing. It is increasingly powerful because it assimilates aspects of the truth into its basic sociopolitical framework. The myth becomes difficult to distinguish from reality and adds to one side's political power.

In the following pages we will expose a worldview that seeks nothing less than the all-out destruction of Christianity in America, a worldview that the modern church is largely adopting. Many Christians are under the influence of a cultural machine. They condemn their other half as idolatrous Pharisees while they think of themselves as more enlightened and living in a deeper relationship with God. But they are often engaging in the same misbehavior as many of the Pharisees were, such as tweaking God's Word to fit better into human philosophies and traditions.

Neutrality is becoming less and less possible in an increasing atmosphere of hostility. It is an illusion. One who claims total neutrality is likely not being honest with themselves. An honest examination of the ideals and values held up by both sides of the political spectrum reveals an obvious dichotomy, with values that are antithetical to Christianity on the one side and values that corroborate Christianity on the other.

Introduction

One of the goals of this book will be to examine the modern attitude toward Christianity. My last book, *The Best Guess* did this through a theological and apologetics approach, whereas this book will examine the "real world," or political viewpoint of the post secular era and how it relates to the faith. It is my suspicion that the visible is linked to the invisible in the matter of politics. After all, politics etymologically falls into the range of the second set of commands—how people are to treat one another and live in a good society. The second set hinges on the first.

The tangible, physical, visible state of the world emerges from how the world sees itself. As the spiritual eyesight of the world fades, so does the world. The following pages will traverse a fair amount of territory, ranging from theology to current events, political philosophy to the advent of the technological age (and more) in hope to bring it all under the comprehensive scope of the Christian worldview, showing that the Christian worldview both presents the best interpretation for the state of things and offers hope for the state. Such diagnoses and prescriptions, which I dare not say are my own, cannot be given without crossing into the controversial.

The modern attitude suggests that Christians have mythologized a real, secular nation. This attitude operates under the assumption that religion and the reality of culture are at odds with one another. In some ways, this attitude is correct. Christians historically have run into problems when they proclaim to have the highest interpretation of reality, whether it pertains to theology or national law, sometimes muddling the two together. The inquisitions and witch hunts come to mind. Whereas culture historically degenerates when it marginalizes, oppresses, persecutes or terrorizes others, including Christians. These cultural and religious dangers present a paradox that this book is intended to clarify.

The puzzle is as follows: can "church" and "state" really be separated without grossly deforming us? Do they depend on one another? Moreover, what exactly is America? Is it a Christian nation? Was it ever? Can it ever be one? What does it mean to be a Christian nation?

The list of questions could meander indefinitely, but we have plenty to work on for the moment. For the time being, we will look at the notion of reality as being either secular and random or God-breathed and structured, as well as the various interpretations that fall into both of those camps. Interpretations of laws, politics, and policies that fall into the first camp have often proven to be based on attitudes that range with the times. But the same problem could be placed in the second camp, as integrating spiritual wisdom often merits interpretation of a religious text like the Bible in order to synthesize its values with the higher laws of society. Misinterpretations could result in a defective implementation of spiritual wisdom by those who are only wise in their own eyes. The result is religious hypocrisy and legalistic authoritarianism.

The American project sought to synthesize these two camps which were apparently at odds with one another in order to ensure the longevity of the nation, as well as freedom of thought and speech. Today, on both sides of the political spectrum, we are faced with the questions of whether or not the American project was a success and what success truly means. The left side questions whether America's foundation was indeed structurally sound. The right side doubts the foundation's soundness less than the skyscraper that is being built upon it.

The topic of the church poisoning the state has found its way into the church. Two theological and unseen camps mirror the two political and visible camps—progressive and conservative. Just like the political progressives question the mythological origins of America's constitutional foundation, the theological progressives question the Judeo-Christian aspects of this origin. Whether or not it is "loving" to advocate for more church in state is up for debate among Christians. The tide of confusion is rising in the church, following rising confusion in the culture. Many want zero church in state. Although this is a popular sentiment, it is an impossible objective with disastrous means and ends.

One stubborn detail stands out in the midst of this problem and ought to be considered by the church, especially before hopping on the "zero church in state" bandwagon: the advancing campaign against Christianity at virtually every level of culture. Many Christians have conceded territory after being intimidated, believing at times that the church's public influence is less important or real than the state's public influence. After all, the kingdom of the state is real and tangible. It's something we can taste, touch, feel, and see, whereas the kingdom of God is still invisible, meriting faith to believe in it. By such reasoning, when one stands in the way of the visible state as a kingdom representative, they ought to be admonished for valuing the unseen more than the seen. Some Christians are told that they are "missing the point" and that they "don't understand the bigger picture," that they are "narrow minded." This could be taken as a compliment as they are called to walk the narrow path and not to buy into hollow and deceptive philosophies.

The rising American campaign against Christianity takes the same form as other campaigns against the Orthodox Church in 20th century regimes, as we'll see in the pages that follow. When the ideas of the times are criticized by churchgoers and the binary political values are spiritually weighed and evaluated, the troublemaking Christian who looks closely at these things is criticized for being overly judgmental or too political. The simple question remains, should America become Godlier or more godless?

Progressive Christians largely believe that the church has no place "judging the culture," or becoming too involved with politics. We should take the plank out of the church's eye before we take the speck out of American culture's eye. The best way to win hearts for Christ is to blend with the culture in a covert way, and win them from the ground up—apologize now, preach the gospel later.

As a fairly new conservative Christian, I believe that we are watching culture deviate farther from anything related to God, and that the consequences of rejecting God as a society are manifesting daily before our very eyes. Either way, one side seems to hold onto a mythological version of America, whereas the other holds onto the real version. Whether we will walk forward into the unconditional mercies of Christ or the relativistic judgement of Pilot remains to be determined.

Progressivism promises to reveal how Americans have been duped into thinking our country is actually Christian in origin. Secular media outlets approve progressive Christianity because it agrees with less church involvement in the matters of the state. The church in effect becomes less of a threat to the various goals and visions of the state. The political and theological left see conservative Christians as wanting to subjugate people under the cruel dominion of religious authority. In reality, we just want to live in peace. The conservative Christian sees the left as moving in a direction that is antithetical to God. The results of this national, spiritual migration do not always remain in the unseen, theoretical realm. Simply put, the church sees more state as harmful to the church and the state sees more church as harmful to the state. There is a clear contrast.

America appears to be at the pinnacle of civilization, the Babylon of its age. But the foundation of America has little to no adequate support, many critics of the American system claim. It is a bed of shifting sand. While it has stood the test of time for a couple hundred years, it is bound to come crashing down sooner or later with a hurricane or a flash flood. Any renovations or feelings of nostalgia that we the people make or have in the name of our idolatrous religiosity are only measures to delay the inevitable, coming from the false hope of a false promise of American longevity. This actually makes sense from a godly perspective. America is just another nation in a long line of nations that have risen and fallen. Nations crumble or wither eventually. History has shown us little to no evidence to the contrary. Whether it is the American foundation or the American structure that is ready to collapse is the main question. The answer will determine the outcome of our future.

The new revolutionists think America is being held together by duct tape and glue. It's time to stop pretending otherwise. Christians have tried to stop America from crumbling, but in so doing they have only served their own self-interest, becoming lovers of self.

If only lady liberty could keep her religion to herself, and not preach the gospel anymore. If only she would have left either religion out of her politics or politics out of her religion, America would be in a very different state. We wouldn't have the muddied past of slavery, genocide, wag the dog wars, and social intolerance. It's time for lady liberty to set down her book of old outdated wisdom, hide her lamp under a bowl, and to rise up and play. If she does not do this, the structure she stands on will be torn down.

There may yet be a way to reconcile lady liberty to her creator. It will take a lot of work, and I don't mean by restructuring her from the feet up as a theocracy. In order to understand our past and our need for reconciliation we may want to look at the Garden of Eden, and what went wrong there.

Every person who's reading this has an imperfect past, yet here we stand, alive and breathing in the future of that past. We are not myths. Neither is the nation that brought us here. It's a country that still exists. Its future matters. Its direction matters to every present and future citizen. As its past mattered to our present, so its present matters to our future. This is why Christians express political concern on both ends of the spectrum, and always have alongside the growth of the various nations they've inhabited. This is their American and God-given right. Our nation's laws protect, at least for the time being, our freedom of speech. They demand that we stand up, speak out and fight back when our individual rights are under threat of tyranny by anyone; the minority, the majority, or the government. This fundamental law, which today's left sees as our fundamental flaw, extends to people in all walks of life. People from all walks of life are free at any time to walk into or out of the realm of politics, even if their political opinions offend others, as they most certainly will in an increasingly hostile political environment. Sometimes people forget that without an offensive no war can be won and no ground can be gained.

This clash of viewpoints is not what lady liberty set out to protect us against, but to protect. A secular person and a Christian person are likely to differ on a good number of issues, and they may agree on some. At the end of the conversation, they can shake hands and walk away from one another in America, free to live their lives. They are both still free thinking and believing men and women. To suggest that one of them ought to leave their beliefs and convictions at the door of the political sphere is wishful thinking at best, tyranny at worst.

America is not an all Christian nation. America is not the manifestation of the Kingdom of God either. America shouldn't become a theocracy. America shouldn't force anyone's hand to believe what any one group of people believes. It is not the Christian's job to fight all the battles of the world in the way that the world fights them. But the Progressive assessment of Christianity's role in the world says substantially more than this. Christianity was always a religion of choice. Today it is being replaced by a religion of forced compliance. The modern left is using the pretext of tearing down an old theocracy, which never was a theocracy in the first place, in order to establish a newer, more rigid, legalistic and unmerciful theocracy.

The freedom of choice appears in the Word of God. It also appears in the bill of rights, in the Declaration of Independence, and in the Constitution. Imagine if the Word of God, or at least the idea of a transcendent standard that was based on the existence of God, was completely removed from these latter documents. We may be living in a very different kind of myth, a deterministic myth—one far less fair, humane, protective of our liberties, and yes... inclusive.

Conservatives who've thought a little bit deeply about their political convictions do not believe that those who differ from them ought to be silenced. Their philosophy is that they ought to never be silenced, but protected from the tyranny of thought policing. They are trying to conserve the framework that provides this protection. But conservatives recognize some ideas to be dangerous. The Christian also enters politics to protect human liberties that the rest of the world cannot see, not to enforce religious edicts for personal gain.

While there may be a myth surrounding the notion that America and Christianity are synonymous, neither America nor Christianity are fabrications. They are real, present, and as necessary as ever. Although America isn't perfect, her convictions have been an asset to her and to the world. Her convictions have contributed to her greatness and aided the world in many ways, even when the world did not agree with her. At times, like any other person or nation she deviated from what she was taught and sinned. It is not wise to expect her to always be perfect as she continues walking. And there is wisdom in considering her to be another mortal nation. Keeping this in mind, we should also remember, "The fear of the Lord adds length to life, but the years of the wicked are cut short" (Proverbs 10:27).

Chapter 1

In the Beginning

Sandcastles and a Rising Tide

God created mankind from the dust of the earth. It's hard for us, as human beings, to look at a pile of dirt and see how it could have become us, or the nation we're in. It is especially challenging to try and grasp how this happened through chance and chaos. This is not a science book, or an exposition on the first chapters in Genesis, or a book that will try to link the two. This book is intended to be political *and* theological through the lens of a novice. Hopefully it will not be idolatrous in the meantime. It is not supposed to be restrictive to one point of view or one area of study, although it will discuss laws both Godly and constitutional. This inevitably leads to certain conclusions. I hope in the pages that follow to provide a common sense approach for Christians who are on the right, the left or in the center. A religious, political person is not an idolater. A political, religious person is not a fool. We need to break out of the bigotry of that thinking. Especially as a church.

Dust itself had no capacity to create us, but was the substance used to create us. Dust is motionless without wind, lifeless without breath, and thoughtless without thought. It has no feelings or motivations of its own, whether it be stardust or earth dust. But when water is added it can become clay. It can be formed into something. Even a child knows this. The mind of mankind is likewise malleable, capable of great folly or understanding as it is formed by experience. Mankind must be swayed in one way or another, whether by wind, doctrine, or the news cycle. It is destined to be shaped by the many cumulative forces, experiences, and influences it faces in a given amount of time. Like ships in the ocean we are swayed with the wind, driven forward in the right direction or overwhelmed by a storm. Good seafarers avoid large storms. They do not forget the maps drawn by seafarers before them. If they go into a storm, they cannot see. If they forget their maps, even if there is no storm and they can see clearly all the way to the horizon, they cannot be sure of where they are going.

When mankind builds things, we show that we are made in the image of God. God created us in our mothers' womb. From an early age we show that we are builders, "built" in the image of God. A child may build what he imagines to be a nation of sandcastles. He must build it on the edge of the shoreline during low tide. The wet sand there holds its form better than the dry sand above it. The low tide gave him the ability to build. It also guaranteed the destruction of his sandcastles. In other words, the conditions provide both vital life and inevitable mortality. The waves make a daily promise. They will soon claim his great nation, just like all the other nations before it. This may take minutes or hours. Construction was permitted only for a time, even if the child saw the sandcastles as eternal. They are even more mortal than their builder.

As his family enjoys a day at the beach, the child watches his sandcastles dry out and begin to collapse as the sun beats upon them. The tide also begins to rise. He occasionally walks back to the shore in order pack mud onto the sides of the deteriorating castles to help them last a little longer. He even tears down old castles and builds new ones on top of them. He does this even though he has come to understand that the tide is coming in. His sandcastles will be wiped away, regardless of his efforts.

Maybe we can look at America a little like an arrangement of sandcastles. It was built out of the mud of a new shoreline on an old horizon, and as the ages go on it is subject to decay like all nations, likely eventually to fall altogether. But what would constitute this fall? What would the wave that wipes it out look like? We can speculate about that all day long. If the child sat there and thought about what the wave of destruction might look like, without seeing that his castles were collapsing because they were drying out, he would not have walked over to fix them. There would have been no point anyway. They would have simply become piles of sand like the rest of the shore around them.

America cannot see what's coming. We can only see where we are, and where we've been. And even those two things are hard to see sometimes. Nevertheless, the sandcastles of America are still standing. It is up to us to recognize where they are decaying and fix them to the best of our abilities even as the tide rises, instead of hopelessly mourning the impending hour of their collapse.

Progressive Christians may see my above metaphors as a bit too simplistic. They may say that I have ignored the ambiguity in how Christians ought to see various "political issues" like abortion and socialism fitting into all the other issues. The political dichotomy in the church calls into question the direction that our nation and church are going, as well as where they came from.

Many philosophers and thinkers argue about the true foundation of a nation. Many argue about the true foundation

3

of a man or a woman. Some might say it is the mind, for from the mind come the motives of mankind. Others might say that it is our bone structure, for our bone structure is our "picture frame" in which the artwork of our flesh and blood is held. Others might say it is our feet, for our feet connect us to the world around us and take us on all our historical journeys.

However, none of these things could exist without a more primary biological foundation. An unfathomable amount of information must first exist that allows all these secondary functions to exist and develop, just like a well-structured constitution must exist for a prosperous nation to develop. The foundation of a house could not exist or develop without a blueprint. Our bodies could not function without a blueprint either: the blueprint for our foundation is our DNA. DNA has in it everything that we are, prewritten and coded; our eye color, hair color, genetic strengths and deficiencies, bone structure, our personality traits and various individual tendencies to some degree. It is a scientific fact that we are meticulously "pre-programmed." When the sperm and the egg cells meet, a new *life* is formed apart from its parent cells. All necessary information of what the child will be is intact. Indeed the breath of life is more than air, it's the incomprehensible wisdom of God.

Today it is controversial to say that the true foundation of life is life, but it still is. Lives of nations and peoples begin at their conception. Life is not a myth. It is not a figment of our imagination. It is real, even when it is the smallest it will ever be. But, just like the sandcastles built during low tide, that life would eventually wear out with age, or be destroyed by the waves, so maybe it would be better for it not to exist in the first place—or so some reductionists may say.

There are different ideas of what a beginning actually is, and then there is the *actual* beginning. And what better place is there to start a conversation about where we are now than at the beginning?

What was the beginning of a beautiful painting? Was it the canvas? The frame? The first brushstroke? Or was it the idea of the artist? The fact remains that the painting would have disappeared without the initial idea of the artist *to paint*. The life of America also began at conception, for it had to be conceived via information before it was able to grow into the superpower it has become. This "single issue" of beginning is symptomatic, if not the definition of our national moment.

The progressive Christian often refuses to take a political stance on a single issue that should be fairly cut and dry, for fear of being controversial. He therefore takes a political stance on the issue. Regardless of his stance on abortion, he tells his church that they shouldn't let single issues dictate their politics or let politics dictate and pollute their church services. When we do this, he says, we are actually fornicating with the world, becoming self-righteous idolaters. Apparently an issue as important as wholesale, state-sanctioned infanticide isn't a large enough hill to die on for some Christians. This is sadly a popular sentiment across modern evangelical pews.

Advocating against "single issue voting" is a strong argument, and it has troubled me, especially as I've become temporarily interested in politics. "Am I still on the right path?" I sometimes ask myself when I consider the many things which led me to my current political stance. Is pledging allegiance to the flag another form of idolatry? Should I stand with my hand over my heart with respect when the national anthem is played, or kneel in resentment? Should I stay silent?

When we seek to mythologize any true definition or undermine a foundation, we ought to take a good hard look at why they are there in the first place. The shifting definition of life can grant a person or society the right to justify themselves as they take life away. In the last century, people with disabilities or belonging to certain races were viewed as less than human. Atrocities against them were justified by the state, at times on national, legal, and industrial scales. To oppose these atrocities was incredibly unpopular. There is truly nothing new under the sun.

When God created the heavens and the earth he *spoke* them into being. Their foundation was God's conception of them, something behind the matter. Their foundation was fixed, as well as the parameters He pre-ordained. Outside of these parameters the universe would fall into chaos or collapse into a singularity. Perhaps this is why a good portion of conservatives walk out of progressive Christian church services. It isn't because they are evil right-wing idolaters, or self-righteous hypocrites. But because they have strong convictions which emerge from a basic fear of the Lord. Their convictions are in many cases simply derived from common sense. Other times they are directly corroborated by scripture. Perhaps they saw that these convictions were increasingly under attack not only by the world around them, but now by their fellow congregants.

Since abortion is the first topic that is thought of as symptomatic of the narrow "right-wing" viewpoint, let's consider why Christians believe that their stance on this issue is one of dominant importance, and why it ought to be considered outside of our prayer closets and in the public sphere.

Playing with Fire

While I hope to move a little more quickly through other issues, I think the issue of abortion is perhaps the most symptomatic of the deteriorating condition of our times. The church that sides with this needs to be confronted.

Some Christians have trouble taking a clear stance on abortion, making it hard to determine whether they are pro-life or pro-choice. They will say that regardless of how we feel deep down in our hearts about such things, we should not muddy our religious feelings with the nitty gritty, real world of politics. At this point in time, our religion is infringing on the rights of women (and men), they say, who deserve the choice to do what they want with their own body and their own future. Christians who want to impose their standard of ethics in this area are wrongly advancing a theocratic agenda. As long as Christians press against these "single issues," they are forgetting the larger scope of the various problems facing us. This results in a neglect of issues such as poverty and climate change, as well as a distorted political viewpoint.

One may say that there are not many Christians who support the pro-choice agenda, but there are. A growing portion of the progressive church has sided with Planned Parenthood, as "the right to choose" has gained more cultural popularity and the pro-life position has become more unpopular. The caricature of the more conservative church that decries abortion is an image that the more evolved Christian would rather not fit into. It's distasteful to the world. Many have rejected the pro-life position for a "more nuanced approach." However, one simple conundrum remains: if abortion is what it actually is, the massive demographic of the American church that supports it is playing with fire.

Many Christians would rebut with the following claims; that it is scripturally unclear what God's stance on abortion is, that it is futile and immoral for Christians to disproportionately hold fast to something that may not actually be that big a deal in God's eyes, that faulty judgment clouds the Christian voter's broader vision and obfuscates their better judgement at the ballot box, and that apparently it is impossible for a Christian to simultaneously hate a thing like abortion and to hate another thing like racism. A common pro-choice fallacy is to think that those who speak out for the voiceless unborn cannot and do not do anything else. It is hard to imagine a more vague, untrue, and unfair accusation.

One problem with this position, as it pertains to the Christian left, is that Christians don't technically need to claim to be pro-choice. They can "have their cake and eat it too." By claiming to be pro-life and supporting abortion in almost all circumstances, one may pose as neutral and impartial. They see themselves as being able to judge more clearly. This is just one example of progressive Christianity's self-perceived neutrality and nonpartisanship. But it is perhaps the most consequential. By maintaining the illusion of neutrality, one may benefit from the church life as they are applauded by a left-leaning culture. What they fail to see is that they are falling into the bygone pattern of the conformist church, which bowed to the wills of socialism, eugenics and progressivism. This pattern was always a result of an immense top-down pressure, whether it was culturally appropriated or enforced by governments.

There is a pretty cut and dry moral case that standing firm on the issue of abortion as a Christian—and even as a single issue at the ballot box—is not legalistic, political idolatry, but the most obvious thing to do. The case is stated as such: infanticide is an abysmal evil, and I won't vote for anyone who promotes it. It's a dangerous game, as a Christian, to support the ongoing campaign of eugenics and genocide in their modern forms.

The Secular Foundation for Abortion

The secular idea of being is growth and achievement based. It cannot be anything else in an existence of chaos. In this lens, the value of the individual grows as they grow physically or socially. The value of their life is merited by factors such as viability, stages of development, and usefulness in society. A new life that consists of ten cells in this respect is worth less than a life that consists of twenty cells, and a human who is "not viable" (an intentionally vague title) is not really a human after all. By this line of reasoning, a five year old would be worth less than a five and a half year old, and missing the arbitrary status of viability can result in the forfeiting of one's life.

The progressive ideals of relative human value and victim status are two mechanisms behind the pro-choice position. The pro-choice position is disguised as scientific and humanitarian. But the science and humanitarianism are both based on eugenics. 20th century pseudo-scientific philosophies like genetic determinism were prevalent on a global scale. Seeing the world in the reductionist terms of survival of the fittest and conflict theory led to multiple genocides, concentration camps, two world wars, and the scorching of a continent. Like today's less visible version, eugenics meshed well with a purely naturalistic perspective. The least fit person is still by nature the least necessary person.

The progressive view of abortion is that when a child is less than a certain arbitrary size, the child has no rights. It is, in the eyes of society's truth tellers, not technically a viable human being. It would not survive apart from its mother. This logic defeats itself. A newborn baby cannot survive apart from its mother. Does it count as a viable human being? How about a two year old? How about a quadriplegic? How about an elderly person who requires full time care? Are they "not viable" or "less human" because they need assistance to live? Progressives have to do a lot of mental gymnastics in order to prove their point about human viability.

In the meantime, while crowds are painting uteruses on cardboard signs and chanting obscenities in bovine herds, children, who do not fit the relative modern notion of life and are smaller than a certain size, are stripped of their value and terminated daily on an industrial scale.

Mothers and fathers who do not want to keep their babies are seen as the true victims because their future is threatened by an *unwanted* child. Neo-Darwinism and its resulting moral relativity affirms the parents in their thinking. By the logic of survival of the fittest and natural selection, the thumb-sized child is the least fit. The "more fit" mother and father's financial, physical, and social status eclipses the baby's right to life. Neo-Darwinism is the engine for justifying abortion to ensure the social evolution of the parents. The industry itself was primarily intended by its founder to control or even eliminate populations of minorities and less proficient people to promote the next stage in the evolution of our species.

There is a condition for these types of reasoning: moral nihilism. Moral nihilism must be consistently upheld in order to make any sense of the pro-choice argument. We must simply brush aside the groupthink and sloganeering in order to rid ourselves of this stain on society.

A Few Quick Points

I wanted to succinctly and parenthetically describe a number of reasons why the pro-choice position is futile. I will provide the conclusions of these reasons without all the arguments needed to establish the conclusions, but the following conclusions should still stand on their own quite well. These points are listed in no particular order.

Human usefulness to society does not determine human value. Abortion results in the death of a human baby every time it is carried out successfully. Based on the scientific fact of when life biologically begins and the legal definition of homicide alone, the act of abortion cannot be reasonably divorced from homicide. Over 60,000,000 abortions have taken place since abortion became legal in the 1970s. Abortion includes brutal practices such as, but not limited to, euthanasia, chemical charring of the baby, crushing the child's skull, dismemberment and mutilation, and vacuuming the child out of the womb. The pro-choice position is reliant on changing words and definitions of words to make sense of its position. Parents' livelihood should never come at the cost of another life, especially the life of their own child. The abortion industry has a large scale propaganda campaign and is incredibly powerful in our modern culture. The abortion industry targets women for abortion, and young children with sexual propaganda to preserve its revenue stream. The abortion industry claims it wants to reduce the number of abortions that occur, but is reliant on abortion as its primary source of income. Abortion is legal in every state, and the industry is pushing for more radical forms of abortion as well as to strike down any restrictions whatsoever. Lastly, not one of you would have been annoyed with this paragraph if your mother did not carry you to term.

Let Your No be No

Can Christians be pro-choice? Though some claim that the Bible does not actually have much to say about this topic, there are a few verses that might shed light on it: Exodus 20:13; Psalm 139: 13-16; Jeremiah 1:5; Numbers 5:27-28; Psalm 127:3-5; Numbers 5:19-22; Proverbs 6:16-19; Genesis 1:27; Job 31:15; Psalms 22:10; Isaiah 49:15. This ought to secure the position of the Christian against abortive procedures. God considers a life to be a life, even when it is really small and is *most* dependent on its mother to survive.

When abortions are pushed up to the point of birth by the left, we can assume that the next step will be post-birth termination of the child. We should also realize that many who made the decision to go through with an abortion were often told something different than the truth. The business model of the abortion industry thrives on "counseling" parents to end the lives of their children.

Can Christians object politically to such progressive agendas? Yes. Christians have the political right and duty to speak out on such issues when others are advocating silent prayer and waiting for Jesus to come sort it all out. The United States of America was founded on the principles of freedom of speech and equality of individual rights, no matter how unpopular the speech is or how weak the individual may be. Christians say that lives ought to be considered as having individual value apart from their parents, even when they are developing in the womb. This does not contradict science, and deserves to be a priority topic in the political sphere. The arguments against the unborn are fleeting and unsubstantial, yet they are the loudest. Through coercion, sloganeering, groupthink and intimidation, these arguments without arguments emerge as the new universal reality. Suddenly the pro-abortion position becomes the position that is on the side of truth, the angels, and science precisely because it is on the side of the religion of progressivism—survival of the fittest. When personal fitness is at stake, one has the *right* to trample the rights of others to ensure personal well-being. The less fit rights of the unborn are thrown out in the streets of America, the epicenter of the "free world," along with their bodies.

The argument between pro-choice and pro-life illustrates the state of our nation and our crisis of identity. The pro-choice arguments rest on the secret subjective knowledge of the progressives, and these arguments are composed more quickly than they can be dismantled. Discovering falsities, tautologies and slogans of the left is always more of a challenge than writing and mass producing them through pamphlets, memes, and cardboard signs.

Abortion lies at the heart of today's big American problems, whether we want to admit it or not. It gets to the bottom of what each worldview perceives to be a mythology. For what can be more primary than conception? There is mythology in many of the stories that make up America, but the myth has never been America, or the people in it. The conception of America and the birth of America as a new nation is not a myth. Nor is the conception and birth of its citizens. The day either of these are dismissed is the day our identity becomes void. The rejection of our national beginning extinguishes the sanctity of our nation. The crusade of abortion and eugenics has smothered life's sanctity.

Foundation is under attack, unless it fits the paradigm of convenience and comfort. Christians should walk out of any assembly that supports, or is indifferent to abortion.

Death Incorporated

This next section is an elaboration on the evils of the abortion industry, Planned Parenthood and the rhetoric of their supporters. The pro-choice position needs to ignore reason, stretch metaphors, abolish definitions, and fabricate circumstances to make any sense of abortion. Their tactics often include cursing, anger, slander, mocking, spitting, chanting in groups, and physical assault rather than logic, reason and arguing their position by use of the Socratic Method.

The basic logic of pro-life arguments hinges on what constitutes a life. The pro-choice arguments say that life's beginning is arbitrary and imaginary, "wherever we want it to be, that's where it is!" They can't come up with a unified conclusion of when a life begins. This is the first of many problems. Some say it's when the heartbeat begins, others say it's when there are brainwaves, and others say it's at birth, when the babies take their first breaths. When they make the claim of when they believe life begins, they also implicitly suggest that all abortions after that point are immoral. They set traps for their own position when they can't unanimously agree on a threshold for human life.

The next problem is that the abortion industry is a truly grisly industry, which must perform its operations in the shadows, protected by the very culture, politicians and media it influences. The philosophical edifice of Planned Parenthood is strengthened by the intimidation tactics they use against their opposition to keep them silent. They are criminals who need to be brought to justice posing as angels who should be worshipped. They attack their opposition with lawsuits and defamation campaigns, and are rarely, if ever, held accountable themselves for countless crimes against humanity. As Christians, we need to remember that this is the most pressing issue of our times. In the future, when darkness is exposed by light, Death Incorporated will be recognized as a great stain on US history, and on world history.

Right down the street, no matter where you live, there

are abortion mills committing heinous crimes, dismembering children, at all stages of pregnancy.

The cutoff for legal abortion where I live in Utah is twenty one weeks, the developmental point when "the science" claims that children can first feel pain. Children have been shown in ultrasounds fighting for their lives against abortive methods a lot earlier than that (apparently against a pain they cannot feel). Abby Johnson, a former Planned Parenthood counselor, recalled witnessing a vacuum style abortion. During the procedure, the "doctor" ended a child's life at thirteen weeks. It visibly fought back against his tools, showing a prenatal defensive struggle for life. The struggle was futile. It always is. What baby can win a fight against such selfishness and brutality?

The modern day Josef Mengele jokingly uttered the words "beam me up, Scotty," before crushing the child in a suction-tube device. There are many modern day Josef Mengele and Kermit Gosner types in America, being paid handsomely and held up as cultural icons, heroes who go into work every day to dismember and char helpless children. They are paid an average of $100,000 per year. How many of those dollars are taken out of your paycheck?

Planned Parenthood is America's largest abortion provider. Even when a child visibly fights for its life in its 13th week, we are told it can't feel pain until the 21st week. Only a fool would disagree! The left said so, so it must be true. It is true, however, that the later the abortion is performed, the more heinous the abortion procedures become; the child's skull is collapsed, it is dismembered, charred, euthanized, or something else (anything they can do to make sure the child won't survive). Meanwhile, abortion supporters become enraged when the practice they wholeheartedly support is described in gruesome detail or revealed in photographs. They often are filled with disgust. This is hypocrisy at its finest. Supporting an industry of death, which thrives on the shedding of innocent blood, a legacy of pain and a modern day genocide, relies on decrying those who aren't afraid to show what it actually is.

Christians can and should expose this industry unapologetically, but many support it or are indifferent. Some states allow abortion up to the 9th month and even partial birth abortion, when a child is killed as it's being born. This is nothing less than collectivized madness and state-sanctioned wickedness. There are some things the land cannot bear up underneath.

Recently a state criminalized euthanizing babies who've survived the abortion process, making it illegal to put down a baby after it's been born. While some may see this as a "step in the right direction," it actually shows that Planned Parenthood is not scrutinized or questioned at all. They are likely behaving outside the scope of what the law allows more often than one would assume. Allowing the baby to die after a failed abortive process is likely a common occurrence, especially since it has been demonstrably made illegal in only one instance. This shows that abortion is a very secretive procedure, and what we are allowed to research and investigate is only the tip of the iceberg. Behind closed doors, the sky is the limit for Death Inc.

This is a present evil in our epoch. Many who are pro-choice may not thinking hard about it. They may be adopting the popular and repeating clever slogans. But that is generally the extent of people's thinking on the subject—autopilot. They don't consider it to be something more, and they operate in ignorance of the biological and scientific fact that a new life begins when the new cell type forms.

If an abortion supporter is asked to point out where a life begins on a developmental chart, it often catches them in their duplicity. As soon as they point to a specific stage, they undermine their own position. According to them, all abortions afterward are *taking a life*. They've made themselves an enemy among their own ranks.

There is a good common analogy for why abortion supporters are gravely incorrect. Imagine driving at night in the fog. As you drive with your high-beams on, you see in front of you something that looks like a person, but you are not sure that it's a person. What are you going to do? No one in their right minds is going to keep on driving in hope that it might not be a person. *They are going to slam on the brakes.*

The pictures of aborted children show little babies, not chopped up potatoes, or heads of broccoli. There are many pictures of dismembered, charred body parts. But people are being brainwashed into believing that these babies aren't babies, but a clump of cells, a type of cancer. The pro-choice position has insulated itself by calling motherhood a state of perpetual slavery and suffering. This idea comes from advanced feminism, where women have been subjected to the cruelty and malice of the male-dominated-patriarchal-system. Women are taught that pregnancy is like a cancer growing inside of them. The *fetus* is going to drain them of their life and forfeit all their dreams. Men are told to shut up if they disagree. Young teenage mothers, (who are often just as morally and intellectually confused as young teenage fathers) who've had sex out of wedlock and are impregnated as a result of dual irresponsibility, travel from home in order to "get advice" from "the experts." These experts are simply on a concentrated mission to sell another $1,500 service. They are well trained on how to sell it. The best salesmen and saleswomen are the most handsomely rewarded.

The abortion industry's business model and revenue stream relies on convincing women that they should get an abortion, even when many women are skeptical about what is in the fog. They tell women, "You're not ready yet. Wait till you're ready. It's just a clump of cells anyways." Many women aren't aware that they and their child are being preyed upon by a cruel monster. Many of the counselors already know that, scientifically, the baby is a baby, not a clump of cells. They have seen firsthand the piecing together of baby parts in the back rooms.

The abortion industry is going to be recognized as one of the great stains on human history. Planned Parenthood needs to be exposed. From its conception it had evil motivations that were rooted in racism and eugenics. Margaret Sanger, the founder of Planned Parenthood, spent her life pushing for birth control and trying to globalize her twisted ideals. She was an outspoken eugenicist and a racist. She nicknamed her goals after a racial slur, secretively wanting to decrease the black population—as well as the sick, disabled, and weak members of society. She was a mighty contributor to the American and worldwide eugenics movement. Planned Parenthood has its origins in eugenics, but is lightyears beyond what even its controversial founder originally intended. Since it is so obvious that Sanger was a vicious racist, in an age when racism is no longer popular, Planned Parenthood has reluctantly denounced its founder. In reality, the organization is carrying her racist, classist legacy to an extreme that Sanger herself may have found distasteful, disproportionately targeting minorities and the poor for abortions.

Margaret Sanger found black spokespeople, ideologues, clergymen, and anyone else she could to push her anti-black propaganda. Her radical goal of eugenics and population control started with small beginnings based on personal bigotry—birth control could mitigate unnecessary populations of people she deemed less fit. At that time eugenics, like racial determinism was popular. One could argue that eugenics is still popular.

The abortion industry has become one of the most radically eugenic institutions ever conceived by man, killing unborn children for profit and personal convenience. The abortion industry covers up its eugenic motivations with the claim that it's not eugenics at all, but "healthcare," "reproductive rights," "just science" or something like that. By doing this, it makes abortion more palatable and demonizes anyone who opposes it as anti-woman, anti-health, and anti-science.

Sanger was raised in a catholic family and rejected the faith. She held resentment for the church and the nuclear family structure in general. She marketed the freedom of total sexual expression for society, without the biological outcome and responsibility of children. Birth control advertised that "you can have sex with whoever you want, whenever you want, and never have to face any consequences." Sanger, like so many who follow in her footsteps, sneered at the traditional notions of God's design for family. The birth control movement was a great leap forward for the sexual revolution. Sanger had to convince a skeptical population to make what was once a controversial idea commonplace. Many today may sneer at the idea that birth control was ever controversial, because it is a fact of life now. But those who initially opposed the birth control movement likely recognized what such a small beginning would lead to for society. They were right. Birth control lost control over the decades. Like Hitler's slow inching toward industrialized eugenics throughout his rise to power was followed by the dominion of a genocidal age in Germany, Sanger's ideas also started small, offering "protection" from unwanted children. Now "protection from an unwanted child" has become the industrialized and monopolized culture of crushing children's skulls, mutilation, post birth abortion, killing children after they survive the initial attack on their life, and various other barbaric practices. Christians need to wake up from their weekly worship sessions and shine a light into this darkness in order to put an abrupt and jarring stop to it, no matter how loud people scream at us or how much they spit at us.

Many of the people I know support abortion, and it is the most controversial thing I could talk about amongst people. People who really stand up and fight against abortion are sneered at, mocked, cursed, spit at, shunned and beat up. They have guns pointed at them and urine thrown at them. They are dragged into court and threatened with incomprehensible fines and prison sentences. They face off with demon-possessed abortion doctors and the church of Satan, which is in league with Planned Parenthood. They are sabotaged, threatened, and persecuted all across the board. This is why Christians are so prone to tiptoe around and compromise on such a common sense issue. The more the church stands against such a popular evil, the more it will inevitably face persecution. The dark deeds of the world do not want to be exposed. Eugenics is alive and well in the western world. If we are consistent with what life is, then we could argue that we are living in the midst of an American holocaust. It's showing no sign of slowing down. It's only intensifying. The sins of Manasseh are mild in comparison to our own. Deep down in America's underbelly, there is an industry of slaughter and child sacrifice that is being propagated and advertised wholesale. It offers "freedom of choice," but there is no choice for the most innocent among us.

Locally, in Utah, a red state, the leniency on abortion is somewhat less extreme. But even our local abortion mill locations reveal the industry's racist legacy. The clinics in Utah are strategically located in lower income and higher minority areas—South Salt Lake with the highest Black population, and West Valley City with the highest Hispanic and Polynesian populations. The modern "fight for social justice" seems to be nothing more than a hypocritical façade, as long as this form of systemic racism remains ignored by today's bored and meandering activists.

Most states and most cities that Death Incorporated places its clinics in are lower income, minority neighborhoods. Such is the case in Utah, and all across the country. I will admit, it is doubtful that targeting specific minority races in particular has any monetary motivations for Death Incorporated. Blatant racism is no longer expedient in the 21st century. Today's racists must mask their racism as "antiracism" and "abortion rights for minorities." Such a clever tactic effectively turns protecting the next generation of minorities from the omens of Planned Parenthood into "robbing them of their reproductive rights." Imagine, being labelled a racist for actively opposing an organization that disproportionately and systemically *kills black and brown babies*. Death Incorporated has simply recognized that preying on the most economically and circumstantially vulnerable people in a society, regardless of the color of their skin, is the most advantageous strategy for the longevity of its business model.

Another strategy that works well for them is to target colleges. In Utah, Planned Parenthood advertises heavily at the community college, which has the largest population of Hispanic and Polynesian students. They also have a strong presence at Westminster College, which has the highest black student population. Planned Parenthood creates specified targeting campaigns not only with race or economics in mind. They are aware of the mundane fact that kids in college have a lot of sex and can be tremendously irresponsible. College students are also uncertain about their future. Planned Parenthood promises that it will be there to help them when they're various dreams and ambitions come under threat after a night of partying and an unwanted child.

Abortion also has negative psychological and physical impacts on women. Some studies show that it is worse for women than actually carrying a child through to term. It results in suicidal thoughts, depression, anxiety, increased chance of breast cancer, infertility, death, PTSD, and many more conditions. It is also a very painful procedure where women are put under anesthetics and operated on. Often these women are put in dangerous situations during surgery. But just like everything else, Planned Parenthood covers up how dangerous the procedure really is and pretends that "everything went great." In reality, these women can be brought an inch away from death. Abortions are extremely dangerous for women, especially when taking into account that the child dies every time, half of whom are little women. This begs the question, what about their "women's rights?" The pro-choice side would have us believe that these women don't have any rights. Therefore the abortion industry is not only the most systemically racist organization in America, but also the most systemically *sexist*, indiscriminately preying on female adults and children alike.

There were two dissenters in the historic 1973 Roe v Wade ruling who acknowledged that legalizing abortion wasn't constitutional, but a reckless instance of judicial activism. Roe v Wade is an illegal law, a shady precedent that has existed as the left's immutable scripture throughout the last four decades. Jane Roe herself, the woman behind the historic ruling, came to see abortion as a great evil later in her life. She joined the pro-life ranks and expressed gratitude that she was legally unable to go through with her abortion. Unfortunately, remorseful or not, she paved the way for millions of others to cash in on government-sanctioned chaos.

Many pro-choice advocates point the finger at men who oppose abortion. They see anti-abortion movements as falling in line with the patriarchy. They yell, "It is so evil of you to speak about this, you misogynist!" But "the science" behind their accusations is highly based on *The Handmaids Tale,* a dystopian science fiction television series. Pro-choice activists often march at rallies dressed in garb worn by the characters in this miniseries. They use arguments based on personal preference, social media, and Netflix. They forget that although they claim that their opposition is trampling roughshod over women's rights, we actually maintain a huge amount of female support. According to a 2021 Gallup poll, 43% of American women self-identify as pro-life. No one wants to restrict a woman's right to choose what to do with her own body, just what she can do with her child's body.

If all men and women were properly educated on what an abortion actually is, we would have even more support. The fact is that pro-life supporters do stand up for a woman's right to choose *not to be preyed upon by a corrupt organization*, as well as the rights of millions of "little women" to life, liberty and the pursuit of happiness. The pro-choice position, however, must manipulate a multitude of definitions and alter reality entirely in order to make itself appear to have some semblance of being on the side of women's rights. These are only rights that are based on the whims of a confused time and culture.

Saying that women "should have the right to terminate their pregnancy" willfully omits what a pregnancy is. By saying that pregnancy is a state of being akin to an illness, where a clump of cells is growing in one's body, the pro-choice position has effectively turned pregnancy into cancer. They also alter the definition of "child," simply by replacing it with the word "fetus," the Latin word for child. If I held up a banana, calling it a banana, and you corrected me by calling it a *platano*, would it stop being what it is because you said the word in a different language?

Another tactic, or argument used by pro-choice supporters is the stage of development argument. They will say a child is not a child until it reaches "x" or "y" stage of development, the imaginary line they suppose makes a life a life. The argument becomes absurd when carried to consistency, as basing value on a stage of development analysis would understandably make new born babies less valuable than one week old babies, two year old toddlers less valuable than three year old toddlers, and thirty year old men less valuable than thirty one year old women.

Along the same vein is the degree of dependency argument: the child is not a child because it's dependent on its mother (i.e. a part of her body). But, again, when pressed to consistency, the argument falls apart. What about when the baby's born or two years old? In either case, the child will die if left alone. It is dependent on its mother. This also carries implications for the elderly and people who are reliant on medical devices to keep them alive. Are they less valuable because they are dependent? Elderly folks are often highly reliant on others for care, should we have the right to euthanize them based on their degree of dependency? In 2012, bioethicists argued, for the sake of consistency with the pro-choice narrative, that women should be allowed to kill their babies after birth (they weren't actually claiming to support this, but pointing out that it is where the pro-choice logic is headed). The arguments all fall apart. It is impossible to divorce abortion from its eugenic DNA. In order for abortion not to be eugenic anymore, it must be euthanized.

Another argument commonly in use is the rape, incest, and life of mother argument, which is fairly easy to refute. Abortion supporters think it's clever to suggest that, because its opposition cares so strongly about abortion, they must not care quite as much about things like rape, incest or the mother's well-being; they think they've won the argument by asking if we support making these special case abortions illegal also. Here's the problem. Less than one or two percent of abortions are a result of rape, incest, or life of the mother, and if you allow those, it is still resulting in the death of a child every time. When the person who brings up special case abortions is asked if they support abortion in all other cases, they usually will say yes. This again catches them in their hypocrisy. They are only using special case abortions as a smokescreen. They realize that if they give up abortion on all other ground, it will demolish their pro-choice position—they will have condemned 99% of abortions. The rape, incest, or life of the mother argument is meant to build a case through an appeal to emotion, but it is another trap for the pro-choice position.

The idea of rape resulting in a harsh penalty is something pro-lifers often support. Many even think rapists should face death if they're proven guilty. Many pro-choice supporters don't think rapists deserve death, but they think the children do. Punishing people for the sins of their fathers is an out-of-date measure. Pro-lifers take rape very seriously. They just don't think that one act of evil justifies another.

The left's manipulation of language and circumstances does not change the nature of what is happening over at Death Incorporated. The church must recognize this. But instead, it is largely complacent. A recent poll shows that 34% of evangelical Christians support abortion. As it becomes more and more popular to support "a woman's right to choose" and more and more intolerable for people to stand against the abortion industry, people who continue to stand against it face hatred, slander, and persecution. For this reason supporting abortion is becoming more popular or a non-issue across Christian pews. Many Christians who don't fall into this percentile may say that they don't support abortion, but are unwilling to speak out for fear of losing congregants or being mocked by peers. For this reason, the number seems likely to go up as it becomes more dangerous to stand against Planned Parenthood and the abortion industry, a multi-billion dollar industry that has overwhelming government and media support. A pro-choice Christian is an oxymoron. We can't support murder, the taking of innocent life, the shedding of innocent blood, or child sacrifice. Based on our religion alone, these are always signs of coming judgment and are not consistent with the Christian worldview at all.

The abortion industry is likely to preserve itself in the coming generations. It is an influential entity in our modern culture, and holds a lot of sway over society at large. It allows people the convenience of sleeping around with whoever they want, along with the right to not face any consequences. It also relishes in the campaign to degrade the morals of our youth, propagandizing children at younger ages through influencing mainstream "sex education," which has really just become teaching children how exactly to perform various types of sexual activity in exhaustive detail. Planned Parenthood also says on the teen section of their website that it's up to the child to decide at what age they should be allowed to start having sex. Parents apparently ought to have no say in the matter. The abortion industry knows that kids will enjoy sex, and that they are irresponsible. These are the obvious grounds for creating sexual addiction in young people, a means that will indefinitely bolster the economic interests of the industry. Irresponsible children will often have the biological result of sex, a child. They won't be ready for parenthood and will seek out abortions. This will insulate demand into the lasting generations.

Another problem is that many who we know and love have either had abortions or know someone who has had an abortion. Abortion is popular and normalized. Those who oppose the abortion industry are likely to lose a lot of friends if they speak out because of the implications of their position, but we can't afford to compromise on our convictions.

Abortion represents something similar to the child sacrificial systems shown in ancient cultures. Sacrificing children to idols and demons became popular in the near east, but was always a disgrace in God's eyes, and a sign of a society's undeniable decay. If we weigh the amount of abortions that happen daily in America against this, it makes those early systems of child sacrifice look amateur. They are dwarfed in comparison.

Planned Parenthood's ability to hurt people that expose them, alongside their ethical and legal unaccountability is truly remarkable. One man who went undercover to expose them for selling baby body parts faces nine felony charges in the state of California for the inexcusable crime of telling the truth. Planned Parenthood is trying to put him in prison, and they may be able to. They have immense power to come after their opposition in whatever way they can. Meanwhile, they are above reproach for decades of crimes against humanity. This shows where we are as a society. As more people wake up to what the abortion industry really is, more people's lives are likely to be destroyed by Planned Parenthood, so that it can preserve its revenue stream and cultural influence. Christians need to wake up to the signs of our times and bring an immediate end to this industry of death and suffering. Every day thousands of little ones are being ripped from their mother's wombs and torn limb from limb. God has started waking Christians up to what's happening. We can't fall asleep again.

～

In Ezekiel, God saw the story of Jerusalem as the story of an individual. She was lying in her own blood, doomed to perish without a father. God adopted her in her helpless state and raised her up to be a great nation, but she sinned repeatedly against her Father. In this metaphor, Jerusalem began to sin against God and prostitute herself to the gods of other nations. The worse she became, the more God's wrath was stored up against her. Like a giant stone rolling down a steep hill, the momentum of her sin continued to increase. There was no human way to stop the stone.

The Case for Conservatism

Some progressive Christians believe that conservative Christians have largely allowed their "Kingdom convictions" to be clouded by an overtly political stance. This accusation comes with a certain lack of self-awareness. Moving forward it will help us to know the basics of progressivism and conservatism. Conservatism is the protection and cultivation of a real utopia. Progressivism is the unchecked travel toward a utopia that doesn't exist, and historically has proven to be a dystopia.

In the church, politically neutral Christians do not want to be placed in a certain political camp, often recognizing the stigma of both sides. One misconception is to say that politically conservative Christians believe their social or economic preferences to be the primary engine for their theology. They don't. It's the other way around. Christians who are warned against economic issues like the dangers of socialism and the communal evils of the above-mentioned industry are driven forward by a very Christian desire for freedom from them. Their political intentionality is determined by unity between an accurate historical perspective and a knowledge of God.

Liberalism and Conservatism are both terms that have shifted over the last century. Liberalism was once connected with a passion for economic freedom and social liberty. When progressivism was linked to the stigma of eugenics, racial determinism, fascism and the holocaust, it fell out of vogue and was replaced by the word, liberalism, to mask the pitfalls of its ideology. Today, people have again forgotten the stigma of the word "progressivism" and have again labelled themselves "progressives."

Both camps see the opposite camp with certain amount of humiliation. Modern liberals see conservatives either as sympathetic to racism and totalitarianism or as capable of radicalism, insurrection and extremism (although all of these are media inventions). Modern conservatism is much closer to what liberalism once meant before it was contaminated by 20th century progressivism, which included the push toward centralization of state in the form of government paternalism, communism, genocide, racism and silencing political dissidents through brutal powers of the state.

The word progressivism seems to have lost its dishonor to the modern left, as liberalism is now interchangeable with the term it once sought to cover up. Today, both terms once again suggest many things, including the shift from a free-market economy to a socialized economy, the longevity of the abortion industry, a reinstatement of genetic determinism in the form of Marxist race theory, the abolition of the church, the punishment and shaming of political outliers, and the deconstruction of the founding documents which insulate our freedoms and make us distinct from negative and oppressive systems of governance.

Modern liberalism is hitting all the notes of totalitarianism, whether it be fascism or communism. Remembering the great pains these systems caused humanity in general and

Christianity in particular, Christians who recognize the warning signs naturally gravitate in the opposite direction from these systems. Our criticism of ungodly belief systems is not what drives our theology. Common sense and the ability to think for ourselves is what drives our hesitancy to bow to the issues that dominate our culture, threaten our spiritual well-being and religious freedom, and cause decay within our national fabric.

If more and more Christians are coerced into passivity by the culture and mandatory church neutrality, the balance of the political spectrum will decrease, giving unchecked power to one side, while contributing to the silencing of the other. The church always plays a role in quelling the fire of the state. The more the American church leans left with the state to avoid controversy, the less chance the church body has at withstanding the radical and dangerous campaign of the state.

If we lean too far toward any brand of politics with the wrong motivations we can find ourselves in danger of idolatry. However, if we lean too far away from politics and avoid taking a firm stance on certain issues we can also find ourselves in danger of being complacent in something that is evil.

William Wilberforce, among other Christians who historically opposed the evils of slavery, had a conflict of interest. At one point he considered forsaking his political career to enter into the ministry, but he was torn by the real-world issue of the slave trade. He soon found that God was leading him to act in the best interest of his nation, his career, and humanity. He made it his life's work to spearhead the abolition of the slave trade in England and succeeded. Imagine if he had exited his career in politics for fear of uttering anything controversial in parliament. Imagine if he had abandoned his life's work because his church taught that any political ambitions were just an idolatrous quest for power.

The Christian's place is not always in the political sphere, but some may serve the Lord best there. Perhaps it is God's intent that certain people engage with the advancing problems of the world, not solely to advance God's Kingdom, but to stand at its front gates and slow down the devil's agenda to steal, kill, and destroy.

In the Bible, nations are sometimes personified. History repeatedly confirms the comparison of nations and individuals. National sanity and prosperity always hinge on national morality. When the latter is confused, the former are confused. Human beings and the societies they populate are susceptible to unimaginable success or catastrophic failure. To ensure success and growth in a particular area, we discipline ourselves and focus on our goals. If we do not follow the teachings of our parents or of certain disciplines it can be nearly impossible to reach our goals. We will undergo some degree of physical, psychological or moral entropy if we trade the desires of the spirit for the desires of the flesh.

Human diets are a good example of the benefits of conservatism. If a person eats multiple candy bars every day and stops exercising, they will probably not achieve their goal of losing weight. Whereas discipline and self-control in these areas will result in the goal being met over time. Our longevity will increase. God designed our bodies to be taken care of, not abused and destroyed—even if that abuse and destruction feels good at the time.

Avoiding temporary pleasures that cause harm may seem inconvenient or difficult, but will have long lasting positive impacts. Delayed gratification is not a conservative construct. It is built into the human design. The echoes of this design are apparent all around us. We see the benefits in our own lives and the lives of the people we know. We also see the detriments of a constant and aimless pursuit of pleasure. This design parallels the truths stated in scripture, but is not isolated to scripture because it is God's design for all of nature, even plant life. One type of seed Jesus talked about in the parable of the sower was the seed that sprouted up too quickly in shallow soil and was scorched by the sun. Individuals and societies can run around aimlessly promoting their virtuosity and self-divinity with a shallow theological, historical, or political understanding in the name of a common goal and a day later be brought to utter confusion.

God gave Nebuchadnezzar the mind of a beast for seven years. Nebuchadnezzar thought of himself as the reason for his nation's triumph and glory, and his own prosperity and power. His struggle between idolatry, self-worship, and the fear of the Lord is some of the most important content found in the book of Daniel. His dreams showed God's plan for the future kingdoms of the world. His personal struggle was a mechanism for the prophecies from God that Daniel found in his dreams. His fate held similarities to our own here in America.

The book of Daniel shows that people are incapable of building nations and making them great without God's stamp of approval. In a spiritual sense, if I start willfully sinning every day, I will suffer spiritual consequences. It may feel good in the moment, but I will become alienated from God and others as a consequence for my disobedience. Obedience to my creator results in true freedom as a creature. By following the parameters of my design in proper relationship to God apart from the presence of sin, I may operate in the Spirit.

Nations function in a similar way. Traits such as discipline and obedience have positive outcomes. Sloth and disobedience result in a lack of identity. Biblical and historical evidence shows that as soon as a culture begins to worship other gods or worship themselves as gods they are doomed to fail.

When the Babylonians desecrated God's temple and ate

and drank, they were overthrown by the Persians on the same night. When nations began worshipping Alexander the great as a god, he was soon to fall. The fall of the Roman republic accompanied the deification of Caesar. Hitler thirsted for the worship of the world, but ended up swallowing cyanide. A torn continent and millions of dead were left in the wake of his hollow and deceptive philosophy. Stalin, Chairman Mao, Pol Pot, and many others fell into this pattern.

There appears to be a similarity between the discipline of a nation and the discipline of a man. Both a nation and a man can destroy themselves and others when they do not realize their limitations. It is man's fallen nature to reach for the pinnacle of human achievement with the knowledge of good and evil as his primary foundation.

In the Garden of Eden, God allowed Adam and Eve total freedom, but there was one law that was put in place in order to protect them from death. They believed the lie that they were actually being kept in the dark by God as to the true nature of freedom and life. They transgressed in the name of progress, with the new desire to become as gods, and received slavery and death as recompense. This mindset has plagued the world ever since, and it is always the reason for many different types of world decay. The attempts to answer the question, "Why?" fill our bookshelves. Every person will grow into a rebel's heart one day in order to write his own law and to be his own God.

Simple History

The Bible teaches us that we do not need to understand the entirety of human history to understand the entirety of human history, we just need to understand the basic condition of humanity. The book of Proverbs reassures us that "the fear of the Lord is the beginning of wisdom." King Solomon feared the Lord and was blessed with great wisdom. The prophet Daniel also feared and respected the Lord, and the Lord blessed him with supernatural understanding, including the interpretation of dreams, depth of insight regarding the political climate of his age, knowledge of God's irreducible sovereignty, and prophecies of the future. Daniel did not only understand the history of the past. He understood the history of the future. The visions and dreams that Daniel was given and was able to interpret show that the various nations and rulers are not under their own control, whether or not they deny the rule and authority of God. No matter how fearsome the beasts become and how chaotic the world order becomes, God's plan will prevail.

I do not dismiss the knowledge of those who have undertaken much study in learning all the particulars of history. In fact, I think that all the things that have led us to where we are today enrich the view of the world through the biblical lens. It is where interpretation diverges from God and from the understanding of human nature that the bigger picture begins to fragment into unintelligible pieces. This fragmentation thrusts individuals, societies, and nations into physical, psychological, and moral confusion, and prolongs our world's impartiality and blindness to the underlying mechanisms of its own decay.

The Two Beauties

Ezekiel 16 tells the allegory of an unfaithful woman. In this allegory, God saw a young child perishing alone in her infancy. He took pity on her and even took her in as his own child. He gave her riches, beautiful clothing and jewelry. She grew in beauty, stature and influence. However, she eventually began to defile herself with carved idols, to worship other gods, and to prostitute herself to other nations. She eventually became even more evil than the nations around her. God gave her many chances to turn from her wickedness and backsliding, but she was finally given over to the natural outcome of her desires and actions. She was stripped of all her riches, fine clothing, jewelry, regal status and glory. She was left naked and alone. Her nakedness and loneliness resulted from her God-given freedom to choose.

The general history of Israel and Jerusalem aligns with the disturbing parable of the unfaithful woman. The nation of Israel was Egypt's slave for centuries. When God finally delivered young Israel from its bondage and punished Pharaoh, He led Israel into the wilderness. Israel was exposed to many perils there in the desert, and submitted many complaints to the one who delivered it out of Egypt. Despite Israel's complaints and vulnerability, God fed and clothed Israel daily.

God showed that although Israel (and later Jerusalem) continued to rebel, He was gracious, patient, and forgiving. He led Israel through the wilderness of Arabia and into the land flowing with milk and honey, Canaan. However, like a rebel, Israel continued to disobey God's commands and show disdain for the prophets God raised up as leaders. As Jerusalem's power grew, her sin metastasized like a cancer within her. God led her to vanquish her enemies, gain riches, and to become a great city as long as she honored Him. At one time she even became the splendor of the world during King Solomon's reign. However, Israel continued to slip into deeper and darker sin. David's adultery extended to the heart of Solomon, and remained long after in the heart of the kingly lineage.

Generation after generation fought hard either to maintain

their idols and demons or to turn away from them and back toward the Lord. God continued to warn the young woman (Jerusalem) through the prophets that if she continued in her various adulteries she would soon be greatly diminished, stripped of her power and exiled among the nations. Unfortunately she became too addicted to her sins and lost her way completely. God had to follow through with His promise. He brought the armies of the great conquering nations, Assyria and Babylon to her doorstep. The armies of Assyria and Babylon eventually broke through and conquered her.

I want to be clear. I don't care that much about the word "conservatism." It's just a word. Like liberalism, it can mean a great range of things. To the Israelites who wanted to conserve their practice of idol worship, the prophets' destruction of the statues of idols likely looked like unhinged progression. However, these God-possessed prophets were remembering the past glories of Yahweh, and acting out of conservative hatred for the new abominations that had been put in His place.

God told the unfaithful woman that He was punishing her because she "did not *remember* the days of [her] youth," (Ezekiel 16:43) but had enraged God with all the evil she had done—which included extortion, political corruption, idolatry, cruelty to the poor, forbidden alliances, child sacrifice, and many other evils. When a nation forgets its past, its laws and the righteousness that allowed it to endure, and "progresses" unhindered into untold new levels of immorality and rebellion, it is usually either destroyed or greatly diminished. Of course, Jerusalem is a different case study than any other nation. It is likely much more important to God than Rome or America. Society may want to double check the template of history as it moves forward, in order not to move forward directly into a trap. The terrifying downfall of God's most treasured nation ought to make us stop and consider the parallels of modernity.

Theologically, the desires to succeed, progress, innovate, compete, and win are hardwired into humanity. These things are not evil in and of themselves, it is the contaminated source of their motivations that cause the injustice and suffering in our world. Greed, selfish ambition, envy, and lust for power are all phenomena of human sinfulness which result in the various pitfalls of society like murder, theft, genocide, slavery, corruption, and systemic oppression. Their true origin is always pondered by psychologists and sociologists. Nations are faced with the choice of how they might progress. Is progression for the good of the people? Or is it rooted in the soil of self-worship and the original desire to transgress whatever parameters may be in place?

Conservatism can be seen as the desire to progress with the healthy, scientific and common sense perspective of cause and effect, and the metaphysical equivalent of choice and consequence. Ambition should not ignore the causes of failures and successes of the past. Neither should it choose to reject the possibilities that emerge on the horizon of the future. The recognition that the past has shaped the present and that the present will shape the future is a necessary first step towards progress of the right kind. God's irreducible sovereignty best explains this recognition.

When I acted out in my youth, my parents were kind enough to discipline me and show me where I so often went wrong. The intensity of their discipline ranged with my patterns of misbehavior. Their authority certainly helped shape my future. We all know what happens to children who never face discipline, or successful adults who only acknowledge themselves for their achievements. The former don't achieve much, and the latter do not realize that those achievements wouldn't have been able to grow without a fertile soil.

Many liberals, and some in the Christian sphere seem

37

to think that America was a product of mindless, chaotic, evolutionary forces. The idea of God's sovereignty simply doesn't click with everyone in the post-secular era. But more people are catching on to the link between societies' moral degeneration and the decline in different types of human prosperity and the social fabric. To draw no distinction between the social advantages of liberal democracy and the consequences of Mao's Little Red Book and the Communist Manifesto would be intellectually dishonest. Our culture has again popularized failed philosophies by boasting to have the ability to finally understand the intricacies of those failed philosophies. It does this in order to preserve chaos theory. The American system was predicated on the freedom of choice and the inevitability of consequence, both Christian ideals which allowed the democratic attitude of our nation to determine its course and final destination. Clarity and focus would shed light on this course. Confusion and chaos would mar the path and make it unrecognizable.

We err when we believe that our national survival depends on the infallibility of the founding fathers. America was designed with the notion that it would only survive as long as it protected the basic human liberties of its citizens. The word liberty itself would come to mean many different things throughout American history. Somehow it became the most difficult to distinguish freedom from tyranny in an information boom wherein a person should most clearly be able to see the chronological and ideological differences between the two. Today, people demand mass obedience to wearing masks and pumping experimental drugs into our children even as they decry any form of restriction on abortion measures. The notion of liberty has been inverted. Media constructed fear and the public desire for a return to collectivization has obtained the allegiance of our entire cultural attitude. They appear to be determining our new course. How can the alternative to such indoctrination be approached without forced thought? The American system demands that our course be determined via persuasion, not coercion.

Many have taken full advantage of the great American choice and created an upside-down theocracy based on puritanical progressivism and relativistic atheism. They have tried to manipulate America to bow to the will of their own choices and perceived rights, largely through top down duress. The true intention for America is sometimes forgotten because people believe that if she grants freedom of choice then she must be entirely malleable and suited to whatever whim emerges in the culture.

Every American generation has the choice to either reshape America into whatever graven image is popular or to allow her to be an effective system of governance, protection, and prosperity for the people. As the checks and balances and small government origin of America comes under increased scrutiny, America is falling victim to a primitive type of progression that resembles Cain killing Abel out of pure envy.

America has myths that are written into it, but America itself is not a myth. It is not an abstraction to be poked and prodded at by sociologists, tech moguls, politicians, and public health experts. It is a nation full of flesh and blood people who depend on the integrity of their leaders. Our leaders so often do not know about their role, their responsibility, or their impact. They see themselves rather as empty vessels to carry out the ideals of their college professors and cabinet members. Many of our leaders desire to build America from the ground up. They see the people they govern as mere abstractions, clothed apes to be corralled and commanded in whatever way they will. As government gains more unilateral power over us, we rely more on the integrity and competence of our leaders, not less. But they see dissenters as obstacles to their vision. Dissenters can be dealt with in whatever way possible as long as they stand in opposition to the new elite class.

America is not a Christian nation in that it is a theocracy that wants to impose its value system on every living person. But it is very Christian in that it allows every man, woman, and child the freedom to choose the path that they want to take. American law was meant to impose on every citizen the responsibility of operating within the nation's parameters as a nation designed to preserve the *rights* of its inhabitants regardless of their differences—a paradox that has led to much confusion. Understanding this responsibility brings a longer lasting and more realistic freedom.

Fulfilling the misinterpretation of the American puzzle is transforming our nation into something else entirely. Like God's single law which warned against the primary transgression, America's laws warned against putting our own temporary desires ahead of the needs of others. These laws ensure the survival and prosperity of our nation. But "law" is an unpopular word nowadays. The definitions of liberty, survival, prosperity, and beauty can all be applied liberally and lawlessly until our freedom becomes slavery and our virginity becomes prostitution.

What Lies Behind Progressivism?

I want to first acknowledge that there are distinctions between different factions of the left. However, each of them have their overlapping similarities. There is no reason to be ashamed if you find certain ideas of yours align with some of the left's values. Many of these ideas and the attitude behind them tie in with the Bible, world history, and the history of our nation.

Notions of equality, charity, concern for the environment, social reform, and other causes are indeed noble. Imagine if America remained stagnant for its entire lifetime out of a fear of moving forward. Imagine if there were never amendments made to the constitution. Imagine if America dismissed any ecological concern, ignored poverty, and turned a blind eye to racism, sexism, and other forms of discrimination. It is not a bad idea for conservatives to acknowledge where there is truth in the opposing philosophy. This makes it easier to identify where movements have deviated from the truth. It would be wise also to apply that same standard to principles of conservatism. Conservatism is not infallible. It is often times muddied out of ignorant zeal or a blind allegiance to a sensational figurehead.

Progressivism in its truthfulness sounds extremely positive. Who doesn't want to excel past where they are right now, especially if they are stuck in a place they don't want to be? People set goals for the future, and successful people understand that social, physical, or economic stagnation is dangerous. However, that is not all that progressivism and liberalism in the modern sense, or in the sense that they were used in the 20th century, have come to represent as their definitions have become more formless. Progressivism is not always a helpful transition from negative to positive, as history has shown. There can be other elements involved, some more sinister and uncontrollable.

Progressivism from a materialist perspective has been reflected throughout history. The world and the universe are indeed always progressing and expanding in the modern paradigm, ever since the big bang, and so is the nature of evolution—if politics is to find its proper form, one may say, it ought to conform to evolutionary doctrine as well. One may also say that the evolutionary progression of *Homo sapiens*, which included various cognitive revolutions and the domination of our planet, has led to the modern ecological crisis, the next mass extinction, weaponized technologies that threaten our planet, and the loss of our ability to think for ourselves. The unhindered progression of humanity is at once an extension of our physical and moral development as a species and an undeniable curse which we are continuously placed under. The progressive mentality is common to all. It makes humanity, in its present form, always superior to its more underdeveloped past forms. This tenet suggests that modern humanity is the judge of outmoded people, places, ideas, and time periods. Such reasoning would render anything written yesterday less true than anything written today. The Bible, the Quran, the founding documents, *The Wealth of Nations*, and *Capital* are all less desirable than today's move toward a common goal. This is also one of the driving forces of "cancel culture," the self-righteous movement of our modern generation.

With the evolutionary perspective in mind, certain "forward thinking" leaders thrust nations, continents, and indeed the world into unprecedented peril. The idea of progress has always led nations to conquer other nations, often as a result of leaders who thought they'd progress directly past their humanity and into godhood. Unchecked progression for progression's sake was what led to the prosperity and collapse of many nations, not to mention their long lasting historical stench. Granted, ancient examples were not following a merely "evolutionary" perspective on progression, but they were following their own desire to become as gods and to ensure the survival of their own fitness and dominant status over other nations. Babylon, Persia, Greece and Rome are a few examples.

In the early 20th century, the world was plagued by war. The rise in technology following the industrial era coupled with ambitions of the powerful ravaged the world and demoralized humanity. These were all things that were done in the name of progress of the wrong kind. Was it mere coincidence that they followed the fusion of Darwinism, Marxism and other theories of intellectuals, so beloved by world leaders? The Nazis "knew" that the more evolved race mustn't only survive, but must excel and assert its dominance over other races. If humanity was to be bettered, men needed to become supermen, and rats needed to be exterminated. Romans maintained the same view of God's chosen people in order to subjugate them, even though their view didn't come about by genetic determinism. Many western intellectuals loved the theory of genetic determinism that fueled Nazi motives and propaganda. Some of Hitler's strategies themselves were derived from American progressivism. Racist American policies such as the Indian Removal Act and the Jim Crow segregation laws were used by Hitler as a template for his military campaign to dominate Europe and for separating the Jews from regular society prior to murdering them.

Social Darwinism was the ideological fuel behind such policies. In the eyes of the cultural elite of Nazi Germany, the survival of their race, on which humanity depended, was under threat by the "weaker" branches and "dissenting" factions. Hitler successfully painted those who differed from him as sub-human parasites. With the convincing theory of evolution as well as the lure of nationalism, socialism, and progressivism as the backdrop, the Nazis were able to manipulate popular opinion largely through information control and to come only inches away from world domination.

Joseph Stalin was another leader plagued by the myth of unchecked ambition and totalitarian progressivism. Stalin, like Hitler rose to power as a tyrant. His party created a disinformation campaign in order to win the hearts and minds of the Russian people. They didn't have to conquer by besiegement. They used the doctrines of Marxism and Leninism to conquer the souls of their people, so that they would war with one another—first psychologically, then physically. Stalin successfully progressed his way to the top. He lived a lavished lifestyle. He was rich, famous, powerful, and worshipped by many. He would hold large banquets for his comrades while millions of citizens starved, froze to death in Siberia, endured unthinkable tortures in prison camps, and ate one another. He had great disdain for capitalist pigs and the injustices of the western philosophies of free trade and individual liberty. Many western progressive thinkers, philosophers, and journalists praised Stalin's courageous leadership, and his real-world implementation of the theories they loved.

Many other nations and powers grew from this Marxist root. In many ways, Marxism is still ruling our world today. It disguises itself under different names such as progress, solidarity, equality of outcome, collectivism, and social justice in order to pretend it is on the side of good. But once it tricks a nation into adapting to its principles, it infiltrates the hearts, minds, and bodies of entire societies, bending the attitudes of nations toward total chaos and self-destruction.

Is Progressivism Biblical?

Does anything resembling progressivism exist in the Bible? If so, where does it emerge and how does it operate? In Scripture, there were many temples to idols and God's, but two in particular bear special significance. One temple was a house of righteousness. The other was a house of idolatry and confusion. Both were examples of progress, one of the right kind and the other of the wrong kind. The tower of Babel, which we will examine later, was built for man's ambition to progress. Idolatry and demon worship were behind the construction of this tower, as well as the desire to lift humanity up to the status of gods. The Temple of Yahweh, however, was not built out of the ambition of man alone, but the ambition of godly men who wanted to honor their God, who'd delivered them time after time, with a permanent home to dwell in. Up to that point, He'd only dwelt in tents. Both of these events could be considered *progressive*. But the architecture of ideas behind the two types of temple construction couldn't be more on opposite ends.

The idea of progress cannot be divorced from human nature, both the positive and negative aspects of human nature. It will be left up to the reader to decide whether the progress we participate in today is of the healthy or unhealthy type. Where they land on this issue will likely reflect their belief concerning the reality or absence of human sinfulness, which obviously relies on their belief concerning the reality or absence of God.

Where does sin start in the Bible? This subject is debatable. Some say that it started with a sweet tooth, others say it started with a powerful angel who hungered for even more power. God forced Satan out of heaven when Satan desired to become God, *to progress past God*. God forced Adam and Eve out of the garden when they desired to become their own gods, *to progress past God's primary law*. This is the essence and longevity of sin, it is self-worship and the desire to move past God in order to be "as gods" ourselves.

Satan did not need to write a long speech for Eve, he just had to plant the seed of "progression" in her mind in order to unify her goals with his. In just a few short words, he made her feel stuck, stagnant, bored, and doubtful about God. He made her question God's motives, as if He didn't have the couple's best interest in mind. He did this by taking the truth and twisting it just so, while hiding the fact that the focus was not on progression, which can be good, but on transgression, which gives birth to all types of evil, injustice, and suffering.

If he could get Adam and Eve to transgress the only law by appealing to their intellectual ambition among other things, he would gain control over them, and their offspring. In George Orwell's *1984*, the communist party maintains control over the people with a tactic called "untruth." Untruth is much simpler than an elaborate lie. It is the mirrored reflection of the truth, but because it is only reflecting truth in a mirror, it is a lifeless lie. When God told Adam and Eve that they were free, this freedom brought life to them. Satan triggered their doubt by advertising a different type of freedom, this freedom brought death to them and their seeds. He implied that God's law was actually a set of prison bars, inverting the notions of law and freedom. In order to be free, they needed to escape the prison of God's parameters. He succeeded in "releasing" them from their "bondage," and forced them into actual slavery. Sin was released upon the world.

The next generation committed the first murder, rising from brotherly envy. Generations after this, humanity had become so evil that God regretted creating it. He sent a catastrophic flood to wipe out humanity. After this, humanity grew once more, resettled, and pushed toward civilization, again without a sound foundation in the plains of Shinar:

> "Then they said, 'Come, let us build ourselves a city, with a tower that reaches to the heavens, so that we may make a name for ourselves and not be scattered over the face of the whole earth.' But the Lord came down to see the city and the tower that the

men were building. The Lord said, 'If as one people speaking the same language they have begun to do this, then nothing they plan to do will be impossible for them. Come, let us go down and confuse their language so they will not understand each other.' So the Lord scattered them from there over all the earth, and they stopped building the city. That is why it was called Babel—because there the Lord confused the language of the whole world. From there the Lord scattered them over the face of the whole earth" (Genesis 11: 4-9).

There could not be a clearer image of where the myth of progress for progress's sake leads. The tower of Babel did not come from mankind's good intention, but from endless ambition and capability fueled by knowledge of good and evil. God created human beings with limitations for a reason. Our limitations remind us of our reliance on our creator. But our desire to move past limitations shows God one thing—we think we don't need him. We just need ourselves, our tools, and our desires. Humans can be their own gods. If God excludes people from heaven because of pride, they can simply build a tower back into it.

We've already touched on the tragedy of Jerusalem who fell into the same trap. Can we see how this myth of endless progress also plagued her until she fell? Yes. The history of Israel and Jerusalem is not a history of a single tragic fall, but of a series of falls, leading to the ultimate fall: when God finally told her that He wasn't going to pick her up anymore. He'd had enough. He finally allowed Jerusalem to be overtaken by her enemies: "I will stretch out my hand against Judah and against all who live in Jerusalem. I will cut off from this place every remnant of Baal, the names of the pagan and the idolatrous priests" (Zephaniah 1:4).

Israel and Judah represent the struggle between two paths, the narrow path of following the Lord and the wide road to destruction that the world tends to take. This is the *struggle* into which Jacob was born. From the very beginning, Israel was constantly in a battle for its soul. Even Moses struggled to trust God at times. Although he learned firsthand of God's immutable power, that obedience and faith would be protected and rewarded, he struck a rock out of frustration instead of speaking to it in the wilderness to provide water to the people. For this outburst, God prevented him from crossing over into the Promised Land. When Moses led the Israelites out from Egypt by God's power, they repeatedly encountered God's hand in their story. As often as they encountered it, they forgot it. They turned aside to complain or obey their sensualities. When Moses was with God on the mountain, the children of Israel fell victim to disobedience—they worshipped the gods of the Egyptians and made a large idol. They somehow *knew* that God was not really out for their best interest. Now that they were free from the Egyptians, they were free to rise up and play. Similar transgressions persisted throughout the generations.

God spoke for centuries through many true prophets about the doom that awaited Israel if she did not turn from her wickedness. In light of the parable of Ezekiel which tells about the kind of woman that Jerusalem had become, we see that it was her own wickedness and rebellion that doomed her to nakedness in front of the other nations who'd repeatedly used her as a prostitute.

Jerusalem's idea of progress is the same idea of progress that has plagued humanity all along. It is the result of being beguiled by slogans such as "come, let us build" and "you will not surely die." These suggestions still confuse good with evil until we engage in the act of transgressing moral boundaries. Jerusalem was not always the way she was. She was once an endangered and innocent child. She was a young virgin. She had to grow up into her evil. She progressed step by step, brick by brick, level by level until she fell. "'Do you see all these great buildings?' replied Jesus, 'Not one stone here will be left on another; every one will be thrown down'" (Mark 13:2).

~

Where does America fit into this notion? How can we simplify the ideas of world history, biblical history, and American history to provide a formula for the complex problems we face? Where does the presence of sin and righteousness underlie all our modernist values? The answers must be weighed carefully on a scale.

America was built on the idea of checks and balances to ensure sound and fair governance. The notion of checks and balances may also be applied to the migration of American values. For example, America didn't want too much religious control or she'd be pharisaical and theocratic. She needed to balance God's sovereignty with the freewill of her citizens. She didn't want too much unrestricted immorality or she'd be just another prostitute. She needed to keep human freewill in check.

This paradox allowed for the beauty of the American system. It also presented a massive problem that would eventually manifest. It seemed that no matter which way America turned she would become a Pharisee or a prostitute. If she stayed in the middle she'd become both. The more she closed her eyes to what she didn't want to become, the more she became both of those things. As a child develops into its physical features, so a nation cannot avoid developing into its mortal, God-given destiny. In hopes of becoming a large immovable tree, America became a great reed swayed by the wind. Her power was not in her indifference to change. It was in her protection of freedom for her citizens in their differences. She knew she was not God. She never could be. She knew she was human and fallible. She was aware of her mortality. But like every nation, she had two warring tendencies within her, one to do good and one to do evil. She was trained by the nations that fathered her in the harmony between law and freedom, the correct interpretation of both. The habits that deviated from this harmony and the forsaking of her upbringing were formed over time.

As she grew she began to be able to distinguish where law became oppressive and sinful, and where freedom became transgressive and imprisoning. But just like Eve, the more she grew in her desire for the knowledge of the world, the more she became confused by the very clear ideas of law and freedom that she had been trained up in. Lady Liberty began to change as all humans inevitably do. We change the meaning of words like "liberty" and "law," which define our essence, to align them with what we believe our essence to be. We forget our own essence as defined by the creator. Nations are doomed to repeat the mistakes of individuals. It is a perilous pattern in which we are caught, proving that America is not the kingdom of God, nor was it ever intended to be. It was intended to act like a Christian individual who recognized fallibility, and humbly acknowledged her need for God. But she did not desire to force her beliefs upon the will of others, although at times self-righteousness and a will to dominate emerged. She did not desire to slip full throttle into the sins of her past, although she intermittently backslid. Her story and the motives behind it are too complicated for anyone but God to fully know. Her story began with the desire to lead by following, and to admit the truth that she still has sin within her heart. Her future is not set in stone. It will be determined by the will of fallible people and by the will of God, just as her past was. This is the American design.

~

There is a myth that fuels the American enigma and it is not where we'd expect it to be. The myth forms when we trade flesh and blood people for the abstractions we've conjured up in our minds. Humans see the world through a series of generalizations. Whether it be history, psychology, race, religion, politics, or something else, people make judgments about such things based on partial understanding. The understanding of some may be lesser or greater than others in one or more of these areas, but it is a partial understanding nonetheless. These generalizations form a comprehensive lens for every individual. Citizens who exist in a nation view the nation, as well as their role within it and the role of others, through a comprehensive lens composed of fragmented stereotypes. American free speech and the liberal exchange of ideas has provided a wide range of lenses and stereotypes to choose from. When looking at religion or politics, one is often dismayed by seeing one or the other as strictly dichotomous, ranging somewhere on a spectrum. If such a spectrum is real, then their notions of the way the world works has to fall somewhere on that spectrum, along with everyone else's. This is the beauty of the political and religious spectrums, they put everyone, rich and poor, foolish and wise, at the same level.

The spectrum itself is just an idea. But the idea helps us all to realize that we have certain biases that determine the way we react when we hear the name of Jesus, when we hear a scientist say that mankind are another form of apes, when we see a social media post from the former president, when we hear the phrase "universal health care," when we are told to wear masks for the rest of our lives, or when we see a family member watching a news channel we don't like. The various "triggers" we experience all hinge on the *fact* that we interpret the world through various generalizations, which may be correct or incorrect, popular or unpopular, simplistic or nuanced.

With this notion of worldview in mind, we turn our thoughts to America, and the way people see American sins. Some see America's sins as pharisaical, a result of people's quest for religious power. The westward expansion and the desecration of Indian people and their lands must have been a result of colonialism, stemming from religiosity. Slavery was also a system put in place and maintained through a biblical framework. But were these sins actually religious through and through? Or we're they more politically motivated? Were they more attributable to church or state? Do our tendencies to view the past through preprogrammed stereotypes in a post-millennial, post secular epoch have any bearing on what actually happened in the past?

These American sins and many others stemmed from a cultural agenda. Like all sins they relied on people's wicked hearts, a lust for power, various ambitions, pride, greed, and other passions. Let's examine two or three of America's most shameful evils and see if they emerged from the teachings of Jesus, or from someplace else.

Three of America's most notable sins are slavery, the forceful removal of Native Americans from their lands, and racial segregation—though there are others which still glaringly exist, but are not commonly unpopular. To say that the former sins are an outworking of the Christian worldview is a stretch of imagination, even if those who supported them tried to manipulate the Bible to fit that image. As long as theism in general or Christianity in particular are commonplace, the powerful will need to appropriate them in order to preserve power, regardless of whether or not they personally agree with theism and Christianity. The evils in America's past were much more a sign of people's selfishness than the selflessness embodied by Christ's sacrificial love and teachings of humility. In the case of each of these evils, and others like the push for eugenics and the longevity of abortion, they were proposed, fought for, and signed into law by progressives.

The following synopsis is not meant to identify any modern member of the Democratic Party today with this behavior, but simply to tell the truth and dispel the myth that the greatest stains on American history originated in Christianity. The president and vice president today claim the catholic faith, but they are also fighting hard to preserve and widen abortion rights, which the Catholic Church opposes. Does this mean that forty years from now people will say that it was Christians who *truly supported abortion*? Granted, abortion will first need to be recognized for what it is before it can be turned around and blamed on the church.

When Abraham Lincoln won the presidency, the Democrats who supported slavery seceded from the Union and formed the Confederate States of America, where they could continue their practice of slavery. This caused a bloody civil war where one side fought for the idea of *Imago Dei*, and the other fought for subjugation and ownership of human beings. The former was the Republican Party, and the latter was the Democratic Party.

While the Republican Party was founded by President Lincoln, the Democratic Party was founded by President Andrew Jackson. Andrew Jackson was a proud slave owner who was notoriously cruel to his slaves. He was also a proponent of "Indian removal," and signed into law the "Indian Removal Act," which resulted in the deaths of three thousand Native Americans and the exodus of many more from their rightful lands during the trail of tears. These actions were denounced by Republicans like Davy Crockett who said his decision to oppose the wicked Act "would not make [him] ashamed on the Day of Judgement." Apparently some political Christians recognized faith alone to be a suitable template for opposing the industry of slavery and the genocide of indigenous peoples.

Segregation was likewise sweepingly agreed upon by Democrats and opposed by Republicans. The laws that segregated people based on skin color were written and signed into law by Democrats. The measures brought forth which opposed segregation were likewise opposed by Democrats.

The prevailing notion today is that there was a massive political shift wherein Democrats and Republicans were reversed. The Democrats became the party for the people and the Republicans became racists who loved to wave the confederate flag. While there is some truth in this assumption, the massive political shift never really happened. The opportunistic Democratic Party simply saw the change in culture and the growing unpopularity of racism, and adjusted accordingly.

America has her sins, and certainly not everyone on either side should be judged based on the history of the party they belong to. But before society casts stones of judgement solely on America in general or Republicans and Christians in particular, it should take a closer look at the particulars of who should be held accountable, and for what. When we condemn many here and now for the sins of some in the past, we are blinding our eyes to reality, and jeopardizing the well-being of society. This fits the definition of suppressing the truth in order to create a myth. After all, in a mirror, left becomes right, and right becomes left.

The modern search for information has become rather divisive, causing a further split in the national psyche. Someone who gives information that is not sanctioned is thought of as a "misinformation super spreader," a "flat-earther," or a "conspiracy theorist." Such phrases are an intentional strategy to shut down counter perspectives. Just like in past authoritarian regimes, anyone who is critical of the party in power is ridiculed and thought of as insane. The errors of history are still there for anyone to investigate who wants to, as long as history isn't willfully changed by the internet. The two-faced behavior of politicians and celebrities, and predominating media manipulation is cause enough for speaking out. We are commanded both by God and by our nation's highest laws to tell the truth, even if it results in being told we are going insane for disagreeing with the progressive party.

In other leftist regimes, people who disagreed with the party were also told they were insane. Many were interrogated for months and encouraged to hand over their friends and families to the secret police. Some were placed into concentration camps for making a joke about a dictator. Many were murdered and tortured in indescribable ways for a slip of the tongue. In America today, the media and academe are creating a new age revolution against the status quo. People are being told to hate those who disagree with the state. Christians and conservatives are being lumped in with Nazis, terrorists, and slaveholders. Are people being categorically trained to take out the garbage of political dissenters?

Hate in Church and State

Why has such an ahistorical understanding come to dominate the way people view America? What is the underlying philosophy? Many believe America's foundation to be a myth. It is the story of a nation that has conquered unjustly and enslaved people in the name of Christ and western colonialism. With such a view, progressives buy the big lie that it was the Christians, not people with a specific agenda and motivation, who are truly responsible for our nation's various sins. By caricaturing history and the Christian faith, progressives have become convinced that sins such as slavery, segregation, and The Indian Removal Act were committed for some vague notion of "manifesting God's will" in the foundation of our country. Such a fallacy, or outright lie, has lent credence to condemn orthodox Christianity for establishing and continuing in this behavior. Suddenly the Christian faith is no longer about God becoming a man to lay down His life for His enemies, but about greed, selfishness, and the desire to conquer.

In other words, there had to be some sort of vague Christian fundamentalism attached to America's slavery and the removal of the Indians. It is an effective tool to attach a limited understanding of history to a limited understanding of religion in order to pretend progressivism had nothing to do with the problem. The hunt for past, present, and future wounds for which progressivist remedies are needed relies on omitting progressivism's invention of and continued participation in the worst problems in our country. It was often the Christians who were able to recognize the evil of thinking other races to be sub-human and the madness of genocide, while the alternative viewpoint wanted to justify such things as circumstantial or explain them away scientifically or psychologically.

Modern skepticism of the church and cynicism toward the state relies on imprecise but popular generalizations about church and state. Armed with such generalizations, the modern skeptic and cynic becomes the intermediary between truth and morality. An increasingly anti-Christian worldview deepens the delusion that Christianity is to blame.

The popularity of secularism, pluralization, and privatization emerged after the Cultural Revolution and have all contributed to the marginalization of Christians, from the academe to the workplace. Under such ideologies, Christians inherently become the alien, the villain, and the fool. Privatization sees Christianity as a myth that is unnatural to the land itself; it was a foreign teaching used as an excuse to conquer the Americas. So Christianity is an alien living on this land, sucking it dry of its resources and shoving all non-conformists aside. Secularism sees Christianity as misleading our comprehensive modern knowledge. It is a predominating modern fear that any form of Christianity, or even an area of study that leans toward the possibility of theism in the sciences, will once again be permitted breathing room in our education system. Pluralization, or pluralism, sees Christian claims of exclusivity as intolerant to the modern sentiment of "do as thou will." The law of pluralization naturally includes everyone's beliefs, as long as they do not have claims to exclusivity, which ends up being everyone's beliefs in one way or another, including pluralism's beliefs. This inclusivity is an illusion.

Such ideologies demand the Christian confession of criminality, and a silence that ensues long after. They contribute to considering America's global and historical presence to be tainted by a religious agenda.

All the wars America fought must have been because Christians considered themselves to be the morality police on the world stage, presumably because they assumed the God under whom America was established to be the source from which morality itself emanated. Those who believe in God know that He is the source for goodness. Christ taught, "There is no one good but God alone." So the modern irreligion sees Christians as fighting real battles with real costs of human life on behalf of an imaginary God. American warfare is largely understood to emerge from a religious quest for power. Though this isn't the case, such sentiment fuels the rage of secular culture against God. The cultural attitude is becoming increasingly hostile to the Christian worldview. They see Christians as crusaders and inquisitionists. As long as America has ties with Christianity, it too must be condemned. America must be secularized or abandoned.

This attitude cannot exist without a certain degree of blindness to the consequences of state-sanctioned progressivism in the States and atheism abroad. Unfortunately the push toward secularism is an attitude that has found its way into the church. Many churches preach the progressive gospel and are quick to admit the shortcomings of orthodox Christianity before they criticize progressivism. Many believe American Christianity has become stale. It needs a newer, more inclusive version. The conservative Christian can now be chided for being too political among the congregation when he casts a vote for private property and the right to life. Apparently it is impossible for the conservative Christian to distinguish the unseen realm of religion from the seen realm of politics.

Many Christians consider the preaching of the progressive gospel a good reason to go church shopping. The progressive church sees this criticism as bigotry, judgment, and narrow mindedness. Both sides see one another as diluting the true essence of Christianity with a political agenda. One side must be if either are correct. The basic question is, which side needs to make more alterations to biblical teaching in order to adhere to the prevailing cultural norms?

The notion that Christianity had a major part to play in the founding, furthering, and betterment of our nation and society has fallen out of favor with many in the megachurch. Certain convictions pertaining to issues such as the abortion industry, socialism, and advanced gender theory are now said to be "missing the bigger picture." Such issues are humanitarian, not political. Those who support the progressive cause in the church see themselves as apolitical, focusing on women's rights, charity, and acceptance. This relies on the progressive politicization of everything—from language to biology—infiltrating church ranks.

"The foundational myth" as it pertains to the Christian realization of the United States existing solely in rightful proportion to God's sovereignty emerges from a basic biblical knowledge of the world pattern and a recognition of the signs of the times. When the people and times become increasingly prideful and rebellious, a fall is usually soon to follow. Progressive Christianity sees such a view as a gross oversimplification. Such an understanding doesn't emerge from a worship of the state, but from a fear of the Lord and a recognition that His standards are applicable to the well-being and longevity of a nation, even a modern nation. In fact, it is the church that continuously integrates the prevailing precepts of the world system that is practicing idolatry. Other church systems that have adopted the state's antithetical standards and held them in higher regard than God's standards include the German, Russian, and Romanian churches of the 20th century. Each endured nothing less than a theological collapse beneath the pressures of totalitarian end goals and the grafting on of demonic ontologies. History now views these churches as non-churches that simply adopted the notions of state. It was dangerous in those days to speak out against such compromise, and was likely also seen to be a sign of great folly to oppose the parties in power.

There appears to be no such thing as a double standard for those on the left. Christians who have graduated the steadfast and stale conservatism of the past believe they are standing on the high-ground of perceived neutrality. In reality, they are simply gravitating toward the belief system of the state— repackaged communism, racial determinism, and the radical neo-progressive movement of the 21st century. They claim that we should keep politics away from the altar, unless they are of a certain type, and keep the altar away from politics, unless it is of a certain type. The politics of the republicans, conservatives, and libertarians are the real "myth" that progressives reject and warn the church to reject as well, if they want things to go well for them for the time being. Liberalism is the truer path of the church, and is more in line with the way many in the American church have come to envision the more inclusive "Kingdom of God."

Many progressive Christians state their allegiance to the left with less timidity, believing that the concept of America as a Christian nation is losing its power. These Christians applaud the advancing pluralistic (multicultural) and secularized (atheistic) cultural agenda, because they mistakenly believe this agenda to be neutral and playing fair. But in politics and religion, there is no such thing as neutrality. In other words, progressive Christians believe there's a secular storm coming and no matter how much Christians preach and pray, they won't be able to stop it. After all, don't we want a fairer, more tolerant society? It would do everyone well to remember, societies that forced Christians out of the conversation ended up descending into nihilism and atrocity.

Many "neutral" Christians clearly sympathize with the

modern secular left, and believe that it has more to offer for the direction of our nation than the principles of our mythological founding. America is becoming less and less one nation under God, and more and more one nation under whatever one feels it ought to be under, depending on which side of the bed they woke up on in the morning. For such Christians, the church's merge with secularized culture is inevitable, even desirable. Christians who still acknowledge God's authority over nations and hatred of evil are conspiring to divide and conquer. Those who believe in the older mythological Christianity are a threat to the advancing utopia, a hurricane of forced speech, pseudo-tolerance, political correctness and social justice for all. They are following a dangerous system which is reliant on the storybook doctrine of original sin. Worst of all, they are contentious. They must be corrected at once and taught to see the various complexities of this newer, realer world. Secularized, naturalistic thought, even where it's found its way into the church, cannot give any ground to Christian literalism. For Christian literalism gives way to intellectual terrorism.

Conservatism hinges on mankind's demonstrable and repeatable corruption, not their inherent god-like-ness and perfection. A literal interpretation of the Bible reinforces this tragic vision. The implications of original sin are staggering for many, and so they are ignored or forsaken. But such a "narrow view" undeniably explains a lot, and provides a comprehensive template for forming a political stance that parallels one's beliefs.

There's much more behind the false perception of the Christian in the foundational myth, but I think we get the idea. America was never on the side of good, until the "woke" generation found its way into history, and its ideology made its way to the altar. We were simply a bunch of pale-faced barbarians who conquered and committed atrocities in the name of our God. In the eyes of so many, and the secular left's vision, the fable of American mundaneness is the truer fabric of our national founding—a fabric which must be torn apart thread by thread before it can be re-stitched into a better, more tolerant fabric. The ongoing rhetoric of the interpreters of the past paints anything positive as a "white-washed wall," painted over a deteriorating foundation. Such rhetoric makes beliefs that are objectively antithetical to Christianity somehow seem more Christian to a large percentage of the church than actual Christianity. To give grace to those temporarily under the influence of such a deceptive system, these creeds are meant to camouflage with biblical truth in order to infiltrate the church, pollute it, and convert it. I was not immune.

A Moment for Reeducation

People must reconsider the definition of freedom. In September 2021, Texas passed an anti-abortion law. The Texas law was decried by millions. It faced unanimous rage from the mainstream media. A group of young women gathered in protest, to support "a woman's right to choose." The group performed a rather weak series of arm exercises in unison to show their "solidarity" in opposition to "the patriarchy." All of them wore masks and stood six feet apart from one another in adherence to CDC guidelines as they performed their dance routine.

Not only were they supporting women's rights, but they were also showing that they are protecting society from a deadly pandemic. These women, and the millions who agree with them, believe themselves to be participating in civil disobedience, challenging the status quo. They see themselves as non-conformists. They unanimously support mandatory mask mandates. They believe that people, in general, should no longer be permitted to show the bottom half of their face. But they should be able to have an abortion in the third trimester, no questions asked!

Meanwhile, the radically left-leaning government has taken further steps to threaten various *actual* rights of the American people, such as the first amendment and the right not to take an experimental drug. Many people's jobs and livelihoods are being taken away if they refuse to get vaccinated and anyone who questions the state is flagged or censored. This government has demonized their opposition in a way that can be described as similar to the Nazi demonization of Jews, Gypsies, and orthodox Christians, prior to the holocaust.

This is only one small sign that the notion of freedom, rights, and the fight for civil liberties has been turned on its head. In America, to end a child's life prenatally is a fundamental human right, whereas to show the bottom half of your face should be strictly criminalized. Those who claim to be "anti-authoritarian" have become the new authoritarian class. They are in support of any measure or policy put forward by the Democratic Party to limit rights "for the greater good." Yet they will only parrot talking points sanctioned by the media and their peers. They believe they are acting justly and wisely in their own eyes, in accordance with science and empathy. Why is this?

The Bigger Picture

We are so often told that we are "missing the bigger picture" when we criticize the Democratic Party and the religion of the left. But what is the bigger picture? Are we ever sat down and comprehensively told what the bigger picture is? Let's see if we can guess at it briefly.

The "bigger picture" is an omniscience that is being instilled in every undergraduate in the United States. It is a comprehensive understanding of past, present, and future, in which yesterday, today, and tomorrow all contain a copious amount of obstacles to be overcome by those who understand the bigger picture. The story of the bigger picture starts 2.8 million years ago.

2.8 million years ago mankind split off from their ape ancestors, and evolved over the course of a few million years into different species of the genus *Homo*. But *Homo sapiens* proved to be the most ingenious and resourceful of all the species. So this species crushed all the other species in order to dominate the world. This crushing and domination was primarily the result of *Homo sapiens'* ability to generate fictitious narratives such as Capitalism, Communism, and various religions. Of course, Christianity was the worst of all.

The fictitious narratives we used to justify our behavior and band together was always a tradeoff. Every society, nation, home, institution, book, painting, monogamous family, technical innovation, and cognitive jump was only a result of the fictitious narratives we play out in our minds and tell one another. These narratives, or myths, were and are our justification for world domination.

Today, we will hold in our hands many benefits of the ingeniousness of this otherwise unimpressive human animal. But we shouldn't be fooled. Humans are evil. We have dominated the world, caused many species to go extinct, and are pushing the world to its tipping point of ecological catastrophe. Moreover, all our systems and institutions are saturated with racism, sexism, homophobia, and many other types of bigotry. We are overpopulated and reproducing at a rate that our planet cannot anticipate or hope to sustain. We need to reduce our population at once or we all will die.

Such measures to ensure that these *Homo sapiens*—who will otherwise continue in their ruthless conquest and creation of mythologies if given enough freedom—are not given *too much freedom* may seem temporarily cruel and oppressive, but are a necessary evil. Human rights are an illusion anyway, a part of the myth we've created for ourselves. Humans are just another animal. Our brains are the most formidable weapon known to creation, not in their abilities to create machine guns or weapons of mass destruction, but in their abilities to write and tell stories and unify behind such writings and stories. If we are realistic, and understand "the bigger picture," we will come to understand that humans must be limited and reminded that they have no real rights or any realistic appeal to morality. All such things are an illusion. We are animals to be herded, corralled, and culled by the elite.

The bigger picture is the only narrative that somehow escapes the fictitious category of all the other narratives it criticizes. It is the underlying justification for the new social vision and the shedding of American rights and values in the name of that vision. After all, "America" is nothing but a vague, abstract idea that sits on top of a stolen land mass, and "rights" are another fairytale. It would seem that humanity itself, in all its glories and failures, is nothing more than a myth that must be deconstructed and reconstructed in order to fit this new social vision.

Conclusion

A nation cannot sustain itself on a myth any more than the foundation of a house can exist on a sandbar in low tide.

Sam Wittke

If the Christian qualities inherent in our nation's founding were simply a mythological cover up, then there is nothing to stop the postmodern deconstructionists from discovering and destroying what they perceive to be the more "mythological" elements of our nation, which end up being the all the elements our nation is made out of, including its people, their dreams, their beliefs, their desires, their unborn children, and their lives. This begs the question, what newer and more innovative elements do the deconstructionists intend to use in the reconstruction of humanity? Their answer usually is that they don't know yet, but will figure out how to build the new utopia when the time comes. First, they must dismantle the old dystopia. The tide of the even more real reality is rising, and Christians don't seem to be ready.

Chapter 2
Hindsight's 2020

The Heresy of Good Vision

Please allow a brief personal digression: I have been blessed with a set of eyes that works pretty well. I have had 2020 vision my whole life. Sometimes I cannot believe my eyes, while other times I am told not to believe anything I saw with them—and sometimes when I talk about what I see, I am told by the news and by my peers that I didn't actually see what I saw. I'm even told that I am foolish for saying that I saw what I think I saw. I am told, in fact, that the opposite of what I saw is actually what took place, and if I disagree with what others told me I saw, it's because I'm evil, or even worse, a conspiracy theorist.

The communist party's slogan in George Orwell's *1984* is "Freedom is slavery! War is peace! Ignorance is strength!" The population's acceptance of this slogan relied on first inverting their notions of freedom, slavery, war, peace, ignorance, and strength, in order to more effectively control them and bend them to their will.

When one sees the world through a purely naturalistic perspective, humankind must always be at once the most evolved version of itself and constantly evolving into its more advanced version. So 2020 was by no accident the year of the clear and untrammeled vision, largely driven forward by a deep understanding of "the bigger picture." Humanity, and America especially, are finally being educated by the real world in order to become the more evolved, more sensible version of themselves.

With the view of America's mythological Christian founding, deconstructionist society may establish the preeminence and dominance of the kingdom of this world's reality over the kingdom of God mindset. After all, one kingdom is seen and the other is unseen. This belief has entered the American church, especially as it has forgotten its basic theology. Belief in the Kingdom of God does require a split between socio-political thought and spiritual-theological thought. This understanding differentiates between the worldly kingdoms, which operate by a power over others structure, and Christ's kingdom which operates by a power under others structure, which Christ modeled in His teachings and His death on the cross. The differentiation between the two kingdom types often translates into a platform for some Christians to judge others for becoming more interested in politics, politically incorrect, outspoken or aware. However, politically interested, active, or aware Christians do not necessarily muddle the two kingdom types in their minds. To say that they do is itself an oversimplification which is very politically motivated.

I agree that Christ did not lord himself over others, even though He is the Lord over all. Christ was indeed the dominant voice among the cultures, cities and nations of which He was a part. Based on His identity, they could not have risen to power without His approval. They would not have put Him to death if they did not see Him as a threat to their motivations, which included the religious traditions of the Jews and the political structure of the Romans. He went to the cross not to prove His subservience to and ultimate defeat by the Romans and Israel, but His subservience to God and His identity. His resurrection showed His power *over* the powers of this world. This act was in all humility and love. Humility is not the same as rolling over and playing dead before the ever-shifting attitude of the times, and love is not another word for compromise and complacency.

Humility sometimes requires putting oneself in a position of discomfort and telling the unpopular truth, even when it hurts one's reputation and well-being or even threatens one's life. Jesus's persecution did not indicate His subservience to the political climate of His time or His political neutrality, but the world system's ongoing hateful disposition toward the true things of God.

In modern times, the most threatening order to the various temporary power structures (cultures, ideologies, regimes, political systems) of this world which are largely operated by the ruler of this world is the order of the eternal power structure of heaven which *only* lives on in the one true church, Spirit filled human beings who are called to be the salt (preservers of righteousness) and light (truth tellers) of this world. But the world loves darkness, and hates when light exposes the reality of what is hidden within that darkness (John 3:20).

Why was Jesus so often threatened with being stoned? The people of Israel thought He was blaspheming, but He also was calling out the hypocrisy of *the nation*. He knew that Jerusalem had stoned all the prophets that were sent there previously—because they threatened the worldly power structure founded on rebellion, extortion, and idol worship—and the way Jerusalem treated Him was no different. Jesus, like the prophets before Him, saw that the political and religious elite of His time had become deeply corrupt. He was not afraid to say so, even if it rubbed some people the wrong way.

Can you imagine what the gospels would have looked like if Jesus simply nodded His head and agreed with every false notion and human tradition put forward by the religious and political elite? What would the Bible look like if He never overtly contradicted their incorrect interpretations of the law? The Bible probably would not be the world's number one bestseller if Christ and His followers had respectfully "agreed to disagree" and bowed out of every controversy of their time for fear of facing ridicule and persecution.

I commend the desire to stick with scripture and to more deeply identify the difference between America and the Kingdom of God. The danger is when Christians allow the culture to absorb our beliefs for the sake of being politically correct, and then ultimately bow to the will of the world. There is a clear cut distinction between lording oneself over another and not conforming to the pattern of this world. This wonderful and liberating paradox was most definitively modeled in Jesus. Jesus's unique ability to identify the pattern of this world in a revolutionary way came at a high cost.

The Most Constraining Religion

America is tearing itself apart from the inside out. People on the left are angry about American sins, and people on the right are advocating American redemption. There is little common ground left, as if the devil had come in to dig another series of trenches between a man and his neighbor.

The various matters of what divides us are based on spiritual matters, not just cultural and political matters. The latter are often dependent on the former, which begin as unseen, and then manifest visually. The spirit of a nation—what the nation worships—becomes what the nation looks like. Then the nation legislates according to the image it has fashioned based on its spiritual condition. All three of these things influence our opinions and worldviews, so our conversations shift between them. It is more than political opinions that are often expressed with great fervor at the dinner table. We cannot bridge the "political" chasm until we see clearly that one's political opinion is often a symptom of a much larger issue, how we have been taught to look at everything under the sun. For many, the year 2020 shed light on some of these differences. For others, the differences are more shrouded after that year. The question is, what really "triggers" us? Is it legislation? Is it a political candidate, or party? Or is it something more primary? The church should remember that political opinion is not always relative or unimportant. The politicization of everything is a result of spiritual conditioning.

It is often the Christian who is accused of "getting too political" when they criticize a political party or policy. But the various evils of "organized religion" can be consistently ridiculed without end. Are those who are drawn like a moth to the glow of Marxism really apolitical and irreligious? Or are they just as political and religious as the ones they accuse of politicizing "humanitarian issues" and believing in outdated religious fairytales? If we recognize the inescapable reality of the political spectrum and the fact that everyone follows some type of organized religion, even if it claims to be disorganized and irreligious, we can more clearly identify the even more constraining orthodoxy of the political and religious left.

Marxism is a religion of rebellion and self-justification by any means necessary. Communism, socialism, collectivism, and fascism take root in Marxist philosophy. Marxism is alluring, especially to those who feel victimized and oppressed by others. This amounts to just about everyone at one point or another. Who hasn't felt victimized by their boss? Karl

Marx founded his religion on greed, envy, pride, and hating thy neighbor for what he or she has. Marxism conceals itself to everyone because it takes root in what is unseen. Human beings are vulnerable to sin. Sin often manifests in one or more of these aforementioned ways—envy, pride, greed, rebellion. Karl Marx, the man, had radically anti-Christian values. He resented his parents and sulked in a victim mindset. His poetry spoke of devil worship. Some who knew him spoke of how he prayed to the devil. His goal was to be as a god walking among those on earth. He is long dead, but many still worship his philosophy as intellectually transcendent and corroborating "the bigger picture." His ideas still plague the world like a cancer. The unseen, religious nature of Marxist theory greatly benefits its political longevity.

People sometimes shrug it off when the dangers of Marxism are addressed in our culture today. But one who is able to see it for what it is, sees that it's manifesting everywhere around us, from our TVs to our city streets. It's even making its way into an elementary school classroom near you. The driving force of virtually every 20th century regime is alive and well in American culture, converting those who either do not understand it, deny its presence, or are impressed by its ideas. Marxism reproduces fear, envy, greed, and hate into the masses. It dumbs down the human senses of objective morality, the divine, and humanity, and instills sentiments of meaninglessness, randomness, hopelessness and helplessness. Marxism is the true constraint of the mind, the more fitting opiate of the masses.

Illegal Laws

When the coronavirus came out of China, it took the world by storm. It had all the symptoms of a new religion. All of the sudden scientists, doctors, and public health experts were running the world without accountability, demanding complete uniformity and solidarity concerning the virus. They authored the new doctrine of fear and isolation, and called anyone who deviated from their doctrine dangerous heretics at best, mass murderers at worst. It was no longer safe for the entire population of the US to leave home, go to church, go to work, run their businesses, give hugs, shake hands, or let anyone come inside their house. These new draconian laws and social expectations permeated the country for well over a year. Many saw nonconformists as dangerous. The virus, which unfairly targeted the elderly, became not only a danger to health, but to the most basic liberties of every man, woman, and child in the US. Liberties were put on hold.

This virus didn't only effect the lungs, but the minds and hearts of people. The media used the virus to give political and moral advantage to those in power. The threat of the virus became primary, freedoms and rights of the American people became secondary. Opinions about the virus became highly politicized. The far left thought the virus was an automatic death sentence. The far right thought it was a total conspiracy. The virus is very real and dangerous. But even more dangerous is how the story of its contagion became a vessel for state control and political uniformity. The left was eager to save the world one restriction and power grab at a time. They'd berate and shame anyone who disagreed.

Many churches were swept up in these waves. And those who expressed concerns within the church were often rebuked by others in the church. The virus caused somewhat of a schism, where some congregants left the churches that feared the virus too much and others left the churches that didn't fear it enough. The church that feared it more saw those who feared it less as reckless and selfish. The church that didn't fear it as much saw those who feared it more as uncaring about the threat to religious liberties. One side saw loving thy neighbor to be masking up and social distancing. The other saw loving thy neighbor as continuing to embrace one another despite government restrictions, despite a new illness that had been released upon the world.

This schism, which is hopefully temporary and futile, begs the question, is the radically countercultural lifestyle of the kingdom of God, power-under-the-government model of submission—as derived from Romans 13—the same as agreement with every edict put forth by our government? Or every popular theory or idea for that matter? What about when lower temporary laws contradict the higher national founding laws and new ideas contradict the teachings of scripture? The constitution and first amendment protect our right to gather and the right to freedom of speech and religion. Why should we stand by the "power under" the government mentality when the founding law designated the American government to be a power which is only to exist under the people? We are disobeying the highest laws of our nation when we go along with the creation of illegal laws. We are disobeying God when we bow to any idol, including the idol of mass-marketed fear.

Our national fabric was woven in such a way as to blanket us from the heavy hand of government. Many believe abandoning this notion will make things go better for us, often under the impression that our rights are only being temporarily borrowed by those who better understand the bigger picture. This is short term thinking. Tyranny, whether it happens all at once or comes in incremental stages, is foreign to American precepts. And it is the Christian who truly understands the bigger picture—it is hell that fuels tyranny and godlessness. Our religious duty to sound warnings is protected under the constitution when the depraved and corrupt are running the show. They've already stripped the right to live from innocent babies. The right to speak openly about the frequent blunders and shady motivations of the powerful is now in question, to the resounding applause of the masses. Complacency for the sake of convenience is not a picture of godly submission.

The beautiful Romans 13 principle shows us how to be representatives of Christ through a life of peace in relation to our society. "Everyone must submit himself to the governing authorities, for there is no authority except that which God has established. The authorities that exist have been established by God" (Romans 13:1). Believers also recognize Christ's enduring sovereignty over nations and governments. Christ calls for those who want to be great to become servants and slaves. Paul calls for servants to obey their masters and to labor as if they're working to please God Himself. Romans 13 extends these countercultural precepts to our governing forces. The church is to act in a certain way in relationship to nations and superpowers. Does this mean we are to conform to the pattern of this world? How could those who conform be distinguished from their persecutors? A servant is called to obey his earthly master. Does this mean the servant is to adhere to his master's worldview if it is atheistic, Marxist, relativistic, or nihilistic? What if it's driven by greed? Or paganism? Paul meant that the servant is to be an example of Christ's love to the world around him, including his master and his nation. If the earthly master is running out of money it would be unloving for his accountant not to tell him. If a nation is becoming morally bankrupt it would be unloving to pretend it isn't.

The progressive vision would see this argument as a bunch

of hogwash. It disagrees with the more "advanced" version of humanity and of modernized American values. That pesky constitution and the stubborn old bill of rights were written by a bunch of older, less evolved people. It therefore must be done away with. These documents of the republic should be disregarded if they go against the new social vision. It would be easier for Christians to go along with this vision, to trade the truth in Romans 13 for its willful misinterpretation.

Trade Off

On May 25 2020 the world watched in horror as George Floyd was killed by police. I heard about George Floyd and watched the video for myself. I could barely keep my eyes on the screen as I watched a man struggle to breathe and beg for his life. A police officer knelt on his neck for about ten minutes, eventually killing him. Throughout the following days, the world was turned upside down. Riots broke out across the country. A mild riot even broke out in my home town under the pretense of protesting police brutality and systemic racism. There were a couple cop cars flipped over, a few fights broke out, a crazed man with a bow and arrow showed up and started aiming it at the crowds before being beaten up and arrested. There was some property damage. Graffiti covered sidewalks and buildings everywhere.

I was disturbed, but was reminded by the mainstream media and social media that the uninterrupted rioting from coast to coast wasn't *actually* that important. The important thing was to rid ourselves of the evil institutions that permeate our nation and our culture. Those who understood the bigger picture had finally had enough. The violence was justified.

As I watched America's turmoil arise out of a painful

circumstance, I began to recognize that very real issues were being hijacked and manipulated to fit into a new national paradigm. These issues transformed a partisan narrative into incontrovertible gospel truth. The theories that had been long hidden within the inner circles of the academe emerged in order to hypnotize the public mind and turn people into soldiers for a new ideal. Many had turned their back to the tide. They were quickly swept up into a wave of intense passion.

Many cities came under attack by zealots. Hate and fear intensified. People became visibly angrier at the wrong word or phrase. Thoughts were being manipulated by every visual and audio platform, by celebrities and politicians, by peers and neighbors. The search for truth and voicing of alternative opinions became suspect. Many sought to abolish Christianity. Many sought to abolish America. Western Civilization was rotten. An innate trust of the media and popular opinion had finally succeeded in sedating the epicenter of the free world. The most sedated claimed that they were the only ones truly awake.

Christians were no longer on the side of good but on the side of evil. It was the secular, progressive worldview that truly desired justice and equality. Christians were greedy, envious, colonialist murderers. They always had been. Except for those who stood in line. They were temporarily tolerable. Republicans were evil racists. Democrats were the party for the people. Every action of republicans was unanimously condemned. No evidence of democratic corruption or hypocrisy could be found anywhere in the mainstream media. Democrats were capable of fixing all systems of oppression in a top-down fashion. Since God wasn't real anyway, they would be the ones to step in and take His place. The almighty state demanded worship. The church could either concede or secede.

What is the monster at our doorstep? Is it the descendent

of Karl Marx's destructive philosophy or is it something more ancient and sinister? God holds power over the heavens and the earth. He holds power over our lives. He could turn off our power and water. He could delete our bank account. He could close our local grocery store. God has control over nations. He allowed the pagan nation of Babylon to overcome Israel after Israel's ongoing pride and rebellion. But as soon as King Nebuchadnezzar gloated over the nation "he had established," God gave him the mind of a beast. God made him crawl on his hands and knees for seven years until he regained his sanity enough to give glory to God. Later, God overthrew Babylon in one night for desecrating His temple and gloating. The message is clear. Bad politics aren't to blame. Cultural Marxism isn't to blame. The complete destruction of the definitions and laws of God is to blame. Our blindness to God will be our downfall. God has been reading us loud and clear.

As I write this, the current climate has not been resolved. And whatever happens will happen by the power of God, not by the power of man acting alone. America could very well crumble from within or be destroyed from without. Can we really complain that we didn't deserve it? Is the solution to avoid this destruction socialism? Is it population control through more extreme abortive measures or eugenics? Is it book burning, uniformity of thought and speech, and cancel culture? Or is it repentance? These are the questions that split our national model.

Again, I am not advocating a theocracy. God values the freedom of choice. But His law is continually inverted and mocked by mankind. Meanwhile, we stand on our rooftops and gloat over the lives we've made for ourselves. Economic theory realizes there is nothing gained without a trade-off. We've gained an era of unprecedented prosperity and self-worship only by trading something else for it.

Looking Forward, Moving Backward

As Israel grew in power and prominence among the surrounding nations, it was always striving to advance. Its biggest struggle was idolatry. Its idolatry was usually practiced for purposes of further advancement. The people of Israel would sacrifice to the gods of other nations that they thought were responsible for things like fertility and wealth. God had to remind them through the prophets time after time that He was the reason Israel was in the high position it was in, not the gods of other nations.

At one point the people of Israel complained to the prophet Samuel that they wanted a king in order to be more like the other nations. God understood this complaint for what it was. His nation was forgetting Him again. Its people had a lofty vision for their nation and they were tired of being pushed around and bullied by their neighbors. Their idea of progression was to look forward to a more sensible form of rule. God's idea was to remind them continually of who He was and what He had done for them. God constantly reminded the people of Israel that He was the one who had delivered them out of bondage and established them as a nation. Yet they were quick to forget these things. Their tendency to constantly look forward ultimately ended with unrestrained worship of foreign and demonic idols, and total transgression of God's holy laws. This system of false worship led them to great evil and oppression, and ultimately to their downfall.

The Rise of Totalitarian Hypocrisy

2020 was either the year of no vision, or the year of clear vision, depending on which side of the ideological spectrum one is situated on. For many, the future has never been brighter. Many who have long held the vision of a socialist utopia have never been closer to manifesting their dream. Others see this unconstrained vision as a threat to the founding principles of our nation, remembering the failures of other nations who've reached for heaven on earth and created hell.

For the new-age revolutionaries, both America and Christianity are dangerous myths that must be torn down and rewritten in order to bring about true change. They have difficulty defining the type of change they'd like to see. Many are looking forward to freedom from the oppressive restrictions of the past. The past is only a hindrance to the new definition of rights and reality. If bringing about the new utopia means "temporarily" placing major restrictions on the population at large—mandatory mask mandates, mandatory lockdowns, blue states restricting family gatherings during Thanksgiving and Christmas, cancelling church and work and weddings and funerals, forcing children to stare at a bright blue light all day, and ruining countless small businesses—so be it.

In the events of 2020 (which are proving not to be restricted to that year alone), the greater good outgrew the lesser good. Those who question the edicts of the experts and the opinions of activists are indoctrinated by the old mentality. The virus and the social justice agenda were two branches of state control and uniformity of thought.

Tensions surrounding the origins, nature, and truthful reporting on the virus, as well as the national response to it increased. Many saw a threat to liberty emerging. We were told that in order to progress we must protect anyone even when it came at a great cost to everyone. The more progressive the state, the more up to date they were on the new moral doctrine surrounding the virus. Some even supported lockdowns for as long as there was more than one confirmed *case* of coronavirus in the state. For some, a less-than-one percent chance of losing one person's life outweighed the rights of millions. Others wore multiple masks on their faces whenever they went out in public. The massive blow to the economy following the lockdowns forced many into poorer circumstances. The lockdowns did nothing to slow or stop the virus. The lockdowns have ended for the most part, but the economy and job market have yet to fully recover. Politicians continue to threaten the public with future lockdowns. They have threatened job losses for tens of millions of unvaccinated Americans. They have threatened to legislate that American citizens must prove vaccination status in order to travel and participate in basic commerce. They strongly suggest we live out the rest of our lives in a faceless society. It is a sad irony that a nation that has long forgotten its spiritual identity is now encouraging its people to hide behind real masks.

The 2020 social vision was the culmination of decades of progressive thought conditioning in the form of political correctness, fear tactics, and media manipulation. The nation has had enough of freedom of speech, it has become too dangerous. When the founding fathers wrote the first amendment they did not take into consideration that some might have their feelings hurt as a result of this amendment. Certain speech became more violent than actual violence. "Micro-aggressions" were finally seen for what they are— nuclear bombs of words wreaking havoc on the postmodern psyche. It was up to the revolutionaries to stop harmful words and ideas. Anyone who stood in the way of thought policing became an enemy of the state, a thought terrorist. Meanwhile, criminals and anarchists were praised and pampered by the media and politicians. The radical left became the new puritans, able to heap burning coals on the heads of mild dissenters, without any fear of backlash. They could shout obscenities and spit in the faces of elderly republicans or smash cops over the heads with bricks and burn courthouses with 24/7 media cover up. Christians and conservatives were demonized as the ones responsible for the violence. They were part of a series of systemically rotten institutions. The truth had found its inverted form.

In the book of Ecclesiastes, the teacher tells us that "there is nothing new under the sun." In 2020 the only people who believe this seem to be Christians and conservatives. The insurrectionists in the streets of democrat run cities are the spitting image of something in our not so distant past—fascist black shirts and Nazi brown shirts. The neo-Marxist group Antifa (short for anti-fascist) is the new democratic paramilitary wing, the new vehicle for fascism. Their strategy is to convince everyone that their opposition is the enemy of the state—Christian capitalists who have maintained a system of oppression since America's founding. They seek to revolutionize the world for revolution's sake. They hide behind their counterpart, BLM Incorporated, hijacking isolated social injustices in order to create a cause which will convert the masses to radicalism. They want to make everyone believe that America, the free market, Christianity, conservatives and western society in general are hopelessly irredeemable. One Minnesota police officer had abused his power. Therefore, white-heteronormative-cisgender-Christian-capitalism needed to be abolished.

These fascists are not concerned in the least for actual issues such as black lives mattering. As one of their thought leaders of the last generation coined, "the issue is never the issue, *the real issue is the revolution.*" If the issue was indeed actually the issue, they would likely be focused on finding realistic ways to solve issues such as reducing poverty, quelling police brutality, and helping out people in lower income neighborhoods. Instead, they march through these neighborhoods under the guise of self-righteousness and equity. Their only true motivation is to get stoned, burn stuff, chant obscenities, rob people, and beat or intimidate those bold enough to stand in their way. The juvenile demand for the abolition of all law comes from those who engage in high levels of criminal activity. They only succeed in convincing people to increase the supply of law to meet the demand of lawlessness to which they contribute. Rioting all across American cities will negatively impact the livelihood of those cities for generations. History has shown minority populations to be disproportionately affected for generations by the various race riots that are so cherished by the left.

The pursuit of power by the political, intellectual, and corporate elite is gaining ground. If certain information is hidden, or simply made less readily available to the public eye, the public may be more readily manipulated. Those who burn churches and police precincts become heroes and icons. Those who understand the least about anything real or substantial, besides the nuances of the Marvel Cinematic Universe, are the new revolutionaries. Those who stood to gain the most political, cultural and financial power watched the tearing social fabric and prolonged coronavirus by-laws with eager expectation. They could almost touch the future of one party power.

It is often the richest and most powerful who claim to be the most victimized in our society. The beneficiaries of our "evil capitalist system" are its most fervent accusers in the West. Multi-millionaire, and indeed billionaire socialist politicians, celebrities, businessmen and athletes have joined the socialist ranks. They are paid handsomely and worshipped for understanding the bigger picture. Their lower-ranking comrades bully friends and family into converting to the puritanical left. Unlike Christianity, the religion of socialism can allow no freedom of choice in matters of conversion or apostasy.

Equality of Outcome, "Tolerance," and Social Justice for... Most

What kind of world do the revolutionaries and ideologues desire for you and yours in the not so distant future? It's hard to tell. Only the prophets of the far left know that. Many who are on the left do not agree entirely with what the left is becoming. They are hesitant to go along with every whim and are critical of where the left deviates from the truth. On the other hand, many on the left do not believe that America is pushing toward some form of communism. They're right, partly. America is not pushing toward communism, *in the same way as past forms of communism.* Newer forms of communism do not take the same exact image as past forms because they can't if they are going to work. Although there are similarities between newer and older forms, people can say that the newer form is not going to be communism. This requires a certain level of allegiance to whatever cause will bring about revolution, without knowing that the cause is only a ploy. Therefore, those who do not see a problem cannot see it because they have become part of the problem.

The far-left system permeates most of what we put before our eyes. It has an immense effect on the way we see the world. Even if moderates claim to reject Marxism, they may not be aware of or immune to its new American brand because it has taken on a new disguise. To those who see Marxism as a danger, it is very visible. To those who are committed to it in one way or another, it is harder to see.

In past communist regimes there were different tears of Marxists. The lowest level often formed the majority—the "dupes." The dupes are simultaneously the *most unaware of* the true nature of the revolution, the *most complacent in* the revolution, and therefore the *most necessary for* the revolution. They form the majority, but do not have a deep understanding of all the motivations, goals, and inner workings of the revolution. If the dupes can be swayed and used properly, the regime, or junta, or caretaker government can come to power. If they cannot be swayed, the regime will fail. The Marxists have to go back to phase one of planning their next takeover, which can take decades.

In this way, the demonic religion finds its way into the hearts and minds of those we hold most dear, tragically. The religion of darkness, fear, and victimization is enough to turn loved ones against one another. This is all too reminiscent of 20th century communist countries where family members would punish other family members for apostasy, whether it was by verbal punishment, shunning, physical assault or turning them over to the secret police. Marxism always begins with hazing, labelling, not taking other perspectives seriously and mild thought controlling. Then it moves to fighting, hatred, rioting, and cutting personal ties with those who disagree. Then it escalates to demonizing any outliers among all their peers. Violent action, whether verbal or physical, taken against those outliers becomes justifiable, and indeed righteous. Purging society of evil capitalists and non-conformists becomes a necessary measure to ensure that everyone can live the best, most fair life possible. If the outliers cannot conform, they must be silenced. Granted, we are only somewhere at the dawn of this new day.

It's hard to believe that such an articulate and observable case study for a total Marxist revolution happened in just a few short months directly in the epicenter of the free world. It's even harder to believe that most of the people living in that society *still* are totally unaware of its presence and complacent in its increasing volatility. There is one way to maintain control of the dupes, keep people hooked on the media like a drug and engaged with the fear-driven narrative at all costs. If necessary ignore the truth, invert it, and lie. Fudge the numbers. Rearrange the science. Don't count the ballots. The greater good will thank you in the end. There is too much at stake to allow for the presentation of counter perspectives. Such behavior is subversive.

Rising from the Ashes

Why do so many Christians willingly participate in Marxist philosophy? Why are those who point out the church's nonchalance in these matters told that they are being political idolaters? Which way should the church lean, right or left? Already across the country the church is becoming more and more divided along these issues. Many within the church are buying into the system of identity politics which degrades the value of individuals to the color of their skin or their sexual identity.

Identity politics is the new-age vessel for communism. It vitiates people of all races and religions by trading the inherent value given to them by God for their group dynamics, as appropriated and defined by the state, and pitting them against one another. Some within the church may be ignoring the dangers of Marxism to avoid controversy, or because they believe that the fight for social justice is the only force at play. The trouble comes when common-sense convictions on issues like racial injustice are overrun by a faulty theoretical infrastructure that associates human beings based on various group dynamics, echoing communist class division.

If this is the route we want to take as Christians we will likely be kept relatively safe from those who hate us for the time being. If we merge with the culture, we may be granted temporary asylum from the culture by the culture. This retreat might cost us less pain and hardship as we conform, stay quiet, and engage with the language of the far left. We may mitigate the risk of angering our friends and family. But what is the ultimate cost? When we look back on the year of the 2020 social vision with a less distorted, more historically accurate vision, where will we see ourselves as Christians?

Reverend Richard Wurmbrand, a Romanian pastor who faced well over a decade of tortures in Communist prisons, rebuked the Western Church harshly in his 1967 book *Tortured for Christ*:

> By [Western Church leaders'] complacency, by their neglect, and sometimes by acting as actual accomplices, some Western Church leaders... help the communists to intrude into western churches and to win the leadership in the churches in the world. They help Christians remain unaware of the dangers of communism.

Richard Wurmbrand was not an apologist for free-market capitalism or the republican cause. He never suggested that Christians combat Marxism and Communism with the same hatred they breed, but with unconditional love. Wurmbrand may be the most authoritative voice ever to emerge in matters of the Church versus Marxism. He faced unspeakable cruelty under the totalitarian rule of atheism and communism. But he saw that meeting hatred and evil with the love of Christ was the only way to save communists while overthrowing communism, so that it remains forever in the ash heap of history, right where it belongs.

A Side Note of 'Solidarity'

Just because someone holds a certain set of political ideals does not mean they are "dupes." I don't want to make people feel bad for supporting certain causes or stepping out and protesting for social issues. I commend those things. I have many conversations with people I love and respect who differ from me politically, and often times we can find common ground.

The political climate is such that two people with opposite beliefs can make the exact same arguments and place the same labels on their opposition. Sometimes both can be right. Other times both can be wrong. And still other times only one side can be right. The left is skeptical about the 2016 election. The right about the 2020 election. The left sees Donald Trump as a corrupt, compulsive liar. The right sees Joe Biden in the same light. The left sees the right as potential extremists or white supremacists. The right sees the left as eugenic supporters and socialists. The list could go on indefinitely. Both sides see tremendous problems, fissures that threaten the structure of American civil society. Both sides usually have enough common sense to admit shortcomings in their own political party, but will attribute the majority of the problems they perceive as emanating from the opposing party.

Something that is not often talked about in the news is that, despite the ongoing division that is hyped up in the media, people on both sides with common sense are largely becoming distrustful of the media in general, and therefore are more willing to listen to one another. Even if some issues like abortion, socialism, religion, capitalism, a certain politician, or racism can cause an unpleasant moment in conversation, just like a bad mood, that moment will pass more often than not. The untold story is that the mass advertised division is not always as intense as the political system and monopolies which bank off of the division would have us believe (sometimes it is). Two people can be miles apart ideologically, and still laugh off their differences over a cold beer. This doesn't undermine the massive split in the American psyche. Nor does it mean that some people on either side aren't in need of major correction. There are simply some people, places, and times around which it would do one well to avoid certain topics, and other people, places, and times around which no topic should be off limits.

People try to pull one another toward their own perspective. This is a primary human fact of life. Sometimes we use words. Other times we use mighty weapons of war. Sometimes obstacles seem far too enormous to overcome. Sometimes they are. Sometimes compromises can't be made. Other times they can. Sometimes repentance is possible, other times it isn't.

The post-coronavirus job market has taken a tremendous hit. Businesses have trouble finding enough employees to meet the demand of customers with the supply of services rendered. It is difficult to divorce this economic phenomenon from bad financial policy and too much government spending. To deny this link would be foolish. However, American government's only responsibility is to protect its people. Many relied on the government stimulus payments or temporary unemployment checks to make ends meet. Many even saw the little they received from the government to be an insult after facing job losses, the forced closure of businesses, and the subsequent loss of livelihood. The argument can be made that the government, in this circumstance, had the responsibility to temporarily engage in financially socialist behavior.

The plain reality is that there was a terrifying virus that no-one knew everything about, to which society had a knee-jerk reaction, for better or worse, and the government sought to do the little it could to soften the blow of lockdown policies. Obviously the efficacy, constitutionality, and ethics of lockdowns are a great topic of debate. But this issue, as well as the government stimulus response, do provide neutral economic ground for determining when the government has responsibility to compensate people during a time of economic uncertainty, which is a direct result of another uncertainty surrounding an infectious disease. In a time of great need, is a certain degree of emergency socialism permissible, at least temporarily?

Although my opinion tends to land around less government paternalism and allowing businesses and markets breathing room to recover, I can certainly understand aspects of why people answer yes to the above question. The economic debate surrounding the coronavirus is almost identical to the two ways of seeing the government's response during the great depression. Some see it as a positive economic policy in a time of great need. Others see it as a negative government interventionism that critically prolonged the depression. Although I believe the facts align more with the latter, this debate has been ongoing for eighty years. It's unlikely the 2020 economic paradox will be speedily solved either.

Differences, commonalities, nuances, and complications permeate each issue that contributes to the "widening national divide," whether it be economics, race, religion, politics, gender, the environment, abortion, or something else. In America, the reality of the political spectrum seems to hold across each of these issues, with the right finding themselves on one side, and the left on another. Generally, a lack of understanding the reason for the opposing position contributes to the stereotypes and generalizations that cause people to see one another in categorical terms rather than as people. Each of these issues contain truths and lies, problems that need to be solved and functions that must be left alone, platforms for commonalities and reasons for cutting personal ties, moments for laughter and moments for tears. There is a time for every season, and an attitude for every issue.

Clearly there are forces that want to divide the American people in order to more efficiently conquer them, as well as things we shouldn't compromise on. Determining what those are and aren't seem only to deepen the matters that divide us. The question is, can American society once again muster the resiliency and toughness for which it is known in order to overcome these forces? Or will these forces overcome us? One thing is certain, the dreary monotony of a world where everyone shares the same monolithic perspective on everything seems dull and uninviting. This is a world where free will is abandoned. This is not God's world.

Chapter 3

Babel in America

The New Builders of the New World

It might seem counterintuitive to write about Babel and America as if they were similar, or even synonymous, in a book that is trying to make a partial case for America's Christianity. The wealth, power, and influence of ancient Babylon are often recognized as symbols of new nations that similarly rise in wealth, power and influence. America may be the wealthiest, most powerful, and most influential nation ever to exist. Like every person, and every nation, Babylon had a spiritual component to accompany its earthly presence. There are obvious similarities between Babel and America on both of these fronts. The left leaning church, to the degree they believe Babel was an actual historical event, would probably agree with me there. However, we would see these similarities through different lenses, with different causes and effects. The story of Babylon, and Babel before it, is a story of mankind's incredible ambition, an ambition which proves humanity can create just about anything, and an ambition which is often in direct conflict with God's attributes in both nature and history.

The notion that Christians should pump the breaks on influencing culture and politics predominates the American sentiment. It is thought that many Christians would use coercion to force people to believe. Some see the Christian politician as a polluted vessel, endangering the social longevity of the state. It's hard to deny that there is some truth in this sentiment. Wouldn't forcing a religious agenda on people be immoral, even ungodly?

Kingdoms and powers have never ceased exercising power over peoples and nations, including their own. America is not exempt. Yet where does the desire to rule over the hearts, minds, and bodies of others come from? Where does tyranny, greed, lust for power, and corruption take root? Is it mostly in Christian influence, or does it come from somewhere else?

The premise of denying our foundation rests on two assumptions, one true and the other false. The first, true assumption is that the kingdom of the world reproduces a power-over-others system because of the seven deadly sins. The second, false assumption is that, in America, Christians who enter the political sphere are largely to blame presently for the power-over-others elements of our society. This is one of the most fundamental building blocks of modern ideology—the tyranny of church over state. But the supply of this Christian tyranny is low in proportion to the left's outcry against it.

Secular or Christian policy can only come to be through the democratic process. If an outspoken Christian wants to become president, he or she may. If they want Christianity to constitute the majority of their platform, they may. They will only succeed if the democratic process allows them to, then they can influence policy from there, which requires further checks and balances. But some have come to believe that they live under a vague threat of a totalitarian Christian theocracy. They see any shift away from the progressive paradigm as a symptom of this advancing theocracy. But the freshest historical case studies show the exact opposite shift. So do the most ancient stories we know.

Let's take another quick look at Genesis for a reference point:

> "Now the serpent was more crafty than any of the wild animals the Lord God had made. He said to the woman, 'Did God really say, 'You must not eat from any tree in the garden'?' The woman said to the serpent, 'We may eat fruit from the trees in the garden, but God did say, 'You must not eat fruit from the tree that is in the middle of the garden, and you must not touch it, or you will die'.' 'You will not surely die,' the serpent said to the woman. 'For God knows that when you eat of it your eyes will be opened, and you will be like God, knowing good and evil.' When the woman saw that the fruit of the tree was good for food and pleasing to the eye, and also desirable for gaining wisdom, she took some and ate it. She also gave some to her husband, who was with her, and he ate it." (Genesis 3:1-6).

This encounter initiated the tyranny of sin, the vessel for all "power over" systems of thought and rule. It was after Adam and Eve fell that they felt shame and realized their nakedness. They were cursed to experience the toil of the earth and the pain of childbirth, along with all proceeding generations. Their child, Cain showed a sinful power over his Brother Abel's life by killing him out of envy. The road of history has been paved with similar bloody stories. Generations later, the world became so evil that God sent a flood to destroy every living thing. Fast forward a number of generations after that, and we still have the mindset of Genesis 3:1-6 alive and well in a place called Babel. Here is the text once more:

> "Then they said, 'Come, let us build ourselves a city, with a tower that reaches to the heavens, so that we may make a name for ourselves and not be scattered over the face of the whole earth.' But the Lord came down to see the city and the tower that the men were building. The Lord said, 'If as one people speaking the same language they have begun to do this, then nothing they plan to do will be impossible for them. Come, let us go down and confuse their language so they will not understand each other.' So the Lord scattered them from there over all the earth, and they stopped building the city. That is why it was called Babel—because there the Lord confused the language of the whole world. From there the Lord scattered them over the face of the whole earth" (Genesis 11: 4-9).

The construction of the great tower began with the words, "Come, let us build ourselves a city." The serpent's temptation of Eve began with words of doubt. This doubt became sin, which became death. The generations that succeeded after the fall experienced the repetitive effects of doubt, sin, and death. Adam and Eve fell because of the words spoken to them. Doubt, sin, and death began with words of deception and the ambition of the tongue. There is no man or woman who can escape from the reality of sin, and the Babylonian construct was built from this condition. It is clear that our words build our ways, and our ways build our worldviews.

God's Word was His manifestation to the world. He created the world and showed the way for the world. All of existence came from His Word. But because we are subject to sin and separation from God, every person sees the world He created through a distorted lens, where the light of day must curve around our own darkened understanding and the blind ambitions of our flesh. No man or woman is always able to see the power over us that God's Word has, apart from God, or that history only happens with God's permission. We desire to demonstrate our own power over our boundaries, over others, over the elements, and over definition. This begins with our ideas and spreads like a plague because of our words—our words then set us on our paths out into the world. We build the world from there. The corruption that is mirrored between societies, individuals and generations is bound to grow always within the kingdoms of the world, as long as the kingdoms of the world are founded on fallible human words which are prone to confusion and language barriers. America is just another system caught in the trap of Babel.

The motivation for Babel was simple, humanity sought to build without a blueprint of limitation. They acknowledged their own god-like-ness. They sought to cultivate a religion of idol-worship and to stand on equal ground with the God who created them and designed their limitations. Babel was unique in that it was the first society to implement unchecked ambition as the new law, and to build a city that was to be their savior. This all started with words. They thought that these words would lead them to a better world, a world of power and fame by creating a way into heaven, but their unimpeded vision doomed them to mass confusion. Their path was scattered to the far reaches of the earth, where they still are today, trying to rebuild that first tower.

The quest for power and unchecked ambition is quite simple in its origin, mankind fell and is trying to pick itself back up—all on its own. Virtually everything we see in civilization is a result of mankind picking up the pieces of a broken past. So many of our achievements, sadly, are built and achieved out of our brokenness. America is not exempt from this condition. But America does differ from other nations that were built out of a pure desire for power over self, others, and God's definitions. America initially acknowledged human fallibility during its construction. Past failure was at the forefront of its mind. America was founded not on unchecked ambition, but on *checked* ambition. This is why America was intended to be precisely the opposite of a nation which governed by exercising power over its people. In order to truly live and be a godly nation, America had to recognize its own limitations and its own mortal condition. This recognition granted temporary wisdom and success. It is the humble recognition of the tragic human condition that allowed America to grow into the world's largest military and economic superpower, and its people into the most prosperous on the planet. But our worldly wisdom and success, both standing as inherently neutral powers, soon became being wise in our own eyes and the love of money and self, which are contributors to the tragic human condition.

America is just as much a reflection of a godless tower as it is a godly picture of perfect submission. The Babylonian condition in America is not all due to its evil beginning, but due to the outworking of our value of individual freedom—a freedom for all people who still suffer from the initial human condition as prisoners of sin, but are often unable to recognize the reality of sin. In other words, instead of exercising unchecked power over the people, America gave the people the opportunity to live freely (which can mean different things) and exercise unchecked power over themselves and others. This would inevitably devolve into the same systems of other nations unless *the people* recognized that they exist only as one nation or *power under God Himself.* These were the terms and conditions for America's spiritual longevity. God's sovereignty over our nation has been widely abandoned as a realistic precept. I wonder what God thinks when He sees a nation that struck hands in pledge with Him renege on its promises. Actually, that's what most of the Bible is about.

America was only another product of a world of failure. America recognized the world's failure in hope that it may find a different path that circumnavigated that failure. But America was doomed to become confused and beguiled along that path. The path to true greatness is always muddied with illusion. America desired freedom for her people and also law for her people. She soon found that people in general had difficulty understanding the complex relationship between those two things. She was bound to become either a harlot or a hypocrite. Or both.

Can we really be surprised that America lost her way? Doesn't everyone? Is there any point in trying to pick up the pieces of our past so we can move into a brighter future? Or should America allow the very people she gave power over her to destroy her? Every man, woman, and child born in the United States still has the freedom to choose the path we set her on. We can choose inebriating fruit and a massive tower, or we can choose to humble ourselves and ask God's forgiveness. The more we choose as citizens to obey our own law and exercise unchecked selfish ambition, the more we will add to the tower brick by brick—this time without straw. The result is nothing we can comprehend or stop on our own, any more than we can stop our own mortal condition or comprehend the will of God.

Say 'Uncle'

The Babylonian parallel to America is striking. America has led the world in "tower building" in many different areas. She led the world in a new form of government, military power, and technological advancement, among other things. When the world steps out of line, America's there to keep the world in check, to the distaste of many. Sometimes it does become confusing in the minds of Christians as to whether they're worshipping God or the tower of America. But the more one studies the Bible, the more one understands that they are a subject of the Kingdom first and foremost, and then a subject of the kingdom. God intends His people to respect their government and follow their laws, for the laws are generally put in place to maintain order. This is why the early Christians fought their oppressors through love, not hate.

Romans 13 tells us that the governments of the world are put in place by God, and so following their law is worship to God. However, Christians ought to think hard about what laws they are to follow in America, and whether it is more important to follow the laws of a nation or the laws of God. When the laws of the nation contradict the law of God or the law of God calls one out into the world to preach regardless of laws of suppression, it is our responsibility to follow God's law, not the world's law, as modelled in the Books of Daniel and Acts, among others. In fact, this was the way America was designed. These precepts went into the first and second amendments. America has travelled far from its original designation. The first primary laws were in the constitution

and the Declaration of Independence, and the first amendment
to the law was specified to protect everyone's freedom of speech
and practice of religion. These primary laws compel us to be
wary of any government or group that threatens these rights,
and recognizes that the people also have a say in what becomes
law and who gets to govern. Indeed it appears the laws of our
nation were formed to *reflect* God's law for the benefit of the
people regardless of their religion. They were formed at once
to appease Romans 13 and the rights of the people to follow
God even when the crowds want to cast stones at them for it.

One could say we find ourselves in a precarious position.
Our system of government is held in place by a delicate
balance, and it is always under threat of tyranny—whether
that be tyranny of one party, tyranny of one religion, tyranny
of one person, tyranny of the masses over the minority, or
tyranny of the minority over the masses. Americans are always
supposed to be aware of this threat, and to step up in speech,
into protest, into government or even to take up arms if and
when the system of checks and balances is about to be cast
aside because the great tower simply must be built. It is when
we turn a blind eye to the collapse of this delicate system in
the name of a misinterpretation of Romans 13—which lets
the Christian off easy for remaining silent—that we actually
disobey Romans 13 as it pertains to the primary laws of
America. The founding fathers designed the law to put us in
a headlock when we started down a counterintuitive path. To
obey Romans 13 does not necessarily mean to obey every edict
issued by the government, if it violates the higher laws of our
nation, or the even higher law of our God. Did Daniel and his
contemporary prophets follow the edicts of the government
when those edicts ran contrary to God's standard? What did
Peter and Paul do when the religious authorities told them to
stop publicly talking about Jesus?

One may say that America was founded to recreate the tower of Babel; one may say that although it wasn't founded to recreate it, it was destined to simply because of human nature; or one may say that it was founded with the very purpose of heeding the warnings of Babel and Jerusalem and to avoid their fate for as long as it could. Whether it ended up heeding the warnings or not is up for debate. To the degree that it did, America stands out among the world pattern. To the degree that it did not, America is just another part of it.

Our founding was intended to reveal the natural capacity to tyrannize and overstep our bounds throughout the generations, and to provide a way for us to correct ourselves if and when that happened.

The more we move toward Babel, the farther we move from our nation's original intent. It might be hard as a Christian to think realistically about American failure, and to come to the conclusion that God is "on our side." Common sense tells us to remember her past and the past of other nations so that we do not presently repeat our mistakes, or theirs. There is another vision that tells us simply to erase that past and move forward as though it never happened. As we do this, we will "evolve" into the higher versions of ourselves. At least that is what the laws of nature and the philosophy of survival of the fittest tell us. We can be sure that this vision, while appearing new and different, is nothing new and different. It is as ancient as America and Babel, and as formidable as the devil himself. This is the attitude of unrestrained progress for progress' sake. The modern Babylonian equivalent can be found flickering in our faces every day.

Tech Gods

Imagine having the ability to share your thoughts with everyone you know instantaneously. As quickly as you think of something it can be published for the world to see. Imagine taking ten minutes out of your day to find out what the people in your life are doing without having to go through the tedious burden of actually talking to them. Imagine conversing with friends and having the movie *The Matrix* come up in conversation or the lead singer of the band, Pink Floyd: they are arguing about what year it is made or who the lead singer was, but you have the power of easy access to unlimited knowledge and are able to tell them both things in a matter of seconds. They are not that impressed however, because access to knowledge is now universal to the human race and doesn't prove much of anything. If you didn't live in the 21st century you may be wondering how any of this would be possible. However, the world we live in has grown technologically so much that tech is forever embedded in most of the things we do. One may say that such power would be a good thing, for it would help us to break past our God-designed boundaries and into unlimited thought and potential. Others recognize an increasing and unstoppable threat to our humanity and a darker aspect to the emergence of the light bearing gods of big tech.

Easy access to information doesn't necessarily mean automatic wisdom. Remember, there are two spheres of knowledge, one good and one bad; the fear of the Lord which is the beginning of understanding, and the knowledge of good and evil which is the vessel for sin. The internet is an amazing tool, so is social media—but they can quickly metamorphose from a tool or a blessing into an addiction and a curse. I have access 24 hours a day to the best movies and the best ideas the world can offer. I also have access to the worst the world has to offer. This is because the internet has the ability to reflect global reality so convincingly that humanity becomes tricked into believing it is real. People can become so addicted to all things tech that their human interactions suffer because they don't feel as real, important, or exciting as the on-screen versions. In many ways "tools" such as social media actually induce effects similar to drugs and alcohol by raising dopamine levels, manipulating emotions, and manufacturing a false sense of validation. When reality hits, it can often be too hard to bear, as rising suicide rates since the invention of social media have shown.

The power of big tech did not begin ten to twenty years ago with social media. It made its way into our living rooms long before that. At first, the television appeared to be a helpful tool for families to get things like the news and to be aware of what was going on in the world, as well as the occasional TV dinner. It soon became more helpful for adapting families to the whims of world culture, specifically whatever entities or agencies were controlling the attention of people's eyes and ears. The television quickly became a false idol, so to speak, a parallel reality that convinced the viewer of its preeminence and omniscience. Families' value systems and morality were like clay for television producers to reform and degrade, molding our minds into complacent products of the culture. Why did we allow this to happen? It was out of our desire for continued knowledge and easy access to entertainment, or unearned pleasure. Instead of playing outside, families gathered around their television sets with buckets of popcorn and watched people live out the adventures and stories they never could. This was much more exciting than any yard game the family could play. This was the new American adventure—one that could be bought and participated in for a low monthly rate!

It is easy to believe that we must be at the pinnacle of technology, perhaps my father thought that when he laughed at *All in the Family* long before I was born. However, technology will not stop advancing in the name of knowledge of good and evil as long as humans have the knowledge of good and evil as they continue to create and innovate technology. Movies and videogames are becoming more realistic and entertaining, more overtly violent and hyper-sexualized. Television is growing increasingly efficient in shaping people's opinions. The news infiltrates every aspect of our culture regardless of its accuracy or truthfulness. Social media becomes a bridge between worlds, which is convenient for an army of trolls to live beneath, ready to devour anyone who dare try to cross the bridge. People can say anything they want to anyone without fear of consequence or backlash, they simply have to turn off their notification bar. These entities are no longer in it to win it for themselves only, but they have joined forces with one another to coerce humanity's return to their basest instincts of lust, fear, anger, malice, slander, hatred, greed, and envy. They do this efficiently by convincing people that they actually exist to promote the opposite, like loving your neighbor.

We may no longer have to pick up our phones and ask when *The Matrix* was made, because we already feel as though we are living in it. The machines are waging war with humanity and trying to bring us to our knees. I do not pretend to know exactly how much influence either God or His enemy have over the things that we put in front of our eyes all day every day. But I'd venture to guess a lot, and God would probably only be involved if we are using technology as a tool to glorify Him. Since that is pretty rare, Satan likely has a lot of skin in the game. He is described as the ruler of this world, the father of lies, and the prince of the power of the air. Tech is emerging as a great "unifier" over all the nations in this world, big tech misinformation is a popular concern, and the various goals of technology move instantaneously through the airwaves unseen through algorithms and data codes. Indeed the presence and implications of tech are a great phenomenological mystery of our age, one that will likely baffle humanity increasingly as it grows in power, efficacy, accessibility, and influence. Our only hope to reduce its influence over us is to assume our own agency and responsibility in reducing its influence over us. Otherwise we will voluntarily become its victims, even as we complain that it is victimizing us. Next thing we know we are no longer living our own lives, but the lives of avatars in a videogame, others on our social media feed, or handsome actors or actresses in a movie or television series. The unpopular truth is that God's plan for our lives is much more real and exciting than any videogame, movie, or social media feed.

America is leading the charge in big tech, and big tech is undeniably similar to Babel. Don't get me wrong, I love the fact that I can pick up my phone right now and call a friend or comment on someone's post with a smiley face or unicorn emoji. I like that I can go on the internet and watch funny cat videos. America made all that possible. American inventors created the first TV, telephone, video game console, computer, and social media platform—as well as the airplane. America's freedom allowed inventors to create some of the most useful things known to mankind. Unfortunately in many cases they become weapons of self-destruction and defamation of others in the hands of those with the knowledge of good and evil. Of course, I don't blame this on the inventors, or even the consumers, but on the same Babylonian desire for humanity to skyrocket forward past its boundaries, without ever pausing to consider its true aim or why those boundaries were put there in the first place.

My point is this; in the age of unlimited information and capabilities one would think that we would finally have enhanced our humanity and entered the age of unlimited reason and heightened compassion. The opposite has happened. I'd argue that in many ways humanity has become more numb, desensitized, bitter, confused, strange, and willing to believe wholeheartedly in whatever meme or headline glimmers at any given moment. In our quest for ultimate reason once again we have sought to become as gods while leaving God behind and telling Him we'll see Him at the finish line. Fortunately (perhaps unfortunately for us) God is *actually* much more omnipotent, omniscient and omnipresent than we are, even if we get the new iPhone. He has the power to use the tech tower we are building for our own knowledge or as a weapon of confusion in order to humble us and scatter us throughout the earth, or throughout the airwaves.

Maybe in all this confusion we can finally recognize that God created us for relationship with Him and others, not with our phones. Instead of finding our validation through Instagram likes, we can find our value in Christ alone. Anything outside of this is just another clay brick in the Babylonian wall.

The Alternative Reality of Modern Technology

As I've mentioned in the previous section, tech is now imbedded in most things we do. Twenty years ago cell phones were optional and were just starting to break away from being a luxury to become a universal commodity. I remember growing up and loving videogames. I watched them develop rapidly from the unrealistic 1990s videogames like *Mario* to the hi-definition, ultra-violent videogames like *Call of Duty* and *Grand Theft Auto*. I also remember watching violent films as a young kid. My first rated *R* film was *The Matrix*, which I was told by a third grade classmate was really good. Some friends and I watched it in secret during a sleep over. Since then I've watched and participated in multitudes of simulated deaths in films and videogames. But haven't we all?

Simulated violence is just a fact of life. Lots of people die in movies. We almost don't bat an eye at it. And videogames like the ones mentioned above can simulate massive killing sprees, where one can kill hundreds and hundreds of people, and then experience the simulated rush of escaping the law afterwards. I hesitate to draw a parallel between simulated violence and actual violence in most cases. Some killers may have been influenced by these videogames, and others may not have. But I'd venture to guess that there must be some impact on our psyche from consuming nonstop violence. In fact, when we are engrossed in these story lines for half our waking life, it's hard not to suggest that we are coming close to constructing an alternative reality, one where violence is an everyday fact of life. Does this quell enmity, hatred and strife in society, or breed more of it?

A growing concern is the rise of technology and its overwhelming influence on humanity. Some speculate that technological algorithms could morph into something that resembles artificial intelligence. This AI, some say, will thrive and grow by understanding humanity, in some cases even better than humanity understands itself. This could lead to some form of technological dominion over humanity, or some form of humanity ruling over itself via technology. Of course, the story of human history is the story of humanity learning new forms of innovation and technology and often using them to conquer lands and rule over people.

Today, however, our minds are being won over by our own lack of self-control. People's noses are buried deep in their phones, either on their social media feeds, checking the news, playing some sort of online game, watching movies, looking at pornography or texting others. This has largely changed the primary dynamics of human relationships. People are in general much more isolated than before.

Social Media platforms such as *Facebook* and *Instagram* were monumental technological achievements. From their conception they had a dual nature, one positive and one negative. They were built to keep people connected and in community. They were also created to circulate within exclusive communities, such as certain Ivy League colleges. They eventually became available to everyone, but just because their availability became more widespread didn't mean they shed all the negative aspects of their exclusivity. People are still allowed to filter through friends and acquaintances in a disturbing way. Think about it next time you scroll through your recommended friends list on social media. You are seeing pictures of people you know and judging whether or not they are worthy of holding the status of your "friend." You are making a split second decision that judges the entire character of another person that is triggered by a photograph and name, themselves generated by an algorithm. The strangest part is that it's not all your fault. This judgement system is designed into the dual nature of social media platforms.

Many within the technological elite have blown the whistle on problems like these and claim that these breeding grounds for envy, exclusivity, flattery, misinformation and rivalry are a big reason why we're seeing so much turmoil in society, such as rising suicide rates, depression, drug overdoses, and various other problems of despair. The plain and simple fact is that social media is addictive because it is an incredible tool. For example, I can pick up my phone and make a movie and share it immediately to an audience of hundreds of people if I desire. I then can have immediate feedback either on a film, a selfie, a status update, or a controversial opinion that I decide to post. I have a small army of "followers" who I can influence in certain ways, regardless of what my motivations may be. On top of all of this, I have a growing wealth of content lower down in my social media feed that I've invested time and resources into. As I add more and more content, I grow increasingly attached to it. In effect, my social media presence becomes a huge part of who I am in my own eyes and in the eyes of others. People don't want to judge themselves or others based on social media presence alone, but this seems to happen automatically on one level or another.

Are human beings "syncing" with technology? It's hard to imagine a more confusing, terrifying and fascinating phenomenon than this simultaneous dystopian and utopian rise of the new technological age. Have these incredible tools liberated us from our bounds or confined us from our liberty? Only time will tell how these questions will be answered. The technology itself is becoming increasingly efficient at reading human emotions and understanding the various binary human belief systems. It is also becoming increasingly self-aware. One fact remains—even prior to the possible advent of *Meta, Neuralink,* and *Open AI*—these technologies are only able to be wielded by us. They are built from copious amounts of two very different types of knowledge.

Superhero Culture

Anyone who studies the Bible knows that there are many false gods or idols, and many principalities and powers that rule over the kingdoms of this world. Even if you were born yesterday in America you'd realize that most people don't believe this is a reality. But it is. The enemy, Satan appoints cosmic mayors over certain areas to make sure people continue suffering, dying, and hating one another. The Bible affirms that there are various spiritual powers, dominions, and principalities that are influencing the world pattern. Our motivations, from the micro of the individual to the macro of national powers, are something more than neurons firing and the pragmatism behind international relations. The secular world has grown too sensible to believe in such nonsense, which makes it a perfect target for these influencers. Nowadays people believe in things that are much more foolish, but with strikingly similar themes as the fallen angels they deny exist.

Superheroes are one of the biggest parts of our culture, and they were from their comic-book conception. They are so loved because of their themes of progressing past human boundaries. They are universally loved not because they are alien to human nature, but because they are familiar to human nature—the desire to be as gods walking on the earth. Many superhero origins actually are rooted in the ancient mythologies of Greek, Roman, and Norse gods.

Some children, or parents for that matter, may be unaware that the content of many superhero movies blatantly inverts the biblical paradigm. Is it fair to ask what sort of effect this may have on the psychological and even spiritual development of young children? Here are some superhero films along with their themes.

Endgame: The Avengers are quite the force to be reckoned with. They are a host of men and women with great powers. Together they are unstoppable. They may even be able to defeat their arch nemesis, Thanos, an evil, maniacal alien who is also "the most powerful being in the universe." Thanos' mission is to collect "infinity stones" (powerful singularities scattered throughout the universe) in order to snap his fingers once and wipe out half of the universe's population. Each infinity stone increases his all-pervasive power. Thanos holds disdain for the universe's ungrateful attitude toward him: "I know what I must do. I will shred this universe down to its last atom and then, with the stones you've collected for me, create a new one teeming with life that knows not what it has lost but only what it has been given. A grateful universe." (*Marvel's Endgame:* 2019). Thanos has minions who are dressed like priests and are joined with him in his campaign to annihilate half of life. As they go about their work they tell their victims that what they've faced is actually "salvation" and that "even in death they have become children of Thanos."

In Sunday school we were taught that God is coming back to judge the world. To make a long story short, it isn't going to be a fun time for everyone. The Bible tells us that people will be hiding in mountains, begging the rocks to fall on them because of the fear that the Lord instills in them. Imagine the author of your reality pulling back reality like a screen and suddenly revealing Himself to a world that has forgotten He exists.

Because the above film speaks so much to human nature, it was the highest grossing film of all time. It is amazingly entertaining and well done, and the characters are likeable and fun, so it appeals largely to children. What might happen when Children are introduced later in life to the idea of a sovereign God? Will they think of Him like a superhero villain? More and more people I talk to see God as a cosmic tyrant who just wants to send people to hell, rather than a just judge who sent His only Son into the world to redeem humanity.

The "Endgame," was the Avengers' fourth film. The first three also deal with inverted biblical themes. In the first,

Thanos sends an army of aliens from the sky to reign terror over New York City. In the second film, the villain Ultron, quotes the Bible multiple times saying "On this rock I will build my church." Ultron's mission is to eliminate humanity by sending a meteor onto the earth and to create a perfect race of robots who are connected to his artificial intelligence system, his will.

Each of these villains contain powers which mimic God's all-knowing, all-powerful nature. The demonic themes come full circle, putting the audience in the judgement seat over God, a foolish place to be.

Guarding the galaxy against God: Peter Quill is one of my favorite superhero characters. He's hilarious, and he embodies the unfathomable power in the everyday dude. He is the leader of a group called "The Guardians of the Galaxy," whose characters have a humor level that is through the roof, and a combined IQ of eighty one. Each of them has a criminal past, and together they are entrusted with the protection of the known universe. In their first film, they are battling another maniacal quasi-religious zealot named Ronin. Ronin, like Thanos is bent on enacting his justice on hard working everyday people like you and me. He can only be stopped by a band of marauders, who at the end of the movie transfer Ronin's absolute power to themselves in order to destroy him and assume a more just power over the universe.

The second *Guardians* film is possibly even more blatant in its biblical inversion. In *Volume Two* Peter Quill (Starlord) is finally introduced to his long lost father. His dad isn't quite human either. He's actually another "most powerful being in the universe," and his name is Ego. Ego is so powerful that he actually created his own planet. At first he seems good, until he becomes maniacal and his true nature is revealed to the Guardians. This sounds an awful lot like the way the world views God—God is pretty cool until He gets all "judgmental and mean." Ego eventually presents Starlord with an ultimatum: follow him and learn his way—how to use "the light"—or remain weak and fallen with his friends. Of course Starlord chooses to remain in his humanity with his friends rather than join forces with his all-powerful father. Again, the Guardians join forces to overthrow another cosmic tyrant.

Analysis

Superhero movies are a reproduction of ancient storytelling and cultural art forms. This may not have been their intent, but nevertheless, they fit the pattern of new mythologies told through advanced technological storytelling methods. The simple question is, could they contribute to anti-Christian indoctrination? If the answer is yes to some degree, what does that mean for the relationship between the massive popularity of these stories and our cultural attitude as a whole? Is there a correlation between films like these, the privatization of culture and the marginalization of Christians?

These films show that people can't escape the reality of God even when they want to pull Him out of everything. Even when stories are told from a "neutral" secular perspective, they are only stories that already existed within the human heart, reproducing the themes of perpetual transgression. For this reason, new age mythologies are related to ancient mythologies. The new age mythologies incorporate aspects of our own culture such as technology, advanced science and social issues to persuade and entertain.

When I was a kid I was much more familiar with *Peter Pan* and *The Lion King* than the prophecies of Isaiah and the Ten Commandments. I even remember sitting in my room as a child after watching the first *Harry Potter* film and trying to cast spells over and over again with a makeshift magic wand, half expecting lightning to emerge from the end of it. There was clearly something deeper operating behind the moving images. Powerful spiritual themes and forces operating behind images that our hands have made fit the biblical definition of an idol. But new age idols are not like the old ones, so calling them "idols" is controversial. In a secularized culture, idols and idolatry is a void concept. But what may lie just behind the things a godless culture reproduces on an industrial scale? Moreover, what effects do they have on our development when they bombard our sensorium from every direction—television, computers, t-shirts and cell phones? Comparing and contrasting certain stories with Genesis 3 is the only way to analyze the relationship between those stories and original sin.

Shows like Disney's *Owl House* (A children's television show about life in hell) and *Despicable Me* (A children's film about glorifying antiheroes) have an intellectual effect even if the children cannot comprehend or articulate the material their minds are absorbing. Hell becomes a place we want to go and the villain becomes the hero. Is it a stretch to imagine that what was once absurd, like teaching children to desire hell and that God is evil, may become commonplace in the next generation? Meanwhile, the Bible is increasingly scoffed at. Children are "protected" from it by their parents. It is becoming offensive to familiarize children with biblical principles and normal to teach people the quantum mechanics behind Thor's hammer.

What happens when a child who has come to think of God as Thanos is introduced to the Gospel later on in life? How much of today's rejection among younger generations is a direct result of things they've learned through the most revolutionary and advanced storytelling methods the world has ever seen? What about the last generation?

Teaching kids that they get to be gods one day and that they may put themselves in the moral judgement seat over God are the two premises in Genesis 3. The truth is that we are not God's judges. We are subject to Him. In fact, thinking of ourselves as gods leads to our destruction. We are incapable of saving ourselves from ourselves. That we can be our own saviors is an eternal lie that is based on the primitive desire for self-divinity. This is still taught to humans by our sinful nature and outside influences in unseen and unquantifiable ways.

New age notions like the law of attraction teach that we can will our own reality and desires into existence. These notions are superhuman and correspond with superhero culture. Some practitioners of the law of attraction have testified to their lives being damaged by thinking of themselves as their own gods. This spiritual pride leads many to a spiritual illness and a moral numbness. Many have been led to depression and even nihilism by following the law of attraction and other new age practices. Ironically, the law of attraction leads people to think of themselves as their own gods in a worldview of methodological materialism, where they are simultaneously nothing more than the most evolved form of bacteria crawling around on a meaningless rock in space.

Every single person purchases a lifetime subscription to sin at some point. This notion is simple, but inescapable. Solomon, Jesus and other prophets saw the ancient shapes and patterns in the popular sentiments of the times as emergent from this lifetime subscription. These shapes and patterns were formed out of the human condition, more specifically the human disposition before God. They were never brand new even if they were "coming soon to a theater near you." The endless reproduction of art forms, governments, education systems, and cultural ideals has some level of futility in the eyes of God and His prophets because they so often signify nothing more than our chains. To us, they signify autonomy and power. Those who see the futility of this pattern are in effect challenging the way the world has come to view all of existence. Such a challenge in effect becomes villainous.

In *Dr. Strange*, the villain is a gigantic cosmic being who wants to bring the earth under his dominion; he also has "zealots" who blindly carry out his will on the earth. The zealots are dressed like priests, with dark eyes, and a unifying objective to aid their master in bringing more worlds under his control. They live in full submission to his will. Elsewhere, Dr. Strange says it is his own job to "protect reality." If we apply this precept to how theology relates to real life, it would suggest that there are certain people who live in one reality and certain people who live in another reality altogether. What is this proposed divergence of reality and what is the dividing line? Is it smart versus dumb, conservative versus progressive, naturalists versus super naturalists, or believers versus unbelievers? Dr. Strange's position is very clearly to protect one good worldview from another evil one. The storyline parallels mostly point to the triumph of new-age spirituality over Judeo-Christian monotheism.

Symbolism is film's modus operandi. Symbolism may even emerge apart from the intent of the writers and directors through the audience's ability to read motifs and themes. People who are well studied in something are likely to catch on to certain themes in film, especially if they continue *ad nauseum,* and people who read their Bibles are no different. Films like *Lord of the Rings* illustrate deep and beautiful theological truths, whereas other films illustrate these truths in reverse.

Many reject Jesus after multiple opportunities. Why? Could it be in part because of the powerful and ongoing reproduction of anti-God themes and patterns within the most popular content in the world?

People have an easy enough time putting themselves in the place of God. Now they are getting a self-worship 101 course from first grade onward. God allows us freedom of choice. But choosing to be our own gods, while providing a temporary splendor in this world and in our flesh, actually leads us into a spiritual trap.

The Gospel still stands in every age. We still need to be covered for when we die and come up before the judge. We have all sinned and fallen short of the glory of God. But Christ came to save us from our sins, to take upon Himself the sins of all humanity. Understanding this requires God's gift of knowledge, partly because the caricature that is drawn of Him is such a pervasive stronghold in the modern mind. Instead of coming to destroy humanity, as Marvel makes it seem, Jesus came to be destroyed by humanity so that our worst parts could die off in Him, and so that we may also be raised up with Him. This is the only spiritual reality that can pull us out of the endless and futile worldly pattern. Jesus is the only true super-hero. Human depravity and rebellion are the real villains. So next time you watch these films, keep that in mind.

～

What do a couple of men in tights have to do with the tower of Babel and the corruption of the United States of America? The three may be more related than you think. The tower of Babel was constructed by the same sinful mentality of man trying to be as gods, knowing good and evil, and tapping into supernatural powers. This sin came from the garden. That sin came from the enemy, Satan himself, who sought to overthrow God and was cast out of heaven. He believes that

God is unjust and *ego*tistical, and is efficient at convincing people of the same things he believes. His desire is to corrupt the heart of mankind in how it views God, and up to this point he has largely succeeded in making the population think of Christians as Ultron's robots and Dormammu's zealots.

All of these superheroes share one thing in common, they cannot shed the things that all people share in common—the desire be as gods, to break past our human limitations into unlimited thought, power and potential. When God scattered the citizens of Babel he did it because he saw that they were becoming limitless in their capabilities. God knew, contrary to their desires, that this wasn't actually a good thing for them.

There is a clear link between what was popular in ancient cultures and what is popular in this day and age. As the wise teacher said, "There is nothing new under the sun." There are only old ideas sold in newer, shinier and more convincing packages.

These stories have a primary and fundamental history, and the etymology of their notions are deeply human. These stories speak into the tragedy of forgetting the tragic element of human nature—we are deeply flawed regardless of how powerful we may become. Instead they focus on the "new and improved" social vision—where we can have hope to move past the prison of normality via technology, our own strength or inherent divinity, and alien spiritual powers.

I do not want to seem legalistic in this section, as though I'm suggesting people shouldn't watch these films. I'm simply looking at spiritual themes behind our modern day mythologies. Many may roll their eyes when they hear a criticism of their favorite story lines, especially when there is a suggestion that these storylines may have real world impact and a deep-seated spiritual reality. I, for one, enjoy these movies. I also enjoy thinking about them critically and not shying away from interpreting what the films *intentionally* suggest. As for whether or not these films have an effect on the way people see the God of the Bible, I'll leave that up to you to decide.

In the following sections we will examine some of the more "real world" reasons why people have come to see Christianity, and then America in a negative light, and hopefully distinguish the myth from the truth, so we can solve our problems together, without burning down churches, supermarkets and city courthouses.

Wolves in Sheep's Clothing

In the Bible, the Lord speaks about separating the sheep and the goats in his flock. He doesn't tell you and me to be the ones to distinguish between them and separate them, but the Spirit. They are very similar in manner of appearance, so we often need God's eyes to see them for what they are. It wouldn't be a stretch to say that, especially here in America, there are false teachers who are beguiling their sheep to trust in a skewed perspective of the doctrine, and believe in a Christ that is not real and cannot save.

In the Book of Ezekiel God tells the people that the food and water that his flock was eating and drinking had been trampled and muddied. Likewise Peter warns us not only of a few teachers here and there that have some wacky ideas—but that a false gospel will make its way into the mainstream church to fester and grow, like an infection in the body. It will be very easy if we are not watching to miss what is happening and fall into its trap. Here are some isolated examples of non-Christians pretending to be Christians and committing heinous crimes or acting in hypocritical ways, examples like these have contributed to the modern anti-Christian sentiment.

Francisco Pizarro: On November 15th, 1532, this Spanish explorer and conquistador lured thousands of Incans into a trap.[1] At this time the Incan Empire was warring within its own members, and the Incan leader Atahualpa had just won a major military victory. He was on his way to reuniting the Incan Empire. After his victory, Atahualpa was invited to a feast with the Spaniards in a small town in a valley in the Andes Mountains. Atahualpa consented to bring five thousand of his men to join, believing Pizarro to be well intentioned. Pizarro had actually set up an ambush in the center of the town square. His men lay in wait in some of the buildings surrounding the town square enclosure for Atahualpa's army to gather. While they were gathered, Pizarro approached Atahualpa and attempted to force him to convert to Christianity and become loyal to the king of Spain by threatening the wrath of God if they refused. Atahualpa angrily refused, and although Pizarro's men were greatly outnumbered, Atahualpa's army could do nothing against their cannons and their cavalrymen, and they could not penetrate the armor of the Spanish soldiers. They were massacred by the conquistadors. This isolated example of the widespread shameful actions of the conquistadors could bring up a centuries-old debate about the true intentions of historically violent Christians. I won't win that debate in this paragraph. I'd rather ask a simple question. Do you think Pizarro's end goal was to see Atahualpa come to know Christ and to join in fellowship with another culture, or does Pizarro's deceptive ambush fit the pattern of virtually every other conqueror who had the basic fleshly desire to acquire more land, wealth, and power?

The Inquisitions: During this same time, across the Atlantic Ocean, the Spanish Inquisitions were approaching their darkest period of bloodshed. The Inquisitions are often cited by critics of Christianity as the most unambiguous example of Christian hypocrisy and evil. So are the Spanish crusades and the conquest of the Americas. These evils are not separate, but intrinsically and theologically linked. Looking at the wickedness of the Spanish Inquisitions actually helps answer the above question and to separate the sheep from the goats, so to speak. Shortly after Pizarro's massacre, the Catholic Church in Spain tortured multitudes of Protestants and burned them alive for heresy. The protestants' "heresy" included owning an uncensored Bible. Some place the number of Protestants killed during the Inquisitions in the hundreds of thousands. Others estimate that millions of Christians were killed under the omens of the Spanish Catholic Church. This rivals the persecution under Nero's Rome and the Soviet and Romanian Communists. Again, I'm not going to spend this paragraph debating whether this Inquisition was Christian or anti-Christian. But I'll leave it to the reader to answer this hypothetical question: if a group of men walked into your home and ransacked it, looking for a Bible, which you'd hidden very well because you know that they were made illegal, and then found it in a false drawer, dragged you and your family outside your home and proceeded to torture and execute all of you for this crime, would you consider in your wildest dreams that those who executed you and your family were *actual Christians* keeping in step with the Holy Spirit? Or were they simply persecutors of the one true Church who viewed the Bible itself as a threat to their own ambitions?

Salem: In the Salem Witch Trials, over 150 people were accused of witchcraft and imprisoned, twenty seven of whom were executed or died in prison. These crimes were committed by puritan religious elites and corrupt government leaders. These events, like the inquisitions, were based on identifying various "heresies," such as the denial of the supernatural realm including ghosts and demons. Somehow, in the minds of the puritans and government leaders, this was equivalent to denying the existence of God. And somehow these denials were punishable by imprisonment or death, as if unbelief itself was indistinguishable from actual witchcraft. These men, like the Pharisees before them, were focused on the philosophies and traditions of the religious intellectuals of their time more than the word of God itself. If they'd taken a look at the Gospels and the Book of Acts, they would have seen Jesus and the Apostles repeatedly reasoning for years with people from different backgrounds *including witchcraft, paganism, idolatry and Spiritism* (Acts 19:8-12). They would have seen multiple examples of Jesus and his followers setting people free from the most extreme forms of demonic possession (Matthew 8) and rebuking warlocks and false prophets *nonviolently* (Acts 13). Never did the fathers of the faith, or Christ Himself, put people to death. Instead, they offered redemption from the empty practices of sorcery, false prophecy and demon worship, and were themselves attacked, threatened, imprisoned, tortured, and executed by puritanical religious elites and corrupt government leaders. What made the late 17th century American religious leaders think that they had more authority than the fathers of their faith to put people to death for religious dissension, unbelief, witchcraft and demonic oppression? Moreover, what reasonable basis do modern secular critics have for drawing the correlation between behavior like this and the teachings and examples of Christ and His apostles, and then using that false correlation to bully and intimidate modern Christians?

American Televangelism: Another big hang up for people is hypocrisy and greed in the American church. Many famous pastors, televangelists, and ministry leaders saturate their teachings with empty messages about health and wealth. They dupe members of their audience and congregation into believing that if they donate a large sum of money to their ministry, God will bless them even more, heal them, or make them rich beyond their wildest dreams. They also intimidate members of their congregation and audience into charitable giving as if it's one of God's commands to hand over your money to an exceedingly wealthy false prophet. They often assure people that these funds will find honorable use, and then they turn around and shove widows' hard-earned money into their own pockets. Often times these people are struggling to make ends meet, then they are told by a sensational preacher that if they empty out their wallets on the altar of the ministry they will be richly blessed. Some of these preachers have tens of millions of dollars that they've accumulated over a career of robbing lower-middle class grandmothers of their retirement funds. Some even have hundreds of millions of dollars, fast approaching the billion dollar threshold. If their ministry is in such dire need of funding, why don't they reach into their own suitcases full of cash instead of robbing naïve people who're living paycheck to paycheck? The answer is simple, their massive portfolio became what it is only by making "the ministry," to which a tax deductible donation can be made, synonymous with their own retirement fund.

It is for reasons like these that the church gets a bad rap today, but the assumption that each of these instances stemmed from real Christianity is refutable on the basis of what the scriptures teach alone. You may have heard the atheist shout, "Countless acts of evil have been done in the name of Christianity!" He's not entirely wrong, and as far as the above examples are concerned, I agree with him. But how many countless acts of evil have been done in the name of Jesus and His true teachings? I have often nodded my head and accepted various instances of violence in Christian history. But it is important for us to make the distinction between things done in the name of "Christianity" and whether or not they were in line with the teachings of Jesus or the teachings of men. Upon closer examination, anyone who looks for truth in historical spectacles like these can see that there is a distinction between Christ's true flock and the wolves in sheep's clothing that have infiltrated Church ranks over the centuries.

Which is Which?

I wonder if America can be viewed in a similar light. Obviously America is not the body of Christ, nor was it ever intended to be. It was intended to be a nation founded on certain ideas that protected people through new methods of rights and governance. However, today we will see people on the left and certain pastors claim that America's history is filled with countless acts of nonpartisan evil. They see the history of America through the same lens that so many see the history of the Christian church. All too frequently the accusers of America, who often include those in the church, are first to summon religion, mainly "Christian fundamentalism," as the entity responsible for the many sins of our nation's past, such as slavery, poor treatment of Native Americans, and consistent warmongering.

There are many tenets of "fundamentalism" in certain religions, sects, and cults that are immoral. Christian fundamentalism, to the degree that it is chosen as the entity to blame for much of society's misbehavior, is only a caricature of what Christian fundamentalism actually is. To separate the caricature from the real thing is important moving forward. The caricature of Christian fundamentalism is often seen as judgmental Christians who shout hateful slogans at certain groups they disagree with, televangelists who rob widows of their life savings, conquistadors who massacre native populations, cult leaders who pressure their members to murder and suicide, puritans who burn heretics at the stake, and inquisitionists who force people to either convert or face grisly execution. Christian fundamentalism in actuality is the belief that Christ was God in the flesh, who died on a cross for His enemies and then rose from the grave, along with the desire to humbly follow His ways and His commands by the power of His Spirit. This fundamentalism is based on the earliest first century picture of Jesus Christ and what His visitation and ongoing rule meant and still mean for humanity. So when we hear blame being placed on Christians or "Christian fundamentalists" for all the evil in the known universe, it is important to make the distinction between historical fables which the critic has conjured in his imagination and the real thing.

In a similar vein, patriotism and love for America, despite its sins, is seen through a caricatured lens, and people who love America are viewed through the deconstructionist lens as propagators of an evil, racist system. They are seen to be complacent in America's historical and present sins. Many radicalized Marxists in America now see the American flag as a symbol of hatred and anyone who flies it as a vehement racist.[2] Just as it is important to make the distinction between what Christian fundamentalism actually is, up against its caricature, it is also important to understand patriotism, as it were, as standing apart from what that word has come to mean lately in the public eye. If Americans are going to love their country without tearing it down to start over, a more in depth glimpse into America's past (and present) is necessary, one that separates fact from fiction, and "America's sins" from the sins committed in America by specific people operating out of selfish motivations.

Should we nod our heads in concession to the sentiment of American evil, without identifying its specific causes, motives or outcomes? Or should we dig a little deeper to see whether those evils were done in the name of America, or in the name of something else—a teaching foreign, and indeed hostile to the original intent of our nation's founding?

Leftists decry Trump voters for flying the confederate flag, but what they do not realize is that the confederate flag was designed by Democrats for very similar principles to what they are fighting for today. Many leftists want to secede from the union and disintegrate America's values and institutions because they are so angry at ignorant republicans, and one of the main reasons for this is our opposition to their child slaughter industry. Leftists believe themselves to be so righteous in their cause that they even marched through the streets of Oakland in 2020 shouting "death to America!" as if America's sins and mistakes weren't a result of one particular ideology that *was not* common to all people in the country.

Andrew Jackson was the founder of the Democratic Party. He was an advocate for slavery and was particularly cruel to his slaves. He also signed the Indian Removal Act into law to the disgust of the opposing party, resulting in genocide and unspeakable injustices like the trail of tears. He routinely thought of people with different colored skin as sub human.

The Republican Party was founded by Abraham Lincoln largely with the sole intent of abolishing the evils of slavery that flew in the face of the foundation of our country. He was met by unprecedented resistance, not by racist republicans, but racist democrats. The democrats split from the union to form the Confederate States of America, where their "right to choose" what to do with "their own property" was no longer under threat. Leftist outrage against the "intolerance" of republicans is nothing new.

Republicans fought for the rights of black people with the 13th, 14th, and 15th amendments, all of which were opposed by virtually every mainstream democrat at the time. The democratic progressives had to fight to maintain their political control as the master party. When black people were granted rights and the republicans pushed for their equality under the law, the democrats fought back hard. The democrats formed a paramilitary wing—the KKK—to strike fear into the black community and anyone else who opposed their agenda. They used intimidation to terrorize opposition and to remind black people that they were still inferior to whites. Woodrow Wilson, an enthusiastic progressive, screened the film *The Birth of a Nation* at the white house—a film portraying the heroism of the KKK.

Wilson and his successor also participated in campaigns against the first amendment, in Wilson's case threatening open critics of his administration with fines or prison time, sometimes with sentences of up to twenty years.

It was obvious at the time that the democrats were more concerned about wins for their party than helping the country rid itself of its immorality. The democratic-party still uses defamation of opposition, intimidation, paramilitary force, and propaganda. Only at that time, unlike now, it was more beneficial for the Democrats to unfairly target minorities in order to preserve a white majority vote, whereas currently it is more beneficial for them to incentivize minority votes by demonizing those within the racial majority who dare to dissent from the socialist worldview (not to mention nonconformist minorities, whom they slanderously label "uncle Toms"). Hollow and deceptive philosophies like racist critical race theory and identity politics are the left's ideological insurance policy that protects against past and present parallels becoming common knowledge.

You might ask, "Why do the democrats have minority votes today?" This is a complex question, but it has a few easy answers. First, the democrats and their intellectual comrades worked tirelessly to hide a fairly simple and straightforward history from the public eye. They also convince everyone that there was a massive political inversion wherein the democratic and republican ideologies somehow traded places with one another.

Second, democrats saw the black vote, among other voters such as Hispanics, women, and the LGBTQ community, as advantageous to their political advancement. They discovered an effective measure of forming a majority out of various groups by creating an onslaught of victim narratives.

Although republicans were the ones to put forward the Civil Rights Act, LBJ—who called it the "[racial slur] bill"—signed it into law, and so he is often seen as a civil rights champion for flicking a pen in front of a camera. But he repeatedly let his true racial views shine through his language, saying things like "I'll have them [racial slur] voting democratic for the next 200 years," and "these [racial slur], they're getting pretty uppity these days and that's a problem for us since they've got something now they never had before, the political pull to back up their uppityness. Now we've got to do something about this, we've got to give them a little something, *just enough to quiet them down, not enough to make a difference.*" Compare that with current president Joe Biden's language when he was on the campaign trail, "If you don't vote for me, you ain't black," and you have a fitting image of yesterday's convenient racism of the Democratic Party transitioning into today's convenient race baiting and pandering.

The democrats maintain control of the black vote largely by bribing black people and incentivizing them to vote democrat through various social programs and by labelling political opponents as white supremacists and neo-Nazis, even when there is little to no evidence to support such claims. But, as

Biden's language shows, they still portray the black population as being incapable of thinking for themselves politically. They routinely label them as hopeless victims of a racist system. This helps incentivize minorities to continue to vote democrat.

In fact, when popular minorities begin to dissent from the left, the left engages in all out smear campaigns against them. The cultural tools that the left influences greatly enhances their abilities to do this, as well as to filter out influential troublemakers who don't fit their paradigm. Here are a few examples:

- Candace Owens, a black American conservative author and speaker has become a major target of the left, mainly because she is so good at exposing their racial agenda, which is really just more repackaged racism. Left-leaning news agencies such as the Guardian, CNN, MSNBC, and others have slanderously labelled her a "rightwing US pundit,"[3] a "misinformation super spreader," and even tried to portray her as a Nazi sympathizer.
- Black celebrities are repeatedly painted as controversial figures, or even insane, if they just mildly dissent from a few leftist talking points or are critical of one or more aspects of the left. For example, after rapper Kanye West outspokenly supported Donald Trump's presidency he was attacked and defamed by the media on a national scale. Comedian Dave Chappelle recently came under fire by the LGBTQ community and the mainstream media for his controversial jokes.
- Black conservative intellectuals like Thomas Sowell, Larry Elder, Shelby Steele, and Jason Riley frequently criticize the modern left, especially the modern left's racial animus and systemic racism narratives. They are therefore seen as a direct threat to leftist ideology.

Interestingly, democrats who supported slavery once used the argument that they were looking out for the best interests of slaves, providing slaves with a higher standard of living than they'd previously known. They'd argue that slaves may lose their livelihood if they were freed. Today's Democratic Party still tells minorities that it is their only hope to transcend a society that is hopelessly saturated in racism, even as the minority population in democrat run cities such as Detroit, LA, Baltimore, Chicago, San Fransisco, New York, Seattle, and many others face skyrocketing crime, drug and poverty rates largely as a result of these ongoing narratives and the rhetoric of virtue signaling politicians. The party in power disguises its true motivation, which is unrestrained and uncontested political and economic power as "racial solidarity." Meanwhile they continue to engage in behavior and rhetoric that objectively harms minority communities and continue to slander unorthodox minority voices. After all, the 2020 race riots, which will have long lasting negative impacts on the economies and livelihoods of the communities they affected, were largely a construct of the Democrat-run media machine, the rhetoric of complacent politicians, and the unanimous support of cultural icons.

Democrats maintain ideological uniformity by employing conflict theory and its various victim narratives. This portrays them as the consistent upholders of social justice. They are able to routinely present their own candidates as salvific figures who have come to rescue hopelessly oppressed groups from the dominion of racist republicans. To whitewash their motives and gain the population's allegiance requires an army of media, celebrity, and academic allies, as well as monolithic control over tech monopolies.

It's clear that the Democratic Party is trying to blind us to their racist history. But is this the only thing that they are known for? Democrats routinely pin the labels "fascists" and "Nazis" on republican candidates, conservative thinkers and Christians. However, the paramilitary wings of fascist black shirts and Nazi brown shirts used the exact same tactics of intimidation, brutality, and gas lighting as the KKK and today's progressive paramilitary wing, Antifa and their counterpart BLM. Fascism and Nazism also are deeply progressive in nature, emerging from conflict theory, social Darwinism, centralized state power, and racial determinism.

The parallels of Fascism and Nazism to mid-20th century American progressivism are striking, if not identical. All three ideologies pushed for eugenics, all three pushed for centralization of the state, all three pushed for socialism, all three pushed for racial segregation, all three pushed for marginalizing and persecuting the non-conformist church, all three threatened and/or took away the rights of their opposition, and all three routinely praised the ideas of one another in the intellectual sphere as forward thinking. There are more similarities between these regimes and their ideologies such as propaganda campaigns by state run media and state control of entire industries and corporations.

Are these mistakes only a thing of the past, or can they still be seen alive today in the 21st century? The eugenics movement thrives in the abortion industry. This industry is arguably more extreme than the eugenics movement of the last century which justified practices such as forced sterilization all the way into the 1970s in California. The centralized state is coming to fruition in a way never before thought possible, with the largest technology corporations in existence, as well as many other corporations unifying behind the philosophies, goals, and ideas of today's ruling class, and the ruling class scrambling to attain one party power in cooperation with powerful corporations. Today's push toward socialism is more palpable than ever, with a whopping 76 percent of Democrats saying they'd vote in a socialist president, according to a 2020 Gallup poll. Today's Democratic Party continues to push against the first amendment of Americans, labelling their outspoken opposition as "dangerous misinformation super spreaders," while using the tools of the state to de-platform troublemaking dissenters. They also greatly suppressed the American people's first amendment right to gather in peaceful assembly, their right to run their businesses without state interference, their right to religious gatherings, and various other rights under the guise of public safety or social justice during the Covid-19 pandemic. The state-run-media is overwhelmingly left leaning. As far as racism is concerned, the past age of racism was based on the theory of genetic determinism. This theory seems to still be thriving in the white-privilege-black-lives-matter narratives, where every person is either good or evil based on race alone, and should be held morally accountable for the sin of being born a certain color. This fits the definition of one's *genetics determining* the content of their character and blatantly contradicts the promises of the civil rights era. It seems the same people who are crying out against past injustices are following a virtually identical ideology here in the modern epoch.

America is not really a myth, even though there are mythological elements that surround America's Babylonian parallels. Progressing past our human boundaries is a universal flaw found in all of humanity, and this sickness keeps returning no matter which nation and no matter which generation. It only finds newer and more innovative ways to disguise itself within the same pattern.

∾

These can be some hard truths to realize. I also want to point out that I do not want to demonize anyone for belonging to the Democratic Party, as I did only a short time ago. Many of my friends and family are democrat. In many respects, I'm still the odd man out. I also don't think republicans are always perfect. Neither am I in my interpretations. There have been lots of mistakes made on both sides. But I think that it is unfair to everyone, even those who belong to the Democratic Party to manipulate the party's true history. If they were open and transparent about their past, they might be more trustworthy in the eyes of the public and more unlikely to fall into the same thuggish behavior in the future. Instead, they hide the truth and filter information about the past and present to showcase persuasive picture of themselves to the people. The bullying and intimidation of anyone who dares to criticize them is just a necessary means to the end of protecting their vision of the future. This casts doubt on their true motives as "the party for the people."

The level of control that democrats and the left have over culture is disconcerting. They dominate the media, Hollywood, the education system, and the academe among other things, and try to push any dissenting voices out. They also seem to have control over the political climate in the social sphere. In conversations, many on the left feel entitled to the position of moral superiority because they are on the side of the entity with the most cultural and political influence. This entitlement can shut down conversation when someone's opinion is contradictory. This level of control translates from the entities of state to common folk, and causes conservatives or others who disagree to tiptoe for fear of being attacked, slandered, derided, or labeled for having a divergent opinion. This social silencing is gradually advancing toward a more uniform disabling or elimination of freedom of speech through political correctness and uniting against various common enemies such as racism, global catastrophism, or an infectious disease pandemic. Nonconformists become the enemies of humanity.

The good news is that among democrats there are many who want to honestly come together with conservatives and work through issues, have good conversations, and remain friends afterwards, which is what our country is all about. As the American philosophies drift farther away from each other, people are able to more easily identify where they fall on the very real and binary political spectrum.

There is still a healthy need for conservatives to have counter perspectives that challenge their assumptions, just as the rejection of any counter perspective whatsoever seems to be destroying the modern left as it drifts into no man's land, plunging our national attitude into a soft authoritarianism that gets a little harder each day.

~

Every week I play basketball with a friend of mine named Nick. Nick is one of the kindest guys I know, but we often see things in very different ways. Nick is not a Christian and he is more on the left, but he is really open minded and loves hearing what I have to say. The feeling is mutual. We have great discussions ranging from current events and ideology to religion and recreation, then he beats me at basketball. Guess what? We're still friends, and he doesn't think I'm Hitler for disagreeing with him. In fact he is often able to persuade me to see certain things that I missed, and both of us usually walk away more enriched and happy after our conversations. Basketball and beer are just icing on the cake.

Religion is the Problem

It can be difficult to see where the root of disintegration philosophy comes from. By disintegration philosophy I mean anything that is destructive toward our nation and bears ill will toward its people and institutions. The chanting of "death to America" by Americans in the streets of Oakland in the 2020 race riots is a clear reminder of some of the celebrations that took place in the Middle East on September 11, 2001. This sentiment is no accident.

These people in Oakland are not Islamic extremists however, but they are radicalized, religious fanatics in their own way. They are neo-Marxist postmodernists. One might say that their beef with America cannot be pinned down to any one issue or set of issues, or anything remotely tangible for that matter. Their quarrel is against everything from the Christian church to western civilization, from the police officer in front of them to the United States constitution, from the person sitting across from them at the table to the Holy Bible. Anything that stands in the way of the progression of their ever-evolving Marxist philosophy is viewed as a direct threat, as *thought-terrorism*. But Marxism's biggest threat and most hated enemy, as often isn't realized until later on in Marxist regimes, is not political dissenters, but God Himself. Anything higher than the state will not be tolerated.

Karl Marx famously declared, "Religion is the sigh of the oppressed creature, the heart of a heartless world, and the soul of soulless conditions. It is the opium of the people." To kill a man, one often targets his heart, the center of his lifeblood. Marx saw the world as heartless, and he saw religion as its heartless heart. But his philosophy, some may say, went deeper than pure old fashioned atheism.

Karl Marx spoke of a deal with Satan in his poetry,[4] and

his father was convinced that he was guided by a demon.[5] His hardcore opposition to religion, free markets and free society in general all are telling of a more specific and deadly origin to his philosophy than pure atheistic materialism, although atheistic materialism was certainly a powerful engine for his economic and sociological motivations.

His philosophy was groundbreaking in its pessimistic malice, and appeared to offer the little man and the victims a way out of their victimhood and imbecility. The way out was rebellion against an abstract enemy who could be anyone the "victim" wanted him or her to be at the time. But the truest enemy always was the individual who claimed to be made in the image of God.

Ideas that forwarded the Imago Dei mentality are always viewed as a threat to the totalitarian rule of socialism; God the creator, the family which was designed by God, and the free-thinking individual with inherent value designated to them by God were three obvious targets of Marxism. Marxist regimes saw no need for any of these things aside from their benefit to the furthering of the revolutionary vision. When implemented, Marxism always meant the preeminence of the state. It meant the centrality of the state. It meant the total authority of the state.

Marxist philosophy has had many branches over the years. Socialism was its economic branch. Communism was a way to control and destroy people through collectivization. Fascism was a hybrid of Marxism and state control.[6] But the cleverest thing about Marx's philosophy is that it is malleable and subjective. Unaware generations of Marxian followers and authorities of various state powers have been able to reform Marxism to align with their own desires. All variations remain united under the common idea that the reason the revolution has failed in the past is because it has yet to be properly and thoroughly implemented. This implementation is to be best decided by the more modernized Marxist—*if they were the leader* of the revolution, then it would succeed. The various uses of Marxism have failed repeatedly in nation after nation even as each leader saw themselves in this light.

For this reason, American Marxists realize that in order for the true revolution to come about naturally it must emerge from the culture organically. Many sought to indoctrinate society so that they didn't need to be forced to believe in a "revolution" that was thrust upon them by a totalitarian government. The hybrid of cultural Marxism when mixed with technology is a deadly concoction, making state indoctrination feel like enlightenment. Thought leaders have spent decades infiltrating and poisoning our education system and cultural institutions. They've taken control of our media and have poisoned virtually every platform we have today as Americans.

In an age when technology is paramount and is connected to everything we do, modern Marxism takes a newer, amplified, and more compelling form. The radical slogan, "death to America!" was not being shouted in the streets of Oakland by accident. This required decades of social conditioning and a power network to unify those under the influence of this conditioning.

Marxism's between-the-lines goal is nothing less than total control over all of humanity. It needs to control mind *and* matter. It needs to control property *and* freedom. There can be no freedom that is not sanctioned by the god of Marxism. It has proven to be like the devil who controls it, relying on the unawareness of everyday people. Those who are unaware of these ideological dangers and are passive information consumers are often the most easy to manipulate and readily convinced of the Marxist cause. Seeing all their friends and family on social media conform adds to this convincing, so does having the opportunity to show solidarity and be a part of a supposedly just cause. People can unite together as heroes against a common enemy. When they are asked exactly who that enemy is, the answer is always problematic, nebulous, and undefined.

These premises echo Genesis 3. People are first convinced that they are victims of coercion by a cruel and oppressive system of government or laws; "Did God really say, 'you must not eat from any tree in the garden?'" (Genesis 3:1-2). He planted inside Adam and Eve the seed of seeing God as an oppressive figure rather than someone who was looking out for their best interest. But the devil doesn't stop there. He supplements his lie with the false promise of personal ascendency and glory that follows rebellion; "'You will not surely die,' the serpent said to the woman. 'For God knows that when you eat of it your eyes will be opened, and you will be like God, knowing good and evil'" (Genesis 3:4-5).

The serpent knew the true nature of rebellion. He had practiced it before. He knew its luster and its pitfalls. He knew how to tempt man to engage in the same rebellion he'd tasted. Marxism, beneath all its elaborate theory, operates on the same basic principles; doubt, rebellion and ascendency. With these parallels in mind, Marx's boasting of striking hands in pledge with Satan doesn't seem like a simple poetic abstraction. Beneath the political and cultural fruit is a spiritual root.

Christians should not shrug their shoulders at doctrines of demons, especially as they violently manifest in the streets of their cities and captivate society at large through cultural influences. We should not think of them as a neutral forces for good or for evil. Neither are they vague abstractions that are nothing in themselves. Marxism's philosophical ties with Genesis 3 are undeniable and its body count is piled higher than the tower of Babel.

The American variation of Marxism also has a diverse appeal that is meant to target the masses for forced conversions. The root is still good old fashioned hatred and envy. American Marxism uses the two satanic premises—you are being lied to and you know better—to create a complex ideology with a vast web of causes. It's really nothing more than the blame game. In the world of identity politics and politically correct thought policing, a lack of personal accountability and responsibility for one's own deficiencies can always be shifted onto others based on group dynamics alone. Rather than the enemy being one's own shortcomings, the enemy becomes anyone and everyone else.

Identity politics is the new vessel for American Marxism. It does not rearrange people based on personal strengths and weaknesses, such as being a lazy slob who only thinks about himself or a diligent, hardworking person who loves his neighbor. Instead, it hones in on perceived strengths, weaknesses and levels of victimhood that are dependent on the racial, social, gender, or economic class any given individual belongs to. In other words, it is all based on the same vague stereotypes it pretends to combat. Human beings are nothing more than their victim status or lack thereof, floating along in a purposeless universe next to other higher or lower classes of victims or non-victims. American Marxism no longer needs a class division based solely on economic status like before. By using the tool of intersectionality it can divide the people in many other unique and creative ways. This hybridized and advanced variation of Marxism may be simultaneously the most alluring, the most difficult to pinpoint, and the most dangerous. If it is not dangerous to our bodies yet, it is still dangerous to our minds and our souls, leaving our society fragmented and without a sense of identity.

Marxism never actually cared for the poor, the oppressed

or the marginalized. It just needed to convince people that it cared. In all its applications it always ended up impoverishing, oppressing and marginalizing everyone involved, besides the ruling class which was tasked with its application. Those in power were always the ones who were able to live lavished lifestyles and have whatever they wanted, like the Soviet "Blue caps." Meanwhile, those in power treated the people they ruled over like abstract ideas and subversive meat sacks that needed to be reeducated in concentration camps, exiled to Siberia, tortured in the iron maiden, imprisoned for decades because of a long forgotten conversation, or executed and tossed in a mass grave. These measures were for the greater good, you see.

The devil always rewraps his old tricks in newer and cleverer packaging. His war is against anything related to God or coming from God. In essence, humanity is God's most treasured part of creation. Thus it is the enemy's primary goal to steal, kill, and destroy it. In the past few centuries, he has presented a simple formula for individuals and societies to destroy themselves so that he could sit back, eat popcorn, and watch.

It seems like there are a lot of enemies that we are being told exist today in America. Ironically the biggest friend to us, we are told daily, is the Democratic Party and the leftist cause. These things are here to save us from wicked western civilization, colonialist capitalism, white supremacy, and "fundamentalist Christianity." The basic reality is that all out rebellion, division, purposeless progression, and mass confusion is the spiritual result of a society that has turned God into the super-villain and inverted all His definitions, even the most basic and obvious ones.

Christians must be warned against participating in rebellion or allowing some of these ideas to infiltrate the church. Especially when these ideas are demonstrably anti-Christian and seem to be tearing away at the very fabric of reality itself. Integrating such a belief system into one's theology may grant temporary asylum from the persecution that consistently arises out of that belief system. Sometimes it's expedient for churchgoers to do just that.

It is the rebels who see the Christian claim on the American territory as abhorrent on a sociopolitical level. Wherever they see a problem, modern or historical, it can somehow always be traced back to the church and the God they worship. The anger and frustration can be aimed no higher than the creator of everything. Therefore the progressive tower keeps climbing towards Him. Humans are simply becoming more and more frustrated with the limitations and slow speed of their tower building. They are working more manically and aggressively. This is not a good sign. I don't have to be a sociologist to tell you that the manifold division and hate in our country is not constructive but destructive. It is not progressive but regressive.

When the tower of Babel was being built, man saw himself as reaching toward the pinnacle of humanity. One day later the people's language was suddenly confused and they were divided to the far corners of the world. All their construction came to a sudden halt. When a similar kind of division festers in the heart of the American people, a division that thrives on the diminution of the law of God and the desire to "progress" past His sovereign will, we can be sure that we are becoming weak and confused. Our enemies, both foreign and domestic, see the weakness and confusion that stems from division. And I believe our spiritual enemy is working to intensify this weakness and confusion domestically in order to magnify it in the eyes of envious nations.

∾

In summation, the mindset of the tower of Babel is nothing new, nor is it only ancient. It was nothing new even as it was being constructed. "Is there anything of which one can say, 'Look! This is something new?' It was here already, long ago; it was here before our time" (Ecclesiastes 1:10). The great teacher of Ecclesiastes tells us that there is nothing new under the sun. This perspective can haunt us or free us. The mistakes of the past will return and this philosophy warns us of the realities of our times. It was from the great knowledge of the patterns of the world that Jesus was able to read the times as easily as you and I are able to read the morning weather report. Jesus was the only one who walked this earth having already seen it in its entirety. He truly knew that there was nothing new under the sun. The trouble with man is that he keeps thinking that everything is new under the sun and that the new man is the one to bring about true change. It is the old man who is wise that must remind the youth of this folly. The youth cannot see it in himself. As the youth rages in his passions and his lust to build something new and become the new man, the father is wise who has searched out those ways and has seen that the selfish pursuit of the "new" cannot bring new life. In fact, it is much more likely to bring death.

When God's a Part of the Picture

We can hypothesize and theorize about the proper proportion of church in state and state in church until the cows come home. Secular folk can guess about the reasons why things are the way they are. Christians can argue among themselves about what God hates more, Marxism or Capitalism, leftism or the right. But what happens when we include God in the sociopolitical debate and various hypotheses? How does He feel about all this?

I don't propose to know the answer to these questions. But my guess is that the American project only happened with his preapproval, in part because of its reliance on some version of His laws and precepts. This was the agreement for which our prosperity was temporarily granted. We were quick to abandon this agreement and worship the American system, among other systems.

The recognition of America as a mortal nation, existing in right relationship to a sovereign God who can utilize the powers of nature, society, and other nations to bring about judgment for abandoning Him is consistent with the biblical worldview. God can prolong our longevity for a few more generations or bring our end about rapidly. He can also remain invisible to us behind the mechanisms He uses. It all depends on our reaction to His warnings.

I am only suggesting this based on my understanding of the way God interacts with nations in the history of the Bible, and on the assumption that God is still the same. It is within His rights to either allow the big American problems to overcome us or to allow us to solve these big American problems with His help.

The Postmodern Babel

This next section is meant to discuss the themes which unite the Babylonian mindset with modern times, largely by identifying parallels and patterns between what happened in ancient times and what's happening now. This discussion is important, I believe, to grasp the overarching intent of this book.

Knowledge of scripture shows that one doesn't have to

be a professional historian, an archeologist or postmodern scholar to grasp history. It is important for Christians and people outside the faith to see why the biblical outlook can provide a depth of insight to knowing why things are the way they are, and to give insight to why things have become so chaotic. The atheist often cites historical and modern chaos to accuse Christianity of being a false religion, imagining a more orderly existence if there was a God; but a consistent reading of scripture shows that the more chaotic and evil things become, the more those things confirm human nature and the tragedy of original sin, thereby reaffirming the validity of scripture.

The doctrine of original sin, human depravity, and the overall propensity for humanity to fall into chaos seem to be reproduced in every generation. In short, light shines brighter against a dark backdrop. The dark backdrop is guaranteed. The light is optional.

Before Jesus went to "wake up" Lazarus, His disciples asked Him why He was going back to Judea after they tried to stone Him just a short time before. He replied with a beautiful metaphor to explain that He was walking in the Spirit and doing what His Father called Him to do. He was not prone to stumble as long as he walked in the daylight.

As Christians, our motivation should be to tell the truth and operate under a constant recognition that Jesus is the son of God and the only way to the Father. He also is God Himself and king over all of creation, ruling in an eternal resurrected physical body. Our interpretation of politics and history should come from His understanding of human nature, not our own.

What am I talking about with postmodernism and Babel? The two are more connected than you might think. When we think of postmodernism as Christians, we should see it through the lens of Jesus's teaching on the two types of foundations, with the recognition that, as Jesus said, there can be only two surfaces on which to build our lives, or our foundations; the rock, which is His word, or the sand, where any weather can blow over our house.

Postmodernism, as I've come to understand it, is the deconstruction of objective truth and morality, resulting in moral or intellectual subjectivity or relativity. It is the closest intellectual precept to a literal bed of shifting sand. On such a foundation, morality and truth are constantly shifting, disintegrating and being reconstituted, whether the whims of the individual or culture (society at large) cause this depends on the issue and the era.

Postmodernism seems liberating and alluring. Reality suddenly is not as "black and white" as everyone supposes. There are many different options, an array of choices to choose from. This perspective causes people to think that there is no such thing as worldview. When I was in college, learning Marxism and Postmodernism, I thought that a "worldview" was an oversimplification for the way things really were and the complex way people really thought and acted. But since then, I've learned that complexity for complexity's sake isn't always a positive thing. For example, Marx's theory was very complex, but did it lead to positivity? No. It led to gulags and concentration camps. This is because it was rooted in its own false dichotomy, conflict theory. It's true, everything is very complicated, including the way we interpret reality, but simplifying complicated things helps us to understand the truth of the world, just as beginning with elementary teachings on subjects like grammar and mathematics helps children to understand those subjects better. Retrospectively, overcomplicating simple, straightforward things like good and evil has proven to be an effective method for making good look evil and evil look good.

One of my first literature classes in college was on prison literature. It was one of my first pieces of indoctrination, compelling me to look at all prisoners as victims of an oppressive system (some are). There was one study in particular that stood out to me as an example of the negative outcome of overcomplicating people's various visions—the Stanford prison experiment. The Stanford prison experiment was performed by a madman intellectual Stanford professor. He simulated a prison environment for his students, showing that when these students were given the opportunity to oppress and tyrannize other students, they would automatically. They acted evilly. Another study corroborates humanity's innate tendency toward causing pain and suffering to others, where an overwhelming majority of participants who were allowed to administer electric shocks (causing pain) to other participants voluntarily administered all the shocks they were able. These circumstances, in my eyes, do not cast doubt on the true existence of evil, but bolster its existence, helping to explain why "normal everyday people" who were involved in the world's greatest atrocities did the things they did.

The basic understanding of Christianity rides alongside the truth in these studies. Evil is not a psychological phenomenon or an aberration but an enduring reality in the human heart. Jeremiah says the heart is deceitful above all things. Humanity at the flood during Noah's time was exceedingly wicked. God almost did away with it entirely, but showed His desire for our continued survival by saving humanity through Noah's lineage. There is also evidence that Noah was blameless for his time, not perfect, but better than the people around him. Society shows this throughout history. People who are men and women of their times need to be brought to an understanding of what is happening around them, before they can stand against the rising tide.

The Stanford prison experiment's goal was to explicate evil and to explain it away as psychological or sociological phenomenon. Such an understanding attributes evil only to an arbitrary existence of chaos in a random universe where struggle breeds greatness, therefore justifying the struggle. Evil is brain chemistry or social interactions somehow going awry, nothing more, nothing deeper or more primary. What wasn't understood by the professor, was that by wanting to explain away and justify evil, he actually expressed his own evil by creating a circumstance in which evil was allowed to flourish under his supervision—a circumstance that was modeled in order to deconstruct the very idea of evil. By creating what he thought to be a moral vacuum to prove his own intellectual pursuits, human nature immediately filled that vacuum. He sanctioned his students to abuse one another, and they did. In effect, he was directly responsible for the abuse.

∽

Postmodernism, in my opinion, is the best word to explain where we're at now as a culture and society. It is also advertised as the most advanced way for the world to interpret and critique where we are and where we've been. The deconstruction and devaluation of any values and definition is what postmodernism leads to. Its evolution is largely attributable to the emergence of cultural Marxism into the western world, which looks at things through a similar lens—overcomplicating and in a way mythologizing reality. Interestingly, Marxism, under the guise of displacing false dichotomies and "simplistic" worldviews, views the world through the incredibly simplistic lens of oppressed versus oppressors. Modern Marxism would say that my work is a part of the system of oppression, as I'm a white Christian conservative male—the lowest rung of the victim status ladder (even though Christians are one of the most heavily persecuted people groups worldwide, and conservatives face the brunt of media slander in America). Such baseless misappropriations, mass produced and amplified through various tools of the state, lead to a thorough indoctrination of society.

Today's indoctrination is less focused on a purely economic status of individuals or groups, but is still focused on various grievances and levels of victim status. The 20th century Soviet "dekulakization" rallied people against one another based on a shifting notion of grievances. This notion was itself based on two premises, the tyranny of those in higher economic classes and the victimization of those in the lower. Definitions were blurred on who exactly the victims or oppressors were, the two were even inverted, as "the rich" were delivered over to the slaughter for nothing more than making their neighbors slightly envious.

One could say that the same thing is happening in America on an intellectual level. Feminism calls for women to displace the male dominated patriarchy. Race theory calls for the minorities oppressed by the white man to overthrow him. Queer theory calls for gay people to overthrow homophobic culture. Those who are not religious are to end the tyranny of religion, etc. By cutting people up into intersecting lines like a pizza, society is cast off in many different directions. This is the notion of intersectionality, emerging from Marxism and leaving people fragmented in a false and belittling sense of postmodern identity.

Today you can be at one moment a hero in the eyes of postmodern neo-Marxist because you are on the side of good fighting against the forces of evil. You are on the side of the victim fighting their imaginary oppressor, whoever he or she may be. You may be the irreligious fighting against the cruel dominion of religion. You may be supporting the feminine campaign against the masculine. But the next day your status may change to one of the oppressors if you deviate from LGBTQ ideology in the slightest, if you express the least bit of doubt of 3rd wave feminism or pro-choice propaganda, or if you doubt the death of bumble bees to be the greatest evil we're facing in the world right now.

There is no drawing a firm line between oppressed and oppressor. This led to the mass slaughter of past regimes who saw things through a reductionist Marxian lens. Such *narrow minded and dogmatic thinking* always leads to the disintegration of our social fabric.

Marxism and postmodernism are first cousins, if not twin brothers, and they are leading the world into mass confusion under the guise of increasing our knowledge. These false religions are leading us to a very real division of languages. Therein (at least in part) lie the Babylonian parallels.

∼

Babylon was at the height of power and prosperity. Nebuchadnezzar wrote a fascinating chapter in the book of Daniel. In a way, we can all look at our story like King Nebuchadnezzar in this chapter, who was humbled when he exalted himself and was exalted when he finally humbled himself. In another chapter, Nebuchadnezzar builds an idol of gold and demands that the entire population bow down to it when they hear music. The prophets reject his edict and are thrown in a fiery furnace as a result. They live. Today we have idols that we are similarly told to bow beneath—perhaps the technology idol, the worship of money, or the blind following of celebrities, politicians, and "influencers" are a few.

Nebuchadnezzar was an instrument God used to

overthrow Jerusalem, but he was not impervious to God's judgement and divine rebuke. Nebuchadnezzar gloated over his empire without giving credit to God. Then God took away his mind and gave him the mind of a beast. He went insane and scrounged in the wilderness for seven years until he recognized that power came from God and not from men. Nebuchadnezzar was the most powerful king yet known, and probably considered himself to be the most intellectual king yet known. He had an army of intellectuals at his disposal; magicians, astrologers, diviners, wise men, and soothsayers. God took away his sanity in a split second, just as He had taken away Babel's sanity long before. He showed that true temple and nation building can only come from Him if it is to have a strong foundation and that human ambition alone is never enough.

These themes of confusion and pride coming before the fall are reproduced indefinitely, and were there from the beginning individual and societal falls—the Garden and Babel. Every person can and will fall victim to this condition, not just Nebuchadnezzar, or those alive at the construction of the tower, or the Soviets, or Nazi Germany. Marxism isn't the root of all evil, but an understandable extension of this very real pattern. It is an example of a miserable man who sought to become as a god, created a vast theory based on this desire, and mass marketed that theory to the world. Marx was a bum who couldn't get his own life under control. How was he going to bring about the new utopia? His philosophy is now being taught to children, a demonic philosophy that resulted in over a hundred million deaths in the last century alone. Quite simply, if your kid is in college, they're being taught this theory to some degree, a theory that always ends in failure and madness. Branches of this theory are spreading to younger ages.

The new process of indoctrination doesn't claim to be making people into Marxists. Marxism thrives on duping people into joining without letting them know that's what's happening. It is not a religion that requires your consent and desire to follow, as Christ's is. Marxism will force you.

American Marxism, like all the various implementations of the theory, is different than the other formulas that arose in preceding nations. That's why Americans can seem so Marxist and at the same time claim to oppose Marxism. It has infiltrated virtually everything, politicizing every issue. When I speak of Marxism, do I always mean the canonical proletariat rising against the bourgeois? Not necessarily. Marxism is more deeply rooted in a vague and imprecise notion of rebellion based on false premises and misinformation than an uprising against one specific group of oppressors. Marx hated God and wanted to destroy the holy family. He recognized that he first had to destroy the earthly family. Today, popular neo-Marxist organizations want to dispel the heteronormative nuclear family and the "cisgender patriarchy." Planned Parenthood wants to normalize sex for younger children to preserve their industry of death, presenting a very real threat to the future of family. They rely on the widespread modern narratives that are driven forward in culture in order to continue cloaking their barbarism.

Marxism is based on two or three basic assumptions even though it is a very complex theory, as discussed. It begins, like postmodernism which arose long after it, first with undermining God's definition. It then says "you know better... than your parents... than your boss... than your God." After this, it deals a false promise of ascendancy and glory—the proletariat is going to rise against the bourgeois, and become them.

Self-deification is almost always a warning of failure.

During Joe Biden's presidential inauguration, the lights that decorated the field of flags were seen by left-leaning news networks to be Joe Biden's loving, omnipotent arms reaching out to a helpless and hurting people after the reign of the evil republican, Donald Trump. Biden was viewed as an almost salvific figure, here to save us from the ruthless dictator who preceded him. He even referred to himself as the "light bearer," apparently without knowing this title was not given to God, but someone else in the Bible. As Americans become more divided, many are recognizing that America is being destroyed because we are pulling God out of everything and trying to build our own tower through things like the state, technological innovation or what have you. America made a deal with God in order to survive. We asked Him for prosperity, then we forsook Him and turned to the devil. I believe His judgement is here, at least in part. Judgment doesn't always look like fire falling from heaven and decimating a city. It sometimes looks like people being given minds of beasts and delivering their children over to the slaughter, or people hating their next door neighbor for standing in a different political aisle. In the last days there will be slander, backbiting, love of self, self-deification, and other signs emerging in the collective human psyche.

We are in the last days. We have been in the last days for a long time now. It is important to grasp that there are patterns and signs which reveal this to every generation. Jesus wanted us as Christians to be aware of the signs of the times and not to conform to the patterns of the world. Progressive Christians may say that He was only drawing an analogy of a more complex reality. But the underlying pattern is still simple, regardless of the design drawn on it. Godlessness reproduces godlessness from generation to generation. True believers have been redeemed from a life of sin and slavery to this pattern.

Marxism, rebellion, and sin offer self-justification only by exporting blame to others. In reality, it is our own human nature that is corrupt. America became prosperous largely by recognizing the visible and political truth in this precept, the tragic vision of humanity. It's not the Christian's fault that we are where we are. It's not the atheist's fault. It's not Marx's fault, or capitalism's fault. The problem is deeper and more primary.

Marxism and postmodernism survive by re-appropriating themes and putting them in shinier packages for the modern age. They redistribute old false ideas, saying "look, here is something new!" But we know as Christians that there is nothing new under the sun. The expressions of human sinfulness are what reproduce the world pattern. We see evil, chaos and destruction, and we bring them under God's sovereign understanding. As soon as we believe that we give ourselves power, we are given the mind of beasts and as a society we are *struck with confusion*, leading to our demise and judgment. We are likely being judged for the things our hands have made, the worship of other gods after the false promise to God that we would be one nation under Him. Jesus knew that anyone who thinks of worldly things as higher than Him is not worthy of Him.

There is an exit off of the freeway where I live in Salt Lake City with a ten story building next to it. It has a massive painting of a corpse and a demon painted on it. It even used to say "666" on it (this was presumably removed because of complaints). The location is a popular haunted house that has been featured in ghost hunting shows, apparently housing a lot of paranormal activity. Nobody complains about the rotting corpse painted ten stories high as a welcome sign to Salt Lake City. People seem to enjoy it. Today, people like to wear clothes with themes of death and Satanism. "The more death the better," says America. The church of Satan has a large

153

presence in Salt Lake, and advertises itself as a good alternative to Christianity. "Hail Satan" has become a popular phrase among the younger generation. But posting the gospel on social media results in widespread slander and ridicule. If the aforementioned building had a picture of Jesus on the cross, what would happen? The painting of Jesus would not last a week before there was a public outcry against it—petitions, protests, and media coverage. The true gospel offends a world filled with lies, a world stumbling in confusion and obsessed with death. Death is the primary lie and was overcome by Jesus who is the embodiment of truth.

I believe that it is wise to gain a local understanding of these patterns, rather than just seeing them in a broad and vague sense. These themes of confusion, of pride coming before the fall, of wickedness, and of rebellion all were present at Babel in the plains of Shinar. Shinar was the first recorded systematic push towards human civilization from an idolatrous mindset. The biblical account is corroborated by Sumerian literature. (There is an archeological and historical goldmine corroborating the building of the first tower—ziggurat or pyramid—right there in the cradle of civilization). This building was made to worship gods, demons, nature, and self. This pseudo-worship displeased God and caused Him to take action. It still displeases God and causes Him to take action.

Ancient alien theorists have long puzzled over the pyramid phenomenon all over the world. The simple answer is that people were influenced largely by their own pride and fallen angels in the construction of the first pyramid. It was for this reason they were scattered throughout the earth to reproduce what little they knew. The first time they collectively made the attempt to become as gods they were confused and corrupted.

What's true about the tower of Babel is also true about the

various branches of postmodernism and themes of rebellion that are emergent today, especially in America. America is at the height of its prosperity to build various towers—intellectual towers, technological towers, and monopolies. America's leading the world in riches. The richest people in the world are right here in America, and are now in an independent space race to fly to the heavens. We also have infinite information available at our fingertips with a click of a button. Yet we seem to be the most foolish, confused and divided that we've ever been as a species, arguably. America was built on a sure foundation, and then it traded it for a foundation of shifting sand—a relativistic, nihilistic, postmodern, post-secular foundation. God allows us to have our way, to follow freedom of choice, to live out the expression of our corrupt hearts. But there is no telling what this will lead to.

There is a pattern to the world and there is meaning to life. The more we forsake that pattern and meaning, the less we are able to identify patterns and the more meaningless everything becomes. Life makes no sense if everything is just random chaos. Christ is sovereign and will allow people to deliver themselves over to their own destruction. It is not always God who's the vessel for our destruction, but it is often our own selfish ambitions, leading to sin, leading to death. I believe that it is for this reason that we desperately need national repentance. God loves us. But like any loving father, He lets us learn the hard lessons on our own, like the prodigal son. Every human being in the eyes of God is like this prodigal son. We are not beasts, but he will let us crawl like beasts and eat out of pigs' troughs if that's what we want to do. America may have darker days ahead, but only if it willingly plunges itself deeper into that darkness.

Many don't think they can be forgiven, many don't think

they have anything to be forgiven for. "All a man's ways seem right to him, but the Lord weighs the heart" (Proverbs 21:2). We can go through life thinking we've never done anything wrong, but for all we've done, one day, we will be brought to judgment—as individuals and societies. This is the basic algorithm of history. But God's hand is stretched to us out still.

Chapter 4
World War, Always

Revolution Will Rise Against Revolution

If the nation of Israel never went to war, but always turned the other cheek, it would not have survived to this day. Indeed God protected Israel, but often he did this by empowering Israel to defend itself and conquer nations. People sometimes don't like to talk about the bloody history of Israel, and how God sometimes forced her hand to drive out nations from the land before them. People think, "Well that was the God of the Old Testament. The God of the New Testament is much nicer." I hate to break it to you, but God has always been God, it's His covenant that was changed.

We tend to forget that when God shows his power over the enemies of Israel in the pages of the Old Testament, He is all powerful, all knowing, and to be greatly feared. The enemies of His people were a threat to His people. God gave them opportunity after opportunity to repent and stop threatening or attacking Israel, to live at peace with Israel. Ultimately He knew how to ensure the survival of His nation. It sometimes involved the sword.

America has some similarities to this story, but it is not God's nation in the way that Israel was. America was founded on a great revolutionary war. America was ready to become her own nation, but England was not ready to let her go. England was much stronger than America, but the Americans showed determination and military innovation. They underwent tremendous sacrifice in order to gain their independence and bring an end to England's oppression over them.

Some deconstructionists speak about the endless wars of nations in a "tit for tat" historical view. They insinuate, and are not entirely wrong, that war is simply the result of nations hitting each other back in futility and never turning the other cheek like Jesus taught us to. This is a point with some truth in it, but I think that it misses a common sense principle about American exceptionalism—other nations often fight in the name of their nation's pride, but America fights to protect her own people. America also fights for its friends, and when it forsakes its friends, it is disgraced. America was founded by the people and for the people, not for America. If she was to always turn her cheek, it would not have been out of selflessness, but out of cowardice and a disregard for her people. Like Israel, we simply would not have any cheeks left to turn.

In this chapter we will briefly explore the true, but less commonly known narrative of American exceptionalism in military affairs, how America has shown that the cause for war may be just. America has its flaws and evils, as well as faulty motivations for entering into and remaining at war, but it is important for us to take a step back and look at the broader history of America before we lump her in with every other nation that conquers for the sake of conquering. America is often seen in that light by modern far-left intellectuals, but there is always more to the story.

Let's look at the revolutionary war as our first example. The revolutionary war was unique in that it was not a war that was based solely on the desire to revolt against some sort of imaginary oppressor like today's revolutionaries, but on the desire for freedom and nationhood, and as a response to *actual* oppression.

There are two ways of looking at this war from a biblical perspective. One may say that this war was just, another may say it wasn't. If we hold fast to the Roman's 13 principle of following the law of our government in any and all circumstances, then Americans had no right to revolt against England. They should have humbled themselves to serve their master, the king. Americans saw that they were not English at all, but American. England thought Americans were not American, but English. Americans desired freedom and England was no longer concerned with the affairs of American people, but how they could continue to benefit from America and exploit it. This was the basis for the Declaration of Independence. English tyranny was indeed a cause for a just revolution. Based on the principles of this revolution, America gave future generations the same right and duty to revolt against any other tyranny that arises, foreign or domestic.

America was not founded with the intent to be a conqueror. America was founded with the intent of bringing about a new form of nationhood and a balance between individual freedom and common law. America was not formed on any one idea by an individual visionary but on the best ideas of successful nations. America's innovation flew in the face of many other nations, and still does. So it was always under threat of nations rising against it and its advanced system.

The pages of American history have shown a relentless list of foreign and domestic wars, beginning with the revolution. Some see all of these wars as emerging from American greed, pride and a tendency to colonialize. Others see most of these wars as overwhelmingly just. Either way, we are where we are today in the wake of a history that proves nothing but

America's development through the knowledge of good and evil. It too was formed out of the human condition. The disintegration philosophy views America as predominantly evil and promotes a mood of national suicide which is destroying our heart as a nation. This philosophy has largely made its way into the American church. However, God never calls people to suicide, but to repentance.

For a long time many have desired a new revolution in America. They see our past, present, and future as hopelessly oppressive. They reap the benefits of being American and loathe the very system that allows them to reap those benefits. To them, American exceptionalism is more of a myth than their newest Netflix miniseries. They know what true exceptionalism is, and are ready to tear America down brick by brick, meme by meme in order to bring about a more fair, more just system. Ironically, the freedoms they claim not to have are all provided under the law. In a way, they blame freedom itself for their lack of freedom. What they would like to see is more government involvement and constraints on the freedoms of our citizens. Somehow, they think, increasing government overreach and reducing various freedoms is the answer to, rather than a major source of all our problems. These "revolutionaries" are nothing like the heroes who shed their blood for the true freedom and independence of our country. They are simply bovine anarchists and Marxists who enjoy burning stuff in the name of "tolerance." If they have their way in bringing about the new utopia, they will find that they are not fighting for American transformation, but American assimilation into a pattern of failure.

The two ideologies of America are becoming more and more at odds with one another. One leans toward true freedom, the other leads toward tyranny behind the semblance of desiring more autonomy.

Any philosophy that discredits the generations of blood that our fathers shed as needless, and views America as not exceptional in any way, is feeding the fire of the new aimless and unjust revolution. We undeniably have our sins, past, present and future, that we must own up to and deal with. But we must face them together and repent together, or else we will be doomed to do the very thing that the disintegration philosophers want us to do—disintegrate.

The view that America is not a Christian nation at all feeds the fire of the new revolutionary philosophy. The refusal of Christians to engage with these ideas and recognize their destructiveness is nothing less than joining the side of that destruction. In the name of tolerance, we leave the side of peace. In the name of social justice, we leave the side of justice. In the name of a vague idea of Christian subservience to government we disobey God's law of being the salt of the earth, and abandon America's first amendment. In the name of turning the other cheek, we join the internal assault on ourselves and others. We can blind our eyes to these things in the name of progressive Christianity, but this will result only in more suffering.

If we ignore or integrate the most threatening forms of ideology, we disobey another one of Jesus's warnings; to watch and to understand the signs of the times. This isn't the same as forcing others to comply with our beliefs.

Regardless of Thomas Jefferson's religion or lack thereof, he echoed the principle of watchfulness quite fittingly when he said, "The price of freedom is eternal vigilance." Jefferson recognized that American ignorance of the forces that would certainly rise against it was a threat.

Today these words have never been more relevant. Many have stopped watching altogether and have mistaken the Kingdom of God for the kingdom of niceness and complacency.

Is it loving to our neighbors to allow them to keep stumbling into darkness, and toward the slaughter?

The best part of the harmony between Christianity and the Constitution is that American Christians can fight this battle, and are indeed called to fight this battle through love *and truth*, without ever having to lift a finger against our neighbor. We are breaking the law if we do not tell the truth. We are participating in the aimless and ungodly revolution of the new age.

One World War

The naturalist perceives humanity to be ever evolving. If this were true, we would be more evolved today in the 21st century than we were yesterday in the 20th century. Likewise, the people of the 20th century would have been more evolved than the people of the 19th century. So on and so forth. We are told that we can trace this lineage of moral and social evolution all the way back to the primordial pond, where the first progressive amoeba grew flippers and emerged onto dry land. It appears that from this point on, humanity was doomed to have a will to survive through domination over its less-fit brethren.

The evolution of man has always been plagued by the evolution of war. It is never a matter of when there is or isn't a war, but only a matter of the differing degrees of intensity and locations of war. The efficiency of war increased alongside humanity, until we finally reached the height of our propensity to kill, steal and destroy in the 20th century, with the advent of industry and technology. The two adages from Paul and King Solomon concerning sin and the world pattern still hold true regardless of how far along we are on the evolutionary path. The mind of sinful man is still death. There is still nothing new under the sun.

The 20th century alone had more combined bloodshed than all the centuries leading up to it put together, with a conservative estimate of more than 108,000,000 people killed in around eighty different wars worldwide. The holocaust, the killing fields of Cambodia, the Russian Gulags, two world wars, the annihilation of two Japanese cities with an atomic bomb, the rise of Communism, and many more wars, genocides, atrocities and famines endured in the last century. The incalculable death count greatly surpassed this mighty number.

If we look at the scale and motives behind the 20th century wars, they appear to in fact be *one world war*, as many of the ideologies and motivations behind each war intersected one another. Imperialism, Communism, Fascism, and Nazism all had similar motivations to expand ideological and national power, wage class warfare and centralize the work force and any industry under government control, to exalt the race and nation above the individual, to implement socialism and concentration camps, and to indulge in extremely racist and authoritarian behavior. America at times crossed the threshold of a few of these attributes, but it was contradicting its own governing system when it did. Even if America temporarily sided with the socialists and fascists (even the Nazis at times), it eventually found its courage to stand against the rising tide of the world system. Even when the beliefs of that system were difficult to understand, the atrocities that emerged from those beliefs became impossible to ignore.

In World War One, the powers of nationalism, imperialism, and military alliances threatened the world and cost many lives. America, along with the other nations involved, sacrificed millions of people to the fires of a war that didn't need to happen. Twenty one years later the totalitarian and imperialist axis powers tried to impose their tyranny on the entire world.

Immediately after this, destructive and global communist powers conspired to take over the world. America temporarily quelled the fire. All three of these epochs left humanity crippled. The world's attitude toward war shifted after each one. The connecting ideologies were present throughout all three of these epochs. For this reason, I make the case that it was, and is still, one world war.

American involvement in the world war enflames the anger of disintegration philosophers. In the eyes of so many enlightened ones, anything we supposed to be a just cause for American involvement in these wars was just a cover up. American greed, self-righteousness and warmongering were the true engines. We were another cog in the global war machine, no different from Nazi Germany or the Soviet Union. These critics draw a correlation between America's involvement in multiple wars, America's prosperity, America's strong military, America's history of slavery, and America's success in these wars to reinforce their assumptions. From this correlation the false conclusion is drawn that America continues to be the colonialist aggressor and the most negative worldly force, and it always will be unless it is halted from within.

This philosophy has become yet another reason for progressives to delete a history of bloodshed and tear down the system which allowed this history to unfold. Both must be rebuilt according to the new humanist vision. This is taught across campuses today. The deconstruction of the American myth is a precondition for American redemption. But the mindset that fuels the desire to deconstruct is rooted in the ideologies of America's enemies. The bitter root which sparked the fires of the one world war is being resewn right here in the heart of the free world. The new American sentiment is to force the free world into conformity with past systems of failure. Each of these past systems resulted in forced servitude, genocide, total state control, famine and thought manipulation. Freedom has become distasteful to the free.

If America refused to fight the world war, the world war would have brought the fight to us. This is not to say that America never had any questionable motives and that everything America did in the world war was right and just. Although it brought a swift end to the Pacific War, dropping two atomic bombs on cities full of innocent Japanese civilians without warning is an inexcusable crime against humanity. Nevertheless it's amazing how quickly philosophers, as well as the children they teach, can forget the simple fact that America was often the water that quelled so much of this fire. Without us, the Third Reich would have succeeded, imperialist Japan's new order in East Asia would have been realized—subjugating millions, the Soviet Union would have maintained control of Eastern Europe and spread communism to the far corners of the world, fascism would have endured in Italy and merged with national socialism, South Korea would be under communist rule today, the Iron Curtain would not have been lifted, and so on. The teachers of the new age are still permitted to "debunk America" in order to stay relevant and earn tenure, even as they enjoy the various fruits and pleasures that were bought and paid for by rivers of American bloodshed.

To the far left intelligentsia, both then and now, America is seen as a negative force of opposition to the rest of the world. In fact, all throughout the world war, western intellectuals frequently sided with the radicalism of the very powers which opposed the free world.

In Great Britain, Winston Churchill faced backlash from the left-leaning intelligentsia when he stood his ground in opposition to Hitler, rejecting appeasement. The US faced similar backlash from pacifists when we entered into war against the axis powers. During our fight against communism an internal moral revolution within America was set ablaze by the American Communist Party. While young men were sacrificing their lives on the battlefield, ideologues were telling us why it was all in vain. They told the real story about needless war, the male-dominated patriarchy, the tyranny of traditional values, the evils of capitalism, and much more. As we now know, the ideas and culture of the next generations were largely structured upon this moral revolution.

The motivations of the communists and socialists today seem to be just as, if not more popular than the permission of the free market to operate and the American system. The progressive ideas of America's communist enemies have seduced our own thought leaders. It doesn't matter to them that these ideas left entire continents starved, ransacked, scorched and butchered.

From their "safe spaces" American Marxists can say whatever they want, whenever they want, without any accountability or fear of backlash. They are above reproach. They can condemn the cause of the fallen. They can enter into American government with a deep disdain for America. They can implement destructive policies and maintain their positions after those policies fail. They can accept bribes from corrupt foreign governments and retain their power indefinately. They can be upheld as warriors for justice and peace for generations for not doing much at all. They can use filthy language to demonize those who disagree. They can flag any dissenting thought for being politically incorrect. They can get you fired. They can spit in your face and cry out in deep inner anguish when you criticize the person they voted for. They can vandalize and cause violence as they are applauded by the American propaganda machine. The list of benefits for being on the American left goes on and on.

Today many intellectuals and activists who agreed with Hitler and Stalin, or helped the Vietcong win the war are still upheld as heroes and visionaries. Their motivations were in harmony with the enemies of the free world. Those whose motivations are similar today are likewise upheld as heroes and visionaries.

(I do not make the accusation that these intellectuals and activists are *directly responsible* for bloodshed because of their ideas. But that they were intellectually irresponsible and reckless, and that they never faced any criticism for this. Instead, for decades they have heaped the blame on their political and ideological opposition, namely "Christian warmongers." This begs the question, if modern Christians can be blamed indefinitely for something centuries old that they were not responsible for like witch hunts and inquisitions, can people like Karl Marx and Fredric Nietzsche likewise be blamed for the barbaric outcomes of their philosophies?)

The forward thinking vision of progressive American ideologues was and is more in line with the forward thinking vision of the central, axis, and communist powers in the world war, although this is buried in the teaching of American history. America's refusal to assimilate was and is still seen as a threat to the survival and advancement of the forward thinking vision.

It is clear that calling every war needless is nonsense. If there ever was a cause to enter into war to quell the spread of tyranny, it was America and the allies' cause in the world war, even if many of the motives of those who led the charge from the comfort of their offices were questionable. The theory of America as the main colonialist aggressor is true for many today. Children of the last generation are now teaching the children of this generation. Their goal is nothing less than total political assimilation into the same radical worldviews that first generated all the chaos. It's difficult to come to any other conclusion than to say that the black-shirts of the academe long for the new utopia, even at the cost of demolishing our way of life and silencing any political dissention.

The one world war rages on in the hearts and minds of the American people today. There is no shortage of theorists, politicians, celebrities and laymen who are critics of America and Western civilization. They promote repackaged eugenics, socialism, and racial determinism. As Americans become desensitized, obedient only to their sensualities, and demoralized by the left's total control over American culture streams, the forward thinking vision is permitted to sweep across our nation at a worldview level. Many who know the power of these philosophies are becoming increasingly concerned about the ever evolving, ever advancing forward thinking vision. As soon as they express any hint of concern or doubts, or draw any connection between yesterday and today, they are labeled as ignorant, evil, or (worst of all) conspiracy theorists.

It seems to be clearer and clearer that the misrepresentation of American greatness is a fabrication that rests on little more than filtered evidence and subjective theory. It is the result of decades of indoctrination and meticulous social conditioning.

We need not use the sword on those who oppose us and those who oppose the free world because of the theories of the world system. But Christians do not need to consider it sinful whenever we choose not to obey the ever-widening laws of those theories. Christians do not need to consider it sinful when we reject outright the filtered news and history which is pushed on us daily. We need not consider it sinful when we do our own research and come to our own conclusions and reject the doctrine of demons.

We ought to hold fast to the truth of God's Word. We ought to passionately oppose lies and hate in whatever form they take. We ought to use our common sense that God endowed us with as we brush up against the war on reality, which is a part of the one world war.

When Jesus taught about turning the other cheek, He may have meant that persecution is a glory to God and that we shouldn't strike our oppressors, not that we should bow to the various idols the world carves out for us. We may not have to fight the world war with our hands but by keeping our ideals and convictions in tact while the war on reality seeks to conquer and dismember them, to put more and more pressure on our faith until it can no longer breathe. The war on reality seeks not only to kill the body, but to demoralize the sanctity of the soul and mind until the body is basically of no use.

The world war seeks to undermine the very structures of the world itself, which God set fixed in its foundations. God called the world important, naturalism calls it a meaningless speck with bacteria on it. God said that when He created man and woman among everything else it was "very good," the social Darwinists deny any exceptionalism in man and woman besides what they may have stumbled on by random chance. God humbled himself and came down to us to fulfill the law and save humanity, the Marxists and Postmodernists seek to build a tower up to God in order to finally destroy His law. Once they have destroyed the world of man there is no more territory to claim but His. This is a fool's errand.

The world war is making its mark on humanity differently in the 21st century than it did in the previous century. It has now realized that the most important weapon is the mind, and the most important territory to claim with that weapon is also the mind. God's law must be forsaken at an early age in order to imbue us with a nihilistic foundation for the tower of groundless self-worship and self-ascendency on a bedrock of moral relativity. America is auctioning herself off little by little to the highest bidder or the lowest whim of the world. Her aging adulterous heart is reflected in the words of a lost friend of mine, "I do not see any reason to go on living." Imagine a world so blinded by transgression that it can't even recognize the gift of life.

The world war was largely defeated by fearless warriors of a free world who forfeited life and limb in order to stop the senseless slaughter spreading from lands ruled by godless ideologies. They were unfortunately unable to quell the dogmas of Satan himself, which seem to be as old as creation, so the heartless heart of the world war went back underneath the earth to return to the drawing board. How could the movement gain more momentum? Today in America we see a growing malice reflecting the same old philosophies of greed, envy, deceit and hatred stirring at every turn. Instead of standing against it, we seem to welcome it with open arms in the name of tolerance and social justice. But like yesterday, the mind of sinful man is still death, and his tongue is still a poisonous root which can lay waste societies, itself set aflame by hell.

We can look at the world war in a broad and baseless sense, calling it a "tit for tat" game and an eye for an eye, but we will have a hard time living in a country that is no better or has never been any better than the bitter foes it faced. Or we can see the world war as an occurrence for which mankind was not ready. The ideas that formed the destruction were common to man even as he went about his day unaware of them. These ideas stemmed from a condition. This condition is one from which we cannot escape. Cain's sin of killing his brother Abel did not begin with the first strike, but with the first idea of envy and hate. Sin was crouching at his door.

World War Won

Did we win the world war? If not, how can we? On September 2 1945, the Japanese surrendered to the allied forces and World War II came to a close. America was united in celebration. It didn't matter at that point what one's religion or political affiliation was, if one was American they recognized the glory of the victory of the free world over the combined powers of tyranny. There was no mourning America's victory in America.

Today in the eyes of many, America is seen as just another tyrannical force in a long list of global oppressors by Americans themselves. But it might do us well to remember the unity brought about by the victory of America, the leader of the free world, against the unhinged ambitions of nations whose only desire was to conquer. The end of the bloodiest war in history finally arrived.

For many in the critical elite class, and to pacifist thought leaders who are critical of any war whatsoever, America had no business defending herself or her allies. To the culturally anointed, the war wasn't won. It could never be won. America was never a real nation to begin with. It was simply a collage of competing people and ideas, with no person or idea being better or worse than another, and therefore no nation and its ideals being better or worse than another nation and its ideals. Whenever America didn't obey the will of the enlightened and turn the other cheek in the wrong sense of the phrase, the enlightened were quick to remind us of the great American myth that stood as the foundation for our beliefs.

America was actually not the United States. It was the

divided states. We had no business coming together in moments of triumph and elation, for American triumph and elation was nothing but a backward sign of our own military and colonial pride, our undeniable oppression. However, despite the critique of the intelligentsia that our nation was a myth, we managed to pull through the times with our morality slightly intact. The common sense American who didn't have the anointing of the intelligentsia was able to recognize true evil in the rise of the third Reich. It was the most scientifically advanced and highly educated who couldn't understand the folly and madness in methods like eugenics and coerced collectivization. It took time and truth to waken us from our sensibilities to the horrors that were unfolding abroad.

Fortunately the vision of American mediocrity within the intelligentsia was not true. Japan attacked us because they saw this supposed mediocrity, a nation divided in its ideals and identity. The American myth was a mirage. America was indeed the United States, not the divided states. And the United States has within its DNA the desire to stand against tyranny within or without. If the myth stood true, we would not have stood together to win the war. As soon as the myth became true among the cultural majority, we were destined to lose. We may be closer than we ever were to losing the war today, even without losing millions of our sons on a distant battlefield.

The world war rages on in the hearts and minds of the American people. It is a war of confusion and folly, meant to keep us bogged down in our sensualities and numb to the encroaching threat of tyranny. The narrative of American mediocrity is gaining ground quickly in order to at last make the myth true. A mediocre America can be changed. A mediocre America can be transformed. A mediocre America can be forgotten. By asserting the premise that there is actually nothing that unites us as a common people, we become unsurprisingly more divided than ever before along multiple intersecting lines—race, class, religion, gender, political affiliation, etc. In the eyes of a rising movement of Marxism and multiculturalism, past victories are now seen as the true mirage. Moments of temporary unity and victory are just crumbling white washed walls meant to delay the inevitable reality that the structure must come down. The America we know must be unanimously reformed. If you disagree in one iota with the neo-reformation, you must be reformed along with the ideas you wanted to protect.

The quickest way to gain ground for this movement is not to burn the American flag, but to burn the Holy Bible. In 2020, neo-Marxist rioters were caught and arrested in Seattle with a Molotov cocktail, on it were written the words "attack and dethrone God." Although the physical destination of this cocktail may have been the backseat of a police cruiser or a city courthouse, one can no longer deny that its truer spiritual motivation was written right on it. The quickest way to win the world war on anything related to God is to "attack and dethrone Him," but also to attack and dethrone any ounce of integrity, patriotism, or convictions in the hearts and minds of the American people. We have no business believing anything outside the orthodoxy of the new democratic paramilitary wing—the inscriptions on their Molotov cocktails tell us as much.

Doubtless the new American league of Marxists see American greatness and history as a sham. America never had the good sense to turn the other cheek in the past, maybe they can intimidate her into turning the other cheek now. Finally America can recognize her own imminent demise and conformity into the rest of the world as a benefit to the rest of the world. The only way to atone for her sins appears to be national suicide. Suddenly the trending hashtag on the 19th anniversary of September 11th became "all buildings matter." Even the grave memory of terrorists hijacking civilian airlines and flying them into towers filled with thousands of people can be hijacked and politicized by propagandists.

If you disagree with the imminent demise of America and the final triumph of the Marxist world war you can expect a figurative Molotov cocktail to be cast upon your "old fashioned" beliefs and traditions. The one world war must be a world war won at any cost!

The neo-Marxists achieve their tyranny and propaganda by inverting the truth, placing shame on the American people, and labeling *them* as tyrants and propagandists. When the truth is inverted there can be no more common ground. Now the wrong words or ideas are considered violence, but violence itself on behalf of the democratic paramilitary wing is considered "mostly peaceful progress." We may as well lionize these anarchists as the Lewis and Clarks of the new age, discovering the new world by burning down the old one. They deserve a Medal of Honor for fighting American tyranny one marijuana blunt and Netflix miniseries at a time. They hit us with baseball bats and tell us we didn't feel anything. They shame us for believing in God and tell us that God hates us. They cheer the slaughter of the unborn and parade slanderous banners against the born again. They force the church to fly the hammer and sickle, and slander any iota of opposition. They fight to abolish any sliver of law and order, and turn red in the face at any deviation from their allegiance to the new world order.

The enemy finally realized that the one world war cannot be won by a show of external force. The primary battle ground is the mind—the conscience. Any beliefs that are held at a higher standard than the state must be done away with if the war is to be won. The secondary battle ground is the family. Just as Marx sought to eliminate the nuclear family and then the Holy family, today's revolutionaries seek to undermine the heteronormative notion of family as well as to "attack and dethrone God." The tertiary battle ground is the state. Once the individual is fragmented from his beliefs and separated from those he loves, his sense of nationhood will become perverse as well. This is the effective way not only to kill the body, so to speak, but to kill the soul. These new tactics have proven to be very effective: sear the conscience and all else will follow like dominoes.

This "tit for tat" game goes on while the church often blinds itself to the increasing polarity and intensity of the revolution. We close our eyes to the threat against the church and the tyranny on the horizon with a vague notion of turning the other cheek. As long as we can be on the side of the angels of light, the intelligentsia, the truth tellers of the world, the myth busters and "fact checkers," the professors, the celebrities, and the politicians, we can finally feel good about ourselves as pastors and sheep when we get the occasional pagan tip of the hat. If we denounce America as a Christian nation and ignore the present reality of the spiritual forces of darkness and light in society we can finally have the stamp of worldly approval.

The god of culture is finally separating the sheep from the goats. The goats are old and weary in their conservative ideals of American exceptionalism, pro-life philosophy, and traditional precepts. Progressive secularism is the new Moses, here to lead us out of the bondage of our definitive past and into the utopian promised land of total relativity.

The War on our Youth

The war on our youth is being waged on multiple fronts. We've already discussed Planned Parenthood's "teen section" of their website, in which various types of sex are described in explicit detail to young children such as oral, sodomy, same sex, and other types of sex. On this section of their website they also have propaganda videos telling teens that it's "their choice," not their parents', at what age and with whom they may begin sexually experimenting. The injustice of intentionally hooking kids on sex to preserve the child-slaughter industry's revenue stream that depends on grisly eugenics into lasting generations is a staggering reality. What becomes more staggering is when we factor in the various other tools that the media, academe, and our culture is currently using to target our children for sexual exploitation, sexual addiction and other attacks on our children's well-being, morality and sanity. Here are some examples.

Cuties: Cuties is a 2020 French film depicting young underage girls dancing promiscuously. The camera angles often intentionally come inappropriately close to these girls' as they dance in sexually provocative ways. It is alarming that Netflix created a film that is as close as one can come to peddling softcore child pornography without ending up in prison. What is more alarming is that the film was almost unanimously applauded by the left as groundbreaking, out-of-the-box, and artistic. It received an 88% on Rotten Tomatoes movie review website, calling it a "thematically bold yet nuanced study of displacement and duty that deserves to be seen as an auspicious and astute debut, not the source of scandal." The apparently less nuanced laymen audience gave it a score of 16%, apparently recognizing its perversity. Other left leaning online reviews and articles applaud the artistic style of this film, and decry those who criticize the film for visually exploiting young girls. They claim that the subject matter of the film is critical of this type of behavior, but the plain fact is that the film mass produced sexual images of children as young as eleven for millions of viewers to see. In effect, the filmmakers created material for any pedophile with a Netflix subscription to watch without consequence.

MAPs: "MAPs" is an acronym for "minor attracted persons," which is the politically correct term that sexual propagandists now prefer us to use rather than more intolerant terms like pedophile, pervert, or criminal sex offender. Many critics of the advanced gender worldview have pointed out that in order for these ideologies to expand any further, they will need to include minor-adult sexual relationships. There isn't any more extreme territory for them to cover. Now there is a concentrated and organized push by some on the left to normalize pedophilia and to recognize sex offenders and perverts as just another community that should be accepted and even treated as victims.

Pornography: Another concern is the widespread availability and easy access of internet pornography to children. Children are exposed to pornography for the first time at an average age of eleven, and some on the fringes even advocate using some measure of pornography to enhance sexual education for children with "sex positive educators" bringing "pornography literacy programs" into schools. Porn literacy is defended as helpful for children to understand what porn is and how it may affect them, but it also shows sexual images and teaches students as young as five years old how to engage in sexual activity such as masturbation.[7] Children's exposure to pornography and other types of sexual propaganda at young ages has immense effects on their psychological development, and can create an addiction that only intensifies as they get older. It should also be noted that pornography itself is a cruel business that objectifies and exploits women and is linked to sex trafficking.

Vermont: In Vermont, a law was recently passed where secondary schools *must* distribute condoms to middle and high schoolers.[8] The "condom availability program" was sold under the pretext of preventing unwanted pregnancies or passing STDs. The bill reads, "School district administrative teams, in consultation with school district nursing staff, shall determine the best manner in which to make condoms available to students. At a minimum, condoms shall be placed in locations that are safe and readily accessible to students, including the school nurse's office." Our culture has become so dilapidated that now it is considered "normal" and "healthy" for strange adults to hand your children tools that encourage them to have more sex more efficiently. I'm not a father, but if a strange person walked up to my child and handed them a condom, I would call the police, and if my child told me that he got a condom from his teacher, I'd be outraged. Apparently now, if your child is not handed free condoms at school in Vermont, that school is breaking state law. Progressive lawmakers believe they are protecting children by promoting safer sex, but in reality they are sexually exploiting children with systemically perverse laws. These free condoms are provided by none other than Planned Parenthood, and this law was introduced by a "republican" representative and passed by a "republican" governor in one of the most progressive states in our country. Often laws passed in deeply progressive states like Vermont or California spread to other blue states before they eventually go federal.

Graphic sexual literature in schools: In the last year, parents in various states have expressed disgust that their children are being exposed to literature containing graphic sexual descriptions, in some cases between adult men and children.[9] These parents often bring concerns about the material being taught in schools in front of teaching boards and are dismissed, laughed off, or even dragged out of meetings like lunatics. The media has undertaken the politicization of this issue as well and continue to smear concerned and enraged parents as potential extremists, even terrorist threats. What is more threatening is that there are many parents who wholeheartedly support academic institutions peddling sexual propaganda to their children.

Masks: Across the United States the CDC recommends that all students older than the age of two wear masks in school to mitigate the coronavirus. Children are beginning to be trained up to uncritically trust the government recommendations and to think of everyone wearing masks all the time as normal human behavior. Like with the previous example, parents who are opposed to the cruelty of forcing their children to wear masks for eight hours a day are smeared by left leaning institutions and the media as "right wingers." In reality, they just are growing increasingly concerned that children are being manipulated and indoctrinated to blindly obey whatever edicts the government initiates, and that they are being forced to have most of their daily human interactions with people's foreheads. Millions of parents still force their own children to wear a mask any time they go out in public. It's hard to see how this won't lead to a nation of people accustomed to wearing masks long into the future, and a moral ground for dismissing, fearing, or hating those who do not wear masks.

Vaccines: Many children are being given an experimental vaccine to protect them against the coronavirus, even when there is virtually no risk that these children will die from the virus. Like so many other things, the media has suggested that this is a good idea over and over again, so parents are blindly obeying state suggestions, lining their fearful and trembling children up in front of partisan doctors in order to get jabbed with an extremely painful vaccine that will likely fade away much faster than natural immunity. For children, there isn't much difference between Covid-19 and the common cold. This cruel measure appears to be another reactionary outcome of a fearful society that sees children as "potential coronavirus super spreaders" rather than innocent children who need our love and comfort most in this time of social uncertainty. The measure may actually be another instance of targeted and deliberate social conditioning coming from an authoritative government, and an increasingly authoritative elite class of commoners.

As if it weren't enough of a war on our youth to obliterate over 60,000,000 unborn lives since the 1970s, the war on our youth is being waged from the other end of childhood downward. Films are being advertised that promote sexual exploitation of children. Pedophilia is being normalized and brought under the LGBTQ umbrella. Dark and disgusting forms of pornography are readily accessible to any child with access to a *Google* search engine. One state has made it mandatory to hand out condoms to middle and high schoolers. Schools peddle books with explicit sexual propaganda to students and dismiss parental concerns about such matters. Children are now forced to wear masks for much of their waking life, and painful vaccinations are being meticulously pushed on children who don't need them by the media and the government. It's safe to say that our culture has abandoned its sanity regarding how to properly care for and teach the most vulnerable among us. There are many more concerns for our youth than this section has the time to investigate. The basic question remains, how will these brand new problems affect the upcoming generations?

A Conflict of Culture

Imagine a world where you can do anything, be anyone, go anywhere with the click of a button. For a low monthly rate you too can have happiness. You can live the life of a movie surrogate—if you're ugly, watch a movie that stars a handsome actor; if you're bored, play a violent videogame; if you're lonely, log onto an adult website. There is no territory that cannot be overcome. American exceptionalism is no longer found in delayed gratification but instant gratification. Tired of staunch religion? Now there is a buffet of religions to choose from—a little of this, a little of that. You can have whatever you need to become the *Übermensch* you've always wanted to be. All you have to do is unsubscribe from the myth you've been living that there is a specific God who revealed Himself in history and the corresponding absolute, objective truth, and subscribe to the Ashtoreth of current culture. It is time for the children of America to set aside their Bibles and to rise up to play.

In Exodus, when Moses delivered the Israelites from Egypt, he went up on the mountain to confer with God and receive God's Holy Law. The Israelites couldn't wait. They grew impatient with Moses and with God and began to lust after the idol of Egypt. After being freed from generations of oppression they began to experience Stockholm syndrome. "Egypt wasn't that bad after all," they thought. This was a constant pattern Moses would have to face as He continued to lead Israel on its perilous journey.

Sadly, the Promised Land was not the catalyst to deliver the Israelites from their tendency to turn after the idols of surrounding nations. They were at a crossroad that lasted throughout their entire history, from the foundation of their country to their exile among the other nations. At certain times Israel was closer to its true identity as God's chosen people. Other times it forsook its identity and was unable to distinguish between God and the gods. It is undeniable that this spiritual deficiency in Israel is what led to its destruction, not the external forces such as war, poverty, natural disaster, disease, exile, or famine that consistently threatened Israel.

In a similar way, the United States is succumbing to a spiritual destruction that is unprecedented. This is partly because much of our culture has alienated itself increasingly from God's intent and His ways. The spiritual destruction is partly because there is no more cultural fabric that binds us together as Americans. Many in the elite class claim that the only thing we have in common is that we have nothing in common. When President Joe Biden was formerly vice president, he stood by this principle, saying, "There's nothing special about being American. None of you can define for me what an American is. You can't define it based on religion, ethnicity, race, culture." So many people who run our country hold the same sentiment that there is nothing special about America. This sentiment tends to get them elected nowadays. Is it really too much of a stretch to say, based on their own language, that they don't want America to exist anymore and that they care more about bribes and self-interest and virtuosity than the well-being and longevity of the people they rule over?

The degradation is a spiritual reality, the cultural conflict is the real-world outworking of that reality. Again, America was never intended to be completely theocratic, but Judeo-Christian values are largely to thank for the creation and cultivation of our national identity, our prosperity, and our cultural texture. The tangible values that formed the premise of America, partnered with other valuable philosophies, were the starting point for the greatest, strongest, richest, and most innovative society in the history of humankind. We have often contradicted these values in our past, and are now wanting to abandon them for their contradictions.

In many ways America's starting point was also its ending point. Our culture was founded on laws guaranteeing the freedom of choice whether it be religion or trade, and where the law did not clearly state the freedoms of Americans, it was amended to insulate them. Those amendments needed to be in line with the values, laws and philosophies that propelled us forward, otherwise new laws could chip away at our social fabric, all too often under the pretext of propelling us forward. In effect, the laws and philosophies that contradicted the foundation of America and insisted America conform into the pattern of failed laws and philosophies of other nations have plunged the cultural, legislative, social, and moral future of our nation into utter obscurity. In God's eyes the reality may be much simpler. We promised Him one thing and gave Him another.

America set itself on a narrow path, and the slightest deviation from that path more often than not proved to be disastrous. Today, respect for this path is in low demand, and trail maps are in even lower supply. As America explores the other paths of the world, it is buying into the myth that there are many paths that lead up the same mountain, "all roads lead to Rome," or in this case the perfect America. In actuality, America exists in its present form as a result of following a very specific set of guidelines, guidelines that were largely founded on the presupposition that there is a Sovereign God who brings about the life, longevity, and death of nations. This is not to say that being American was dependent on a monolithic allegiance to one religion, obviously. Human free will was implicit in the American structure.

America's culture was always meant to consist of a mutual respect between people within society regardless of their various beliefs, as well as a common bond surrounding a national attitude which one did not have to forsake their individuality to join—this was the condition for becoming an American. America was founded with the intent to protect individuality, not rob us of it. Today our culture has found itself travelling on a much wider path that is easier to navigate, often in the name of individuality. But to those who stand in opposition to the path it often looks more like we are constantly being told to ditch our own individuality and conform, or else. In other words, this wider, "more inclusive" road looks to us like a new theocracy, where an elite class of priests rule over others in the name of the god of post-modernity.

We have effectively stood the principle of a common bond that respects individuality on its head. Individuality is not permitted outside of what is sanctioned. Today, all the windy paths that supposedly lead up the same mountain of national prosperity seem to outweigh and outperform the original narrow path that was intended at the beginning. That path has become overgrown with thorns and is increasingly difficult to find. But as Jesus taught, "Narrow is the way that leads to life and only a few find it." We can rest assured that the few who do find it will be laughed at and mocked by those traveling nearby, on more obvious paths.

How to Make a New Man

It is becoming clearer and clearer that our greatest enemy is not foreign, but domestic. This is not to say it's our neighbor who disagrees with us, but it may well be their blind faith in a radicalized leftist ideology. We live in a world where we are told we can be anything, do anything, and go anywhere. We ought to have no limitations, and we are destined to surpass the ones we do have. Rather than protecting our basic freedoms under law, our law is being reshaped to fit a culture that demands access to new rights as quickly as it can invent them. Now the positive rights of the few outweigh the negative rights of the many. We have the right to become our own gods, to reconstruct the law to fit our own malleable attitude, and to supersede the rights of those who stand in our way. Old man America had his time. Now it is time to create the new man. But the new and the old cannot exist in one man. There is always a tradeoff. Here is how you make the new man.

First, you must remake the mind of the man. In our culture today there is a disturbing amount of control and filtering of information that we receive. We may not always be aware of it, but there is almost always a political spin every time we turn on the news, and news agencies are more than 90% left leaning. 20th century fascist, Nazi and communist regimes understood that they could greatly influence the masses by controlling the media. The media, especially when under total government control and incentivized to abandon factual or journalistic integrity in order to enhance the power of the party, can become an agent of effective indoctrination, polarization, intimidation, fearmongering and political advertisement. The media is historically able to manipulate a people little by little, through incremental steps, in order to push them closer to a threshold of total conformity. One hopeful difference between those regimes and the media in America is that Americans still, at least for the time being, have the freedom to both disagree with the party narrative and to seek out information from opposing or nonpartisan sources, although these sources are becoming more difficult to find, and less reliable. This benefit is indeed on shaky ground as one cultural/political system assumes more and more power and influence over virtually every medium. Under the pretext of helping us know stuff, this medium makes us unable to think for ourselves.

Second, you must reshape his passions. Once you have control of someone's head, it's time to move down to his heart. The heart expresses itself through laughter and tears. God created us to have desires that ultimately prosper us and point us to Him. However, Satan is an expert at inverting those desires to harm us and point us in the other direction. His influence over the patterns of this world (culture) is undeniable. Earlier we discussed the inversion of biblical principles in certain superhero movies that we love to sit our kids in front of. That is just the tip of the iceberg. From Hollywood's conception, culturally and politically partisan influencers like writers, producers, and actors have infiltrated, occupied, and come to dominate 99.9% of Hollywood. There is too much to get into here, but what you must remember as a general rule is that Hollywood holds large sway over our nation's passions and is greatly responsible for shaping the attitude of our culture via TV and film. They are experts at keeping the masses entertained, eating popcorn, and becoming desensitized to their often radical ideals, as well as over-sexualizing culture, and showing nonstop violence. Under the pretext of making us feel something, this medium numbs us.

Third, you must control the work of his hands. America didn't invent the principle of free labor, private property, and economic liberty—God did. God taught mankind that if it didn't work, it didn't eat. God told everyone to work their own land that they may prosper. God recognized that we had the freedom to become laborers in different trades and professions. God knew the benefit of hard work both for the laborer, the business man, and the consumer. Naturally, we understand via the common sense that God endowed us with that the laborer, his boss, and the consumer all engage in mutual agreements and transactions. For example, you set the price, I buy if I think it's fair, I don't if I think it's not. Or you set the wage, I work for you if I think the wage is fair, I don't work for you if I think it's unfair. Negotiation in both instances for both parties is possible. Such basic economic principles are as ancient as humanity itself, but we are taught today that such ideas are simply a newer invention of the western-colonialist-capitalist paradigm. It is the unnatural inclination of slothfulness to invert common sense and real world principles such as ownership and free trade into Marxist economic philosophy, which basically boils down to "give me that for free, just because I deserve it." The more the culture is able to convince the old man to set aside his trade and pick up his iPhone in order to read and repost Marxist tweets, the more the old man is convinced that he has no business working unless his work is sanctioned by a higher authority. He then becomes the new man in opposition to free labor, and can rely on payments from the government to reward his opposition. Under the pretext of granting us liberty, the abandonment of free trade and labor actually enslaves us.

(The new man now has a new mind, a new heart, and new hands. He is ready for a new mouth. He is ready to become a voice for all the things that influenced him into this new life.) He is ready to point out the deviations of the old man in others.

Fourth, you must control the people he associates with. When the new man meets with the old man there is often a hand shake, some mutual banter, and maybe a cold beer. But it is an inevitability that conversation will cross into no man's land, especially as more and more topics become no man's land in the new age. For example, one often cannot have a conversation about current events or the weather without crossing over into political territory that is often a touchy subject for the new man. If your perspective on nonpartisan issues deviates from the orthodoxy of the new man, you can expect to be corrected for your mistake, often with a deep level of derision. In America this is becoming more and more common and is alienating many conservatives and Christians from speaking out for fear of being judged, labeled, slandered, attacked, or losing their jobs because they have deviated from the orthodoxy of the new man in one way or another. Pretty soon, unless he joins the religion of the left, he will have nothing *left* to talk about except for what he had for breakfast, and if it's sausage and eggs he may not be able to talk about that either if the new man is also an animal activist. Under the pretext of unifying people, political correctness divides us.

Handshake

The handshake between the old and the new man can often be a bridge between two worldviews or two conflicting cultures. And even that can be stripped away by a government edict that prohibits handshakes as a public safety measure. The larger point on an American cultural level is not which side is right or which side is wrong, but that the American people are becoming more alienated from one another in general. The political sphere is only the surface level, as we dive deeper into the conflict of culture we find that the root is in the spirit of humankind, the spirit of America. As a spiritual issue, the division makes sense when we see the actual source of the issues being a result of sin, and a redemption from it. We experience division from others as a natural outworking of who or what we worship and which ideas and worldviews we seek to cultivate.

Jesus Himself said that He did not come to bring peace but a sword, and that if mankind hates His followers, it hated Him first. This doesn't mean that we need to bring the sword of the flesh to our neighbor who disagrees with us, but the sword of the Spirit. It is not our job to divide ourselves from others and alienate ourselves from those who are productive in the world pattern. It is our job to be among them and love them in truth even as the spiritual issues often divide us. We extend the hand of love to the new man without participating in his ways.

The New World

In summation, wars happen. Nation will rise against nation, and it is in our vested interest to prevent conflict both internally and externally. Sin effects the mind, heart and work of mankind, then it moves on from inner anguish to societal turmoil and erupts as conflict abroad. There is a fine line, a narrow path so to speak, between cowardice and promoting the kingdom of the sword. The battle is between the old and the new man, but the old and the new man are not who we think they are. The new man is the man who has been born again of the Spirit, he has died to the old man. The old man is the man who claims to be the new man, but is still caught in the pattern of thinking and the temptations of this world—the same attitude that was present in all the ages before him. He can only mimic the mind of Christ, but has become increasingly convincing in his interpretation of biblical precepts. In the new world, ownership and trade become greed, faith becomes self-righteousness, free speech becomes a danger to society, rebellion becomes a just measure, sinfulness becomes industrialized, and mentally unstable fools are seen to be wise men and are given power. The old man becomes so convincing that he is able to trick new men into thinking that they are the old and he is the new.

I don't have all the answers on what the Bible states is a just cause to take up arms versus when we ought to turn the other cheek. I think it was left out with a clear intent to allow us the freedom of choice on the matter. Perhaps God knew that Christians would struggle with this conundrum as history unfolded and left it in the church's hands to learn the balance between promoting peace and defending against tyranny. Christianity has had a past of glorious triumph and shameful bloodshed. When we look at the church we ought to see it just as fundamentally human as God knew it would be. Just as a believer grows into deeper faith, and fails at times along the way—occasionally revealing blemishes and hypocrisy—the church has not mastered perfection, nor will it until the end of the age. To be fair to the Christian, the critical historian ought to hold the legacy of atheistic materialism to the same standard and ask himself what the world would look like without the church standing boldly against evils such as slavery, Nazism, and communism. What would America look like without her Christian founding? Moreover, without the ideological checks and balances between progressives and conservatives, what might our laws and legacy look like today? One may engage in speculation, but an honest evaluation of our history, our laws, and our philosophy will likely show that both Christians and conservatives were not here to restrict our nation's truest liberty but to enshrine it. Without American Christians our nation's past would be dark and its future darker.

The world system points the finger at the Christian as the culprit for all the world's suffering. This is a lie and a longstanding part of the myth. The Christian simply is one who has acknowledged his or her own fallibility and turned to follow Christ. The obedient know that they have freedom even in slavery, riches even in poverty, and joy even in suffering. Nothing in heaven or on earth can tear them away from the love of Christ. The Church has an inner joy and peace that no war, or famine, or persecution, or prison cell, or op-ed could ever revoke, even if the world was pulled out from under its feet, and a Spirit that all the forces of hell cannot prevail against. The enemy hates joy and peace, it makes sense that he is trying to take this away from the new man who is truly made new. He knows that when the new man becomes old again the world war will rage on in his heart, and when the old man becomes new he will find longstanding and eternal peace, a peace that transcends all understanding and that has stood as the biggest threat to the world war for two thousand years.

America's Intellectual Dekulakization

The dekulakization was the state-sanctioned targeting of group oppressors in Soviet Russia. The Russian government encouraged its citizens to turn over other citizens who were perceived to be victimizers. This began largely from economic motivations, then spread to all out social and ideological warfare. The results were catastrophic, millions dead. The ensuing discussion of modern intellectual or ideological dekulakization in America is not without reasonable basis.

As Christians, we must recognize this discussion as less of a political observation, in the way that has evoked negative connotations among nonpartisan believers, and more of an ideological explication through a biblical framework. The examination should begin with what victim-mindedness has turned into historically, and what power the state can have when it is able to harness and mobilize human nature for its own ends.

Alexandr Solzhenitsyn's Nobel Prize winning work *The Gulag Archipelago* exposes much of what happened in the Soviet

Union during the hunt for perceived "oppressors" as well as anyone who disagreed with the party in power or held a belief or value in higher regard than the state. A biblical worldview provides an understanding of the source and presence of evil. When the Soviets pulled God out of everything, the humanity of that country was stripped of any moral grounding whatsoever. Without biblical understanding, this makes no sense. How does this same understanding correspond to seeing our day and age, when we don't yet have soldiers in jackboots coming into our homes and hauling us off to concentration camps for subversion, one may ask?

Marxism was the driving force behind the Soviet dekulakization, and many who participated in the dekulakization were not Marxian scholars, or consciously operating from an allegiance to the men, Karl Marx and Stalin. People today don't see Marxism as an objective threat either, or consider themselves to realistically be under its influence, or some version of it. Neither do they consider themselves to be operating under the influence of various modern thought leaders, but doing what they feel to be right. Many who do not see Marxism as a threat or an evil, do see Christianity and Christians as an evil, as well as a threat to the common good and the forward-thinking purpose. Many caricature Christians who oppose them as desiring to put the world under a cruel and imperialistic theocratic dominion, a "handmaid's tale." It has been this book's endeavor to explain why that caricature is an overused fallacy, as well as why it's dangerous to marginalize Christians and silence them for the sake of self-virtuosity and buying political power. This caricature stems from a simple resentment of God for standing in the way of one's sinful desires.

Today the "Kulaks" of America who are standing in the way are Christians and conservatives—generally white, straight, male, Christian, conservatives (although the shapeless targeting system of cancel culture is not restricted to any one of these categories). Today's dekulakization is not always a matter of physical or geographical segregation (exile), imprisonment, or torture as in the Soviet Union—yet—because people would likely catch on and reject such measures if pushed farther than intended too soon. Instead, we see the dekulakization happening in short incremental steps of social conditioning, fear mongering, and demonization of certain people. People are told to fear and hate their neighbors little by little for whatever new reason may be invented by the minute. Social conditioning must first take baby steps before it can learn to take full strides.

The state uses these measures to ensure that people will begin believing whatever the state sanctions, and rejecting whatever it does not sanction. The state is not necessarily the party in power, or one branch of its ideology, but rather the convergence of various ideologies under one umbrella with incredible power at its disposal. The words of the state have become the theology of the left. This theology deems any dissent from the environmental, LGBTQ, pro-choice, social justice, and Democratic Party narratives (among other bedrocks) to be a dangerous heresy which needs to be forced out of society.

It is for this reason that "Democratic" people in power are actively trying to silence our freedom of speech. Like so many other things, they are doing this through incremental steps, and to the degree that they are able, they are trying to make us believe it isn't happening. In May of 2021, Facebook bragged that it was going to start limiting the reach of its users who repeatedly post "misinformation," or "hate speech." Initially this was to be related to misinformation connecting to the election results and Covid-19. More recently this has spread to any criticism of or dissent from the Democratic Party. In July

2021, two months after Facebook's decision to crackdown on troublemakers, Jen Psaki, Joe Biden's press secretary, openly admitted in a press conference that the Democrats were actively monitoring and flagging any problematic posts. This is an authoritarian move, which fits the definition of the party in power using unprecedented powers of the state (big tech monopolies) to force its agenda on an entire population and to shut down counter perspectives and criticism of their policies. This is likely the greatest threat to our first amendment we've faced in generations, if not in the history of our country.

Moreover, Facebook recently began sending out notifications to users about their being exposed to "potentially extremist viewpoints." The problem with words or phrases such as "misinformation," "hate speech," or "potential extremism," is that these terms are incredibly vague and can easily be shaped to describe any counter perspective or political opinion. Misinformation can become a criticism of some of Dr. Anthony Fauci's latest recommendations pertaining to the virus; hate speech can be applied to disagreeing with one or more aspects of the LGBTQ or social justice dogma; the notion of *potential* extremism can lead to *actual* suppression of various freedoms, including the right to criticize certain policies imposed by the party in power. The party in power uses isolated occurrences such as the January 6th 2021 capitol riot to justify their attack on free speech under the guise of "preventing potential extremism." The big tech platforms, the most powerful information systems on the planet, are complacent in bringing these unconstitutional measures to fruition.It will mean more power for them.

When concerns are expressed about the crackdown on free speech, many on the left claim that they are being "gas lighted," that we are imagining this problem, or even that their freedom of speech is being threatened just as much as ours, even when there are multiple instances of a partisan crackdown. It's pretty simple, the elite class does not want to allow any information that is not sanctioned by them or that disagrees with their narrative to be disseminated, and by labelling anything they disagree with as misinformation or hate speech, terms so vague that they can be anything anyone wants them to be at any time, they are able to scrutinize and threaten the first amendment. As soon as they are told that this is what's happening, they use the grade school "I'm rubber, you're glue" tactic, convincing themselves that the same unconstitutional measures are being used against the leftist belief system. The founding fathers saw anything that threatens the first amendment as a direct threat to our freedom and our country. Now our first amendment rights are questioned on a regular basis. The political establishment sees the first amendment as a direct threat to its independent power, because it is.

These measures echo progressive era presidential policies, such as Woodrow Wilson's and FDR's crackdowns on free speech, in some cases threatening fines or jail time for anyone who criticized the administration. These measures were the closest we've come to government instituted fascism, other than right now. The only difference was that fascism wasn't seen as a great evil then as it is now, which is why the party in power and its black-shirt paramilitary wing "antifa" must pin their own title of fascists onto their opponents.

Many claim that their opponents are "being too political" whenever they express concern about the suppression of basic freedoms or the increased radicalization of the left. Many say that Christians and conservatives are "gas lighting," meanwhile anarchists are applauded for dumping cans of gasoline and burning down churches in Canada. Many want this phenomenon to move south into the US. Hatred of the church is in vogue. It is largely an effect of an anti-religious media and academic crusade. The population has been socially conditioned to see one type of violence, discrimination, and persecution as perfectly acceptable, even admirable. They see the church as falling into the system of oppression that must be overthrown. Ironically, they do not see the similarities between their own beliefs and actions and the beliefs and actions of *actual* past systems of oppression.

Many regimes held disdain for various religions because those religions had transcendent beliefs that the state could not touch. In America, Christians are allegiant to a God who is sovereign over the state. The state cannot have that. Since the state influences the masses, the masses can't have that either. But even if the state was to outlaw and suppress our religious freedoms, we would still be commanded by God to stand up for the faith in the midst of a hostile climate, regardless of whatever unconstitutional edict is hurled at us.

Today, the state believes their greatest enemy to be the GOP. They may catch on that their real enemy is actually Christianity and the God of the Bible. Already believing the Bible to be a book of "misinformation" and "fairy tales," perhaps only time will tell when they will label it "potentially extremist misinformation" or "dangerous fairytales" that must be silenced and suppressed. Christianity, as long as it has beliefs that make the state's agenda seem foolish, futile, and wicked, is a direct threat to the state.

Americans should concern themselves with this absurd campaign against misinformation, and see the term for what it really is—a politicized weapon to coerce people into uniformity, one that can be re-adjusted to harm or force into exile any teaching, term, opinion, belief system or story that the elite class doesn't like.

The presuppositions that contribute to the intellectual

dekulakization include considering outside opinions to be dangerous, considering oneself to be a victim for whatever reason, and considering different people with counter perspectives as being oppressors. This gives the victim the senses of moral superiority, mission, and fighting for justice that it takes to leave the victim class to join the class of *tangible* oppressors. The party in power has recognized that it cannot go all out yet in its campaign against our basic freedoms. Instead they are mastering the art of implanting these sentiments into the minds and hearts of Americans so that the campaign emerges organically—by making people "hate thy neighbors" because they are seen as "oppressors." Thus action can be taken against them by the "victims."

∽

Ensuring division through Media manipulation: CNN, The New York Times, NPR, ABC, and MSNBC willfully ignore certain *real* news such as developments in the situation in Afghanistan following America's retreat and the crisis on the US southern border, while focusing on material that will make people think of their political opposition as oppressors who must be overcome, and demons that must be cast out. On the day I write this, out of twenty nine CNN headlines, only one includes a pointless story about Afghanistan which questions whether a soldier that Donald Trump commended actually hoisted a baby over a wall in Kabul—the implication being that a "Trump supporter" would be incapable of doing something compassionate. There is no way that this news sheds any light on what is happening in Afghanistan. Neither is there anything about the situation on the southern border, in Texas, where an unprecedented amount of immigrants are making their way into the state, many dying of exposure, not to mention a corresponding upsurge in drug and human trafficking (among other crimes) in that area. The majority of the October 1 CNN headlines were focused on coronavirus fearmongering, the right-wing movement against abortion, propaganda to keep people "masked up," negative opinions on various conservative voices and politicians, op-eds in support of massive increases in government spending, and defamation of everyone who doesn't want to get vaccinated, among other hyper-partisan propaganda. The headlines of The New York Times and NPR were not quite so hyper-partisan on that particular day. But MSNBC's headlines were even more so.

My aim in the above paragraph was to provide a quick glimpse to show that a mendacious sentiment fills the majority of news stations daily. It is clear that the media's purpose is to deepen and widen the social divide, even as it pretends to wonder why the divide is deepening and widening. This purpose isn't accidental. One can only imagine how learning about national and world events in depth from the twisted, hateful and conspiratorial perspective of MSNBC and CNN would affect the way a person comes to see people who have a different set of opinions—as morons who need to be laughed at, conspiracy theorists who need to be silenced, knuckle draggers who need to evolve, and even evildoers who must be barred from regular society.

Media manipulation, filtering, control, and outright lying have proven to be useful propaganda tactics in past authoritarian and totalitarian regimes as a means to an end indistinguishable from todays' means and ends. The above news agencies would consider this chapter to be "political propaganda," "conspiracy theory," and "right-wing extremism." The difference is that I'm not willfully hiding anything like the Afghan situation created by the president or knowingly filtering out certain information like the conflict at the southern border (also created by the president) to achieve an end result. I am saying everything I know pertaining to the issue at hand to the best of my knowledge without holding back for the sake of personal gain; I will likely face more backlash than praise for doing so. Whereas the modern left willfully filters out certain information to achieve their only goal of demonizing their opposition. This filtering has become an effective instrument of the state.

Information filtering has the same effects as a flat out lie. It is necessary for making the party's never-ending power-grab more palatable. Power grabs become necessary measures when a population is driven by fear. Anyone who sees a power grab and contradicts the fear driven narrative becomes a danger to the left. In August 2021, Florida Governor Ron DeSantis spoke out against the government recommendations to reinstate mandatory mask mandates which followed a nationwide rise in coronavirus cases. CNN and other news networks portrayed DeSantis as a knuckle dragging GOP member who simply wanted to ignore public safety measures and allow the people in Florida to die as a result. These major news agencies neglected to show that although there was a large rise in cases, there was virtually no spike in coronavirus deaths at the point of their reporting. This knowledge was easily accessible for anyone with access to a search engine, so why didn't CNN choose to show that there was not a corresponding rise in death rates at the particular time they labeled DeSantis a mass murderer? They wanted their viewers to believe that the new round of mask mandates, which would force over one hundred million Americans to muzzle themselves, were necessary. This example is one of many which shows that CNN often filters out certain information in order to defame their political opposition, from high ranking politicians to the average Joe. Most people who are viewing their channel are likely not going to nit-pick details. They will trust CNN to give the full story. After all, they are the most trusted name in news!

Here are some fair questions to ask. How much of the modern division is a direct result of daily propaganda peddled by politicians, mainstream media, social media, and our favorite celebrities and icons? Who or what is the entity or entities behind this modern division that pervades our lives? What is the end goal?

The sad fact of the matter is that people nowadays want the government to have more control over them. Government paternalism necessitates power grabs. Many revere the state as God-like, attributing to it the highest moral and intellectual authority. Thinking thoughts and uttering words not sanctioned by the state becomes a dangerous and suspect heresy, not only to the state, but to commoners. In the early stages of this modern intellectual dekulakization, the state consists of a political elite class as well as this class's belief systems. These belief systems include the correct Covid-19 attitude, uniformity of thought about the environment, LGBTQ doctrine, pro-choice (eugenics) brainwashing, advance feminism, and etc. All of these work together, and are contributing to one another in an interlinking fashion. They also benefit the feeling of a superior moral status of those who hold to them. Therefore, the state is not reducible to "the Biden administration," or "the Democrats" or "the Republicans" because the theology of the state is more important than the entities who run the state. Their theology gives them a transcendent purpose. The motivations become deeper, more widespread, and are said to rise above matters related to politics and culture. One may even say the state has a larger spiritual agenda. Christians can make sense of why this is with the knowledge that spiritual neutrality doesn't exist. But for non-Christians, to suggest that there is a deeper motivation or spiritual agenda working behind these things sounds like a conspiratorial fairy tale. There can be no overarching meaning, no enemy of our hearts, no God who opposes the state paradigm, and no identifiable political spectrum on which to place people. This spectrum, just like the spiritual dichotomy implied by Christianity, is simply an oversimplification. Anyone who tries to connect the dots, warns people, disagrees, or challenges the state becomes a "dangerous misinformation super spreader."

There is an alternative "connecting of the dots" for those in the political elite class. An example is as follows: the conservative becomes a conspiracy theorist, the conspiracy theorist becomes a potential extremist, and the potential extremist becomes a racist neo-Nazi. Anyone who does their own research and comes to their own conclusions that deviate from the theology of the left is seen as an evil oppressor. They are not believing what has been sanctioned by the state. They are simply dangerous because they have gained a deeper understanding of the real motivations that function as the engine of the state behind the façade of social justice, fairness, tolerance, and eco-awareness.

Christians are likely not being heavily persecuted here in America yet because we are a little afraid to fully express our beliefs, and to stand against the rising tide. But many are catching on that pulling God out of everything results in chaos. This falls into the basic pattern of the world, a pattern which has been operational since ancient times, and was recognized by most, if not all prophets. God allows a nation to exist, the nation rebels against God, the nation stops existing. If we are unable to recognize any spiritual danger in the modern system it may be an indication of our own desensitization, which can cause Christians to come dangerously close to conforming to and participating in the intellectual dekulakization. Sometimes if we are unaware, actively sinning, not reading scripture, not praying, or not doing our own research we can be susceptible to being duped by the state—integrating ideology into our theology to conform to the pattern of the world. How is church camouflaging with the various aspects of the post-secular paradigm any different than the countless biblical case studies of God's chosen people engaging in idolatrous practices?

Many who are under the influence of social conditioning have been taught to carry with them a sense of victimhood, or a noble sense of fighting for helpless victims. This falls under the same Marxist principle of the proletariat rising against the bourgeois. Like today's use of certain arbitrary identity labels such as "privileged," "heteronormative," "patriarchal," etc., the Marxist economic labels of proletariat and bourgeoisie were also vague titles. They were so arbitrary that they plunged society into chaos, pitting everyone against one another. Many perceived oppressors and subversives were delivered over to the slaughter.

In the Russian dekulakization, the government told people to expose whoever their perceived oppressors were, or those who sought to subvert the state. Many were tortured and imprisoned for the simple goal of getting them to tell on friends and family. It got so out of control that no one understood who the enemy, oppressors, and victims were and weren't. Many believed that they were fighting an actual oppressor, which was only a specter drawn by the state. Today's push against Christians and conservatives echoes these measures. People have a picture drawn up in their heads of what the oppressors look like. It can become you if you disagree in one iota. Many are witnessing friends and family alienate and shun them for political disagreements, or for standing up unapologetically for the faith. Christian conservatives know that their position offers little moral high ground, no "yay me" moment for telling the truth, but rather will be slandered, mocked and derided for speaking out against the state. There is not much glory nowadays for exposing the evils of Planned Parenthood and the abortion industry. In some cases it ends in lawsuits, fines, and jail time, as well as mass shunning from pro-choice peers. There isn't much glory in asking fair questions about the various population control solutions proposed to solve the ecological crisis. This usually results in being labelled "anti-science" and being seen as someone who doesn't care at all about the state of our earth. Neither is there much glory in questioning advanced gender or race theories, for one is quickly called a racist-homophobe for doing that. However, posting a black square or a rainbow on one's *Instagram* feed will always result in unanimous applause and a free rise in popularity among one's peers.

Today, Christians are high up on the target list of oppressors and "kulaks" because we have a God that is higher than the state and the various belief systems sanctioned by the state. Many do not perceive Marxism to be a real threat to society. They do not see Marxist behavior present in their own self-perceived victimhood, as well as the corresponding valiant battle against the ever-changing list of invisible oppressors. Many are growing tired of being warned about the dangers of neo-Marxism, even in the church. They think anyone who sees communism creeping in to be a conspiracy theorist. However, when Marxist education is offered to your children, when its motifs pervade Hollywood, when its theories are driving all the corresponding theories such as advanced gender theory, eco-critical theory, and critical race theory which are being utilized by the state, it is not conspiratorial to recognize that a new version of Marxism is still the penetrating conceptual force directing all who are "fighting oppressors" and that it is the primary engine for today's "Democratic" Party.

Many who read this may take offense, and pin the very

accusations of what I'm writing about on me. However, the simple fact is that many on the left, who agree with weaponized politics, are not having their first amendment rights come under heavy scrutiny for saying what *they* believe. Moreover, media agencies, big tech monopolies, and the administration they support are burning the candle at both ends to figure out how they can unify and censor opposition, limiting access to the few alternative information resources that remain unauthorized. Just as preaching the gospel is considered "hate speech" nowadays while blasting music about using women, drug abuse, murder, and devil worship is celebrated, so telling the truth about what is happening in the world and reporting the news without the appropriated spin is becoming more and more of a "danger to society."

One of the Ten Commandments tells us not to bear false witness. Another tells us not to have any other god before our God. Still another tells us not to covet. Another tells us not to murder. Another tells us not to steal. Another tells us not to make any graven images. All of these commandments are blatantly contradicted by our state. The information we rely on to tell us what is happening in the world cannot be trusted. The left has formed its own religion to fit in the place of God. Many people are coveting what their neighbors have, judging one another on social media, and demanding "equity." Socialism teaches that it is alright to simply take from those who have more than you. Our next generation is being raised, influenced, and shaped by images on screens. Moreover, we are being taught to reject God by the academe and to fear our neighbor by the mainstream media. The undesirable economic, social, and governmental powers at work in our nation can be seen as an outworking of a long lasting and repetitive spiritual condition of any civilization. The state has risen against God.

Chapter 5

Stick to Scripture and Shut Up!

Keeping the Silent, Silent

It is plain to see: Christians do not belong in the sciences, media, Hollywood, or politics. Evolution is a fact, Genesis is a myth! Christian conservatives are too bias and numb to real world sensibilities to report the news factually. If Christians keep ascending politically we will soon have a theocracy on our hands. Christians should stick with what they know over there in la-la-land and allow people in the real world to operate over here. This is the basic sentiment of religious privatization, and it pervades the American ethos.

The New York Times and far left magazines like *The New Yorker* unapologetically hate real Christians: especially when Christians make noise or, much more dangerously, make sense. *The New York Times* frequently writes op-eds about Christian "radicalism" or "fundamentalism" and the clear and present threat of Christian voters—unless of course they vote the way the left wants them to vote. Christians who agree with the left are praised as intellectually and morally superior to Christians who still are "stuck" in an old-fashioned, traditional mindset. The latter are a threat to life as we know it, while the former are the future of the church.

When Christian voters help elect someone the left doesn't like, they suddenly become the living manifestation of all the evils in the world. Don't believe me? Read the 2020 *Times* article *An Open Letter to my White Fellow Christians* by Margaret Renkl. In this article Renkl writes, "We used our Christian faith as a justification for killing… every month, every week, and every day we have been setting new fires… White Christians who came before us captured human beings and beat them and raped them and stole their babies from them and stole their husbands and their wives from them and locked them up in chains and made them work in inhuman conditions." She goes on to say that Christians are responsible for police brutality, and even the murder of George Floyd. Her article is filled with much more hate driven rhetoric toward the intolerance and racism of Christianity. There are other *Times* articles that condition the masses to hate Christians as long as they do not conform to the left.

If Christians are all wicked, murderous racists, analogous to Nazis and white supremacists, then wouldn't it make sense to enact verbal or physical violence against them? History tells us that the first step toward violence or oppression against a people group in societies is rhetoric like Margaret Renkl's. Organizations like *The New York Times* are still revered as honest and bipartisan. The general population considers them to be the absolute standard of truth. Meanwhile, the Bible is seen as a little book of lies.

The New Yorker is even more intolerant toward Christians that do not adhere to the value system of the left. With headlines like "The Radical Origins of Christianity," "American Christianity's White-Supremacy Problem," "Evangelicals of Color Fight Back against the Religious Right," "A Sociologist Religion of Protestants, Porn and the 'Purity Industrial Complex'," "The Unlikely Endurance of

Christian Rock," "How Black Lives Matter is Changing the Church," "My Childhood in a Cult," and "Christianity gets Weird," it becomes clear that mainstream Christians are being painted with the broad brush of everything evil and taboo by the more popular cult of the left. The only Christians who will be tolerated are those who bend the knee to the anti-Christian, Marxist ideals of the *Times* and *The New Yorker*. There are many other media outlets that help the masses reach the same conclusions about your local racist, warmongering churchgoers. Christians are now to be blamed for every sinister aspect of America's past, present, and future—they must be silenced at any cost.

Many Christians are becoming skeptical of any left-leaning Christian teachings. For my part, I am becoming weary of any Christian material that is praised by left-leaning media. After all, why would the left praise anyone or anything that goes against the grain of culture, or confronts some of its more insane ideas? Some Christian authors are praised by organizations like the *Times* for the reason that they repackage in Christian terms the narrative of all Christians on the right being closed minded bigots. "Progressive Christians" promote a type of Christianity that can camouflage silently and complacently with the culture, agree with the secular disdain for our values, and confront the noisy, far right, white-supremacist churches that step out of line. In other words, many Christians themselves believe in the left's derogatory caricature of Christianity. It's quite simple, when Christians quietly pray in their closets to their make-believe God that's fine. But as soon as they step out into the public square there is a problem.

History is being rewritten in order to tell the tale of the glorious heroism of secularism in opposition to the vicious villainy of Christianity. Again, modern society's problem is not with conservatives, policemen, prison systems, or western civilization, but with God Himself. Every media and cultural drawing that distorts the nonconformist Christian, portraying him as something he's not, is another step towards silencing him and perhaps persecuting him. Every weapon in the arsenal is being used, from making fun of our beliefs as childish and imbecilic to labeling every one of us as rotten to the core. Many "Christian" teachers help further the leftist agenda by sympathizing with this unfair falsification of our people. Some claim neutrality. Others agree that the negative aspects of historical Christianity outweigh the positive. Political "fence-sitting," when one side is clearly out to get us, has become common in modern churches. Conformists are praised as proper Christians in the eyes of modernity. Such Christians may be permitted to keep their church doors open, at least for the time being.

The only weapon against such weaponized rhetoric is the sword—not the sword of the flesh but the sword of the Spirit. Jesus taught us to love our enemies. But as Christians we should never bow down to such hate, participate in counter-spiritual activities, believe wrongheaded ideas, or remain silent on such issues. Speaking out and standing our ground is not the same as picking up the literal sword and striking an enemy with it, just as being nice all the time and never telling the truth is not the same as loving one's neighbor. It is clear that what the left really means when it praises people who "stick close to scripture and shut up," is really praise for the ones who are not a threat to the left's ideology and tolerance only for those who are willing to compromise on their values.

Complacent Christians have come to the knowledge of many of the left's more anti-Christian intentions and still refuse to reject such intentions, integrating these intentions into the church. By taking this stance, many leave the pews and pulpit to become pundits for the party. Pandering may serve them well short-term, sell more books, and increase audience numbers, but it also weakens church awareness of a system that deeply desires to silence the Christian voice.

Many don't mean for any of this to happen. Most aren't intentionally pandering. But Christians that align themselves with culture do believe that other Christians ought to stay silent on certain issues if their stance is unpopular and that left leaning Christians have a firmer grasp on scripture. Such a stance can be dangerous when the water temperature is increasing for Christians everywhere in the western world, especially Christians who refuse to compromise. Today the left wants to eradicate the myth of our nation's Christian foundation and tear down history inasmuch as it pertains to the Judeo-Christian worldview.

If Christians and their worldview make up virtually all of that mythology and history, and are one of the only remaining obstacles to the various progressive objectives, then what's to stop the progressive system from eradicating us—our churches, our Bibles, our voices, our history, our traditions, even our lives? When past regimes finally understood that it was the church that stood most fervently against the ambitions of total state control and worship of the government system, being a Christian suddenly became much more dangerous.

The rhetoric of the *Times* op-ed article is greatly enflamed and clearly untrue. Such rhetoric cannot be without consequence when it's read by millions. Many people who go about their daily lives are growing increasingly impatient with Christians. Many believe assumptions about the church's evil on a daily basis. If the content of the above op-ed replaced the word "Christians" with the word "Progressives," however, the article would be more historically accurate. After all, evils like slavery, segregation, fascism, the removal of indigenous people, and eugenics were theorized, propagated, enacted, legislated, enforced, promoted, and some are now being repackaged by progressivism on the broad world stage, not by Christianity. Granted, many progressives did claim Christianity publicly to help their cause (even Hitler did to some degree), but they only did this to maintain church support for as long as they needed it. Christians often opposed these evils and saw through them even in their infancy. It is the progressives who have the more accurate history of intolerance and injustice, for which they are seldom willing to learn about or admit, much less answer for.

My aim is not to slander anyone who belongs to the progressive left, but simply to tell the truth and to warn the people of yet another rising progressive tide against the Christian. The modern progressive notions are once again in support of eugenics by means of abortion, repackaged communism, fascism through the elite class's use of various tech corporations to gain mass support, leftist propaganda being taught to our youth, media filtering and manipulation, racial determinism, and various other means and ends. It doesn't take an epistle to the American church from Paul to recognize that we shouldn't be participating in such an atmosphere of ideas.

Hide in Your Holes

I recall a magazine article wherein a "pastor" wrestled with what he thought the place of the church should be in America today. This "pastor" was convinced that the church had lost the culture war in the emerging secular age. The article is a series of merciless self-flagellations on the part of the pastor as he seems to recall everything wrong he's ever done in his life. The writing shows a clear picture of how the narrow minded system of Christianity itself—not the pastor's faith crisis—is really to blame for all the failings of his past. Recognizing that Christians have "lost the culture war," the pastor suggests retreating back into our closets and building isolated Christian communities so that Christians can keep their futile religious system out of the way of the real world. Many Christians are beginning to sympathize with the notion that the gospel must be hidden in a hole. It is not politically correct enough.

The unnamed pastor's lack of faith and assurance in the gospel is disturbing, but even more disturbing is the conclusion this brings him to—Christians in general ought to hide in their holes and advance the kingdom only amongst themselves. In this article the thesis seems to scream, "Yes! This is what we've been telling you all along," from the leftist shadow. Again, the underlying narrative castigates uncompromising Christians for being responsible for the majority of the evil in the world. The proper Christian lifestyle is to be one of segregation and perpetual shame. The pastor bows his knee and confesses not only his own sins, but the sins of the entire church against righteous culture, and then vows to leave everyone else alone. It's a win, win right? We leave the world alone and the world leaves us alone—the world doesn't want to hear about Jesus anymore, and Christians don't want to be polluted by the world. The way we are to best love the world seems to be by removing ourselves from it.

When Jesus taught us to pray, he taught us to pray to our Father in secret and not to make a big show of it. So I can see the argument for praying alone in our closets. What I can't see is the argument for living alone in our closets, but apparently what is best for the world is if we all bow before the world and scourge ourselves for our many sins against it. Then we must put prison bars on our home windows so that we can't get out and the world can't get in. The gospel may only be proclaimed after prefacing it with a self-loathing apology.

The modern mood is quite clear. It is through with having its daily entertainment interrupted by the Christian. The gospel makes people uneasy, and so it must be taken "in the most delightful way," with a spoonful of sugar. We are no longer called to be the salt but the sugar of the western world and to bury our light under a bowl. If you try to live your faith out loud, you will soon see the negative effects of having too much salt. You must bow the knee, cross yourself, say ten "hail Mary's," then return to hide again in your hole.

This is the current cultural temperament. The good news is that this means the church is doing something right. Christ told us that the world would hate us because it hated Him first. This hatred becomes especially apparent when any idea is introduced that would prohibit the world from some of its practices—such as the multi-billion dollar child sacrifice industry. The problem with allowing the world to remain as it is while we remain segregated from it, is that the world will eventually cross over to conquer what little territory we hold onto if we don't allow the gospel its freedom. This is why the gospel is offensive to so many, because Christ calls us to die to ourselves and to the things of this world in order to follow Him, thereby recognizing the things of the world pattern to be a futile vapor. This recognition may hurt a person's feeling who is immersed in the world pattern. Of course, this means everyone at one point or another. Christ stands in the way of the deepest desires of our flesh. He was crucified, in part, because He became a stumbling block to the various ambitions of sinners. He didn't hide in a hole, and He commanded us not to either.

It is no wonder that the ideological war is becoming so tense that mainstream articles suggest that Christians pander to culture and apologize for being outspoken. They see our agenda as a threat to their own, and they should.

In the last section we talked a little about an op-ed that blamed Christianity for everything evil under the sun, old and new. We also talked about how if they replaced the word "Christians" with "Progressives" the op-ed would make a lot more sense. Christians have a rich history of refusing to hide in their holes and standing up to rising tides of tyranny and injustice. Dietrich Bonhoeffer refused to keep quiet and be passive. He stood against the Nazis from the beginning. He was ultimately executed for his "saltiness." He said "no thanks" to the sugar. William Wilberforce spent his entire life fighting against the evils of slavery because of his firm grasp of God's law of human equality. He was fiercely ridiculed by his opposition in parliament for his countercultural "political opinion," which presented itself in stark contrast to the subjective "rights" of the cultural majority. Abraham Lincoln's faith drove him outside his private prayer closet as well, and we all know that story! Similarly today, some Christians think that we should step out of hibernation and into the real world—unfortunately we cannot walk too far in this real world before we enter the cultural and political spheres. Christians seem unanimous, besides the ones who pander and hole-hide, in their belief that there is always evil in the world. It's not God who's bringing it there, but someone else.

It seems ridiculous that I should even have to write this book and feel it in any way to be controversial—but such is the case when the truth, both past and present, is being efficiently suppressed, filtered and inverted to fit the godless paradigm. I want this to be a wakeup call. We do not need to pander. We do not need to exit the political sphere. We do not need to hide in our holes and be ashamed of our faith. We do not need to make sure the kingdom stays invisible. We are called to be bold and courageous. This doesn't mean hacking away at people with the sword of the flesh, but hacking away at deceitful ideas with the sword of the Spirit of truth. There is no way around this. Christ founded his church with the intent that the gates of hell or even of political correctness would not prevail against it.

"Alright," you may be saying, "you're being over dramatic. The evils of slavery were vanquished and the Nazis were overthrown. The world today is in less need of Christian political interventionism than it was then."

To that I'd respond that we are all men and women of our times. Satan's schemes are no less present in 2022 than they were in 1922, they are simply *craftier,* and in other words, more appealing to today's sentiments. Evil does not go away even when we close our eyes and tell ourselves it's not there, but it does grow in its ability to cover itself up among the current eras in order to more easily influence them.

Let's do a thought exercise: Let's say that there is an objective morality or a law of human nature, and that there is a transcendent source of that morality and law—a God who holds high expectations, but allows us to make our choices either for or against that law of human nature. Each day, our decisions reflect either a rejection or a desire to follow this law. Let's also suppose that this same God is the maker of all things, including you and me. But He didn't make us when we took our first steps or our first breaths or when we were delivered from our mothers' wombs, but before that. He formed us *in* our mothers' wombs. He knew us before we were born. The information coding in DNA would later prove this. Now let's suppose that as a society we reject this notion of the sanctity and brilliance of human life and advertise the "right" to dismember and rip children from their mothers' wombs before they are born because they may be an inconvenience to their parents. Not only that, but this senseless evil is increasing in its scale and leniency as it is industrialized and praised as an act of courage. In fact, some on the left are promoting an even more radicalized form of infanticide, babies being euthanized after birth. This activity is being advertised and pushed farther and farther into our culture, and it is now considered evil to call this evil "evil," even for many in the church. Voices against this "fundamental human right" to snuff out life are demonized. Many Christians shut their eyes and ears and say "I'm not listening," and "I can't see it, so it must not be there." But when they open their eyes, it's still there as a stain on present society, millions of babies dead and dying, all sanctioned by the state and our tax dollars. It is not hard to see for the Christian why this is an abomination to the Lord, but also for anyone with a shred of common sense to recognize that it flies in the face of the laws of human nature and basic decency. This evil is happening *now.*

Yet Christians are still preached against by hidden pastors when they step up to speak out against such evil or vote a certain way strictly because of things like this. We are "rebuked" for not loving our neighbors enough, for posting insensitive and unpopular opinions on social media, for allowing the gospel to make its way into the public and political sphere, for single issue voting, and for disobeying Romans 13—which they suppose protects the unlawful laws of man even when they blatantly transgress both the law of God and the nature of reality. Abortion isn't the only topic that the "hidden ones" are closing their eyes and ears to. In the name of a vague notion of Romans 13 we have enshrined every edict of man and made *them* an idol for us. Satan, in his craftiness, has made his way into the law of man in order to pull the wool over our eyes— fortunately for him, he doesn't even have to do that. He can just tell us to close our eyes and stay hidden and we'll listen to him. As soon as we step out of our holes we are promised persecution.

"Alright," you may now be saying, "I may concede that there is still evil in the world and that the church has an obligation to stand up and fight, but what makes you think that our voices are being silenced by culture?"

The state's threat against our religious liberties is very real and present, and has metastasized since the pandemic began. The coronavirus took the world by a storm of insanity. It turned normal people into imminent threats and neighbors into diseased aliens. Handshakes were forbidden, hugs were considered attempted mass homicide, and the bottom half of the entire population's face was strictly criminalized. The pandemic rolled through the US and seemed to give the government the opportunity to create a prototype and preview of all out psychological and sociological persecution of the American church. Churches across the board were immediately deemed nonessential by the US government, mainly democrat policy makers, but also spineless republicans. The bad news is that many, myself included, fell for this ploy. The good news is that many more are now waking up to it and realizing that totalitarian edicts are not about public safety measures, but about finally bringing the dream of Christian segregation to fruition. We were actually told by the US government to hide in our holes, and to trade church indefinitely for an internet livestream. Those who opposed these draconian edicts were mocked, punished, arrested, fined and labeled as enemies of the state.

As I write, this has been going on for a long time. In red states many churches still have the option to meet. But many churches, mainly in blue states are still having their first amendment and God-given right to public worship and gathering either questioned or revoked outright. In Canada, the government built a fence around a church that refused to stop meeting. Many brave churches are refusing these edicts, recognizing their true demonic motive, and meeting anyway. They are being punished legally and financially for their rebellion against the principalities of the state. Other churches are trusting in the law of man to look out for their best interest. They continue to avoid meeting. Some churches are even refusing to meet in states that allow meeting. And some are waking up to the *fact* that this is not right and beginning to meet after many months of hiding from the dictatorial edicts of the radical left.

I want to give grace to pastors all across the board, many were looking out for their congregation's safety. Many were believing, at first, that the government was acting altruistically. Many are still wrestling with this issue at a moral level. The answer however is clear. Give your people the option to meet, as well as the option to meet with or without masks as they please, regardless of the punishments you may face as a result. The church does not consist of a bunch of little children, and this rising tide of culture against church needs to be addressed *in church*. I commend the leaders who woke up to this yesterday, are waking up to it today, and will wake up to it tomorrow. The coronavirus is teaching me, as well as many other Christians, that the world thinks we are nonessential, and just how essential we really are.

Maybe we should be thanking the left for in many ways waking the American church up from a deep sleep. They told us to hide in our holes, and after we hid in them for a while and watched the world around us, we recognized why they told us to hide and why we ought not to. They told us to close our eyes, and after they were closed for a time, when we opened them, we were able to see much more clearly. They told us to stay silent and we found our voices. They told us we were insane and we regained our sanity. They convinced the world that we were unnecessary, and the world fell apart as soon as we left it. We listened and adhered to them for a time and walked away from them because of our humanity, and then turned back around to go and love them because of Christ's divinity. We emerged from our hibernation, and we are done apologizing for it.

Big Christian Problems Abroad

Christians are heavily persecuted abroad. From the year 2019 to 2020 the global persecution rate jumped by over sixty percent. The former ambassador for religious freedom claims that we are seeing the highest amount of persecution in the history of the Christian faith on a worldwide scale. In western churches it is sometimes easy to become comfortable on our padded pews and forget about the pains that our brothers and sisters around the world are facing for the name of Christ. The simple fact is that Christians are being targeted by militaries, governments, societies, and ideologies worldwide. The daily news of what is happening to our brothers and sisters abroad is staggering, but it almost never makes it to the front page of US newspapers.

This section will be lengthy, but is meant to provide a slight glimpse into the various recent evils that have befallen the saints, as well as a brief historical estimate of other staggering statistics regarding Christian persecution in the not so distant past. One should note that this is not meant in any way to downplay other religious groups who have been targeted and persecuted. I hope, space permitting, to include some accounts of their suffering. But my main goal is to show how the world seems to be objectively rising against Christianity in a multitude of ways.

Myanmar (Burma): For decades in Myanmar, the Burmese military (Tatmataw) has violently oppressed various religious minorities including Muslims (thousands of whom fell victim to unspeakable atrocities in the 2016 Rohingya genocide) and Christians. The Chin Christians are among other religious groups that are heavily persecuted by the Tatmataw: On September 18 2021, the Burmese army bombed homes in the Chin state and shot a pastor who was trying to put out the fires; another Chin pastor was abducted by the Burmese army on September 16; on September 22 the Burmese army shelled and attacked a Catholic Church in Chin; thousands of Chin Christians are fleeing from this territory; on September 29 two elderly Chin Christians were murdered by the Tatmataw. The Tatmataw junta has killed over one thousand civilians and imprisoned over seven thousand since the February coup. The Tatmataw continues to gain economic and military support from Russia and China. Following the Rohingya genocide of 2016 carried out by the Myanmar military, and the ensuing displacement crisis of 2017, Rohingya Christians now face a violent binary threat from the Myanmar military and their Muslim neighbors,[10] including a militant group which specifically targets Rohingya Christians, seeing them as traitors especially when they profess their faith openly. Following the coup, the majority of Myanmar Christians live in high conflict zones.[11] Out of the six territories where armed conflicts most frequently break out, only two do not consist of a Christian majority. General Min Aung Hlaing has bluntly stated his plan to enforce his religion of Buddhism on the entire population. The evils carried out against Muslims in Myanmar are incomprehensible, considering they are the most targeted religious group and Christians are also considered second class citizens, carriers of the "C-virus" ("C" stands for Christian). In total, the military "caretaker government" in Myanmar barbarically oppresses various religious minority groups including Muslims and Christians, Rohingya Christians face threats from militant neighbors and a military government, and a majority of Christians occupy the majority of conflict zones where towns and villages are raided daily by Tatmataw oppressors.

India: In August 2008, anti-Christian riots erupted in the Kandhamal district, after Christians were blamed for the murder of a Hindu nationalist leader, a crime perpetrated by Maoists. These riots resulted in 39 Christians murdered and over 3,900 homes destroyed. Although this is seen as the worst instance of persecution in modern Indian history, the pressure is still deeply felt by Indian Christians. In June 2021 an Indian pastor from Bihar state and his family received death threats from Hindu nationalists who came to their home, demanding the family renounce the faith, leave the village, or be burned alive. The following day they were summoned to a village gathering in order to participate in a Hindu worship ceremony, again facing the above alternatives from their neighbors. The following morning the family fled the village.[12] Anti-conversion laws have been legislated in seven Indian states. Once these laws are legislated, Hindu nationalists can claim that conversions are "forced" as opposed to voluntary. Christian proselytizers and converts are often assaulted and then arrested following these "forced conversions." Another state is moving to introduce these laws, which enforce religious oppression in a top-down fashion.[13] In September 2021 five Christians were arrested during a house church service after activists forced themselves into the home and called the police, claiming the church was participating in "forced conversions." Since June 2021 over seventy Christians have been detained under similar circumstances.[14] In central India, notices, interrogations, threats from neighbors, spying on church activities, anti-conversion laws, and physical violence have forced a large number of Indian Christians underground. Activist groups have presented the local government an ultimatum to either crack down on Christians or to allow these groups to enact their own brand of violence against them. These Christians continue to meet in smaller groups to avoid being seen praying together.[15] In Odisha state four Christian homes were set ablaze by radical nationalists because the owners refused to renounce their faith. Christians were denied access to water from the village well, perceived by locals as a just measure to meet the refusal of village members to renounce Christ. In mid-September (2021), four women were harassed by a crowd for trying to use this well. After this, their homes were broken into, they were assaulted, and forced to leave their homes. About a week after fleeing into the jungle, the displaced families found that their homes had been burned.[16] Politicians are using anti-Christian narratives to force anti-conversion laws on the country, under which they may more efficiently silence and oppress the church. In late September, six Christians in Yadagiri District were arrested; four were attacked as they walked on the street by a mob and then arrested, and another couple was assaulted by a mob and arrested for the crime of speaking with a railway station worker about Jesus and handing her a copy of the New Testament.[17] On August 11 a Christian man in Bihar was burned with acid. He succumbed to his wounds forty six days later.[18] On September 29 in Madhya Pradesh a Christian wedding was ambushed, and the couple was arrested along with their families.[19] Christians in India are targeted, assaulted, spied on, displaced, interrogated, intimidated, systemically oppressed, arrested, jailed, and murdered for nothing more than believing in Christ and doing what He commanded them to do—tell others about Him. The love of Christ in India cannot be suppressed by these evils.

Egypt: Although legislative measures for Egyptian Christians are shaping up to look brighter for the future, the future still looks uncertain for them. Christians in Egypt still face systemic discrimination and are treated as third class citizens in almost all areas of life. There is a debate concerning religious freedom and a push to recognize the plight of Egyptian Christians on the part of the Egyptian government. However, advocates for human rights and religious freedoms remain imprisoned indefinitely, and the decision to protect human rights and religious freedoms remains a controversial topic among Egyptian leaders and community members. Persecution happens mostly at the community level, rather than by government-sanctioned persecution. In Upper Egypt, Christian women are often harassed and entire communities of Christians may be driven from their homes by extremist mobs. Educational institutions knowingly discriminate against Christians, and Christians are restricted from building churches and other church-based organizations. Many face more imminent dangers from Islamic extremists. There has been a long history of persecution against Coptic Christians in particular, and often when a Christian is murdered, attacked, or driven from his or her home, the Egyptian state-run media warns that it was likely not solely because of their Christian identity. The Egyptian media and authorities have a history of silencing Christian accounts of persecution happening directly as a result of their faith.[20]

Nigeria: Although Nigeria is technically a secular country, in many ways it operates under Sharia law which includes punishments derived directly from the Quran such as beatings for drinking, amputation of limbs for stealing, and execution for apostasy.[21] In one Nigerian state, in one month, Fulani militants attacked a Christian community, killing fifty people, destroying well over two hundred homes and seven churches. In this area over 80% of the community is Christian.[22] A twenty-seven year old man was recently arrested in Nigeria. He explained that his boss gave him a gun with the intent that he'd specifically target Christians. He admitted to killing five.[23] In late September, suspected Fulani militants murdered over thirty people in two villages and burned 15 homes,[24] immediately following an attack on an Evangelical church where a gunman murdered one worshipper and wounded several others after entering a church service and shooting sporadically.[25] On the same week, a mob attacked and killed a minister and burned down a church and a Christian school.[26] Nigeria is at a height of persecution in 2020-2021. In these two years alone, over 3,000 Christians have been killed, according to The International Society for Civil Liberties and the Rule of Law.[27] There is an incredible amount of violence against Christians in Nigeria, and many of the surrounding countries. Christians are seen as less than human, and this sentiment is growing, presumably as Christians grow bolder in their representation of Christ and fearless delivery of the Gospel. Western Christians have a lot to learn from such incredible people, who face life and death circumstances every day for the crime of trusting in Jesus's name.

China: The Chinese Communist Party (CCP) has recently been condemned by US department of state for its restriction on religious freedoms and all out persecution on various religious groups such as Falun Gong practitioners, Protestant Christians, Uighur Muslims, and Tibetan Buddhists. The CCP's persecution has been dubbed a genocide against Uighur Muslims and other religious minority groups. Multitudes of Uighur Muslims are detained in secretive concentration camps under the auspices of socialism. China's violent suppression of Falun Gong and Tibetan Buddhists is a crime against humanity. The CCP is also intolerant of Christians who don't attend the only two state-sanctioned churches. They have effectively forced the church underground and frequently storm homes that host church services. Like other communist and totalitarian regimes, the CCP looks only to accept religion once it has been synthesized with the belief system of the state.[28] Many persecuted religious peoples, including Christians and Muslims from Myanmar, are barred access to China in order to protect China from "religious infiltration" by 372 miles of barbed wire fences. Their concern is that Myanmar immigration will also give rise to establishing, arming and aiding anti-communist militias in China.[29] The Chinese government recently cracked down on the dissemination of Christian social media content in hopes to limit the reach of the gospel via the internet.[30] The CCP threatens parents with their children's education if they continue certain religious practices. They use children to spy on their Christian parents, asking specific questions about their parent's religious beliefs and activities. For fear that the CCP is indoctrinating children with communist propaganda, many Christians have placed their children in Christian home schools, which are illegal. The CCP sees any religious education as a threat to childhood educational development in accordance with CCP values.[31] The CCP pairs the holes in its religious freedom laws with "sinicization" laws to undermine religious autonomy. These laws aspire to force religious beliefs under the authority of the state. Using these powers, the Chinese government shuts down and demolishes churches, restricts religious gatherings, detains Christian leaders and pastors for state subversion, and treats Chinese Christians like second or third class citizens. Much of what happens is no doubt underreported, ignored altogether, or filtered through the CCP propaganda system, and then double filtered through the American propaganda system. The CCP's tight grip on technology and their worldwide ambitions and influence should be a major concern for Christians everywhere who still have access to their religious freedoms. The year 2020-2021 saw a massive increase in Chinese persecution with the new "sinicization" efforts. In China, there is no longer any "safe-space" to be a practicing Christian.

The Middle East: Christians are unwelcome in the Middle East. They frequently face persecution, silencing, death, and exile in order to bring about a fully Islamic rule in the Middle East. Turkey has had a long history of atrocity dating back to the Ottoman Empire. Today, the Turkish government maintains major religious freedom restrictions, continues to oppress religious and ethnic groups outside its borders in a genocidal fashion, and has links with Afghan terrorist groups such as Al-Qaeda and the Taliban who routinely target Christians. Syrian military hirelings including ISIS are deployed by Turkey to target and conquer areas like Nagnoro-Karabakh (An area with an Armenian Christian majority). They are advised to slaughter Armenians for extra payment. Syria has active Islamic religious police and a Syrian Christian home was recently bombarded by Turkey, killing four family members. Syrian militias supported by Turkey terrorize Afrin villages and Assyrian villages are often caught in SDF and Turkish conflict zones. Christians face frequent persecution in Syria. There isn't much to report on Christian persecution in Iraq, considering that Iraq has all but eliminated its Christian presence. Iranian religious freedom is worsening as Christian converts are imprisoned. One prison where Christians are sent for conversion is basically a torture chamber. In Israel, a Christian cemetery was recently desecrated. The Israeli government recently shut down a Christian television channel and rarely allows the Christian faith any breathing room. An Israeli man recently killed his mother for converting from Islam to Christianity. Christians in Palestine frequently face religious persecution from extremists. It is a sad and terrifying fact that Christianity is being driven so forcefully from its homeland. There are a few Middle Eastern countries that deserve their own sections.

Pakistan: Pakistan was considering an anti-conversion law in order to prevent forced conversions. These laws would be different than the Indian "forced conversion" laws where the laws are often misappropriated to prevent and punish regular voluntary conversions. Young women in Pakistan are frequently kidnapped and/or forced to convert from Christianity or Hinduism to Islam, so many Christians saw these laws as protective measures for their communities. The laws were shot down.[32] As of late September 2021, Pakistan refuses Afghan refugees asylum in their country following the Taliban takeover of Afghanistan. This deeply affects the heavily persecuted Afghan Christian community and further leaves them at the mercy of the Taliban. This is a complex situation however, as Pakistan has welcomed so many immigrants in the past without international assistance that it now claims to be unable to bring in another massive influx of oppressed people. However, the Pakistan government, including the Prime Minister and other senior officials, has repeatedly shown support for the Taliban.[33] (The Turkish government also supports the rise of the Taliban.) In July and August, a disturbing rise in incidents of sexual assaults, abductions, and forced conversions of Christian women in Pakistan has happened.[34] Pakistan courts recently refused to return a fourteen year old girl to her parents after she was abducted, forcefully converted, and required to marry her abductor. [35] Pakistan has laws that make the crime of blasphemy punishable by death. These laws have been used as an excuse for religious retribution and all out persecution on the Church. In 2018, a Christian woman was released from death row, where she remained for almost ten years as a result of blasphemy laws. International outcry against the injustice of her circumstance was a large reason for her exoneration. 29 Christians are now in similar circumstances, charged, convicted or imprisoned as a result of Pakistan's inhumane blasphemy laws.[36] Due to these laws, and the violence and persecution enacted on the Christian community by their society, Pakistan is considered one of the worst countries for Christian persecution. Pakistani Christians are treated as less than human. In January 2021, a nurse was falsely accused of blasphemy and tortured in a hospital room by her coworkers prior to her arrest. She is facing the death sentence. Blasphemy laws include killing citizens who deny Muhammad's status as a prophet and are often wrested by people to get even or to condemn someone with a different set of beliefs to a horrible fate. There are little to no rights for religious minorities under the Pakistani constitution. Christians are not allowed higher up positions in the workforce, but are usually forced to become sanitation workers. Christians comprise of 80-90% of low down workforce positions despite making up only 2% of Pakistan's overall population. This is practically slave labor. Any neutral or secular laws are synthesized with Islamic jurisprudence and, just like in every nation where Islamic doctrine is the law of the land, this means persecution of other religions in general and Christianity in particular. An example of this injustice, again, is the forced conversions that take place when Christian women and girls are forced to marry abductors and convert to Islam: Pakistan's secular law doesn't allow this, but Islamic law says that young girls can be married off, and so the Islamic law often prevails. About a thousand of these crimes happen every year according to a 2014 study.[37] This hardline persecution extends from the government to the education system and trickles down into the communities, where a fierce hatred for the Christian faith pervades the Pakistani atmosphere. Just like so many of these other nations discussed, much of what happens in Pakistan is likely not reaching our eyes and ears.

Afghanistan: The Taliban terrorist organization took control of the country following a botched US withdrawal in August 2021. It has brutally cracked down with Sharia law on various identity groups such as women and Christians. Women's rights activists are targeted by the Taliban and Afghan Christians are considered apostate under Sharia law, a crime punishable by the death sentence. Taliban leaders want Sharia-style brutalities and killings to come back to Afghan communities. Atrocities such as beheading Christians take place, and the Taliban searches through peoples' phones to find Christian content in order to accuse and sentence them. Even prior to the Taliban gaining power, Afghan Christians were the second most persecuted people on the planet. Now, under the Taliban crackdown, the heavy-handed threat Christians live under is greatly multiplied. Like so many other instances of global Christian persecution, what is happening in Afghanistan is largely ignored and filtered through our media by "independent fact checkers." However, it is difficult to fact check videotaped beheadings and reports coming from on the ground. Many Afghan Christians are turning off their phones for fear that the Taliban now has the technology to track them. There are many reports of Christians who are hunted down for their faith. In some cases, phones are reportedly searched for Bible apps; having these apps is a crime punishable by death in the eyes of the Taliban.

The West: Anti-Christian sentiment seems to be growing in the west, as it has been this project's intent largely to show.

The church of Satan is growing in popularity in the US and Canada, and is unified with the pro-choice ranks against innocent life. In Canada, the church of Satan supported the 2021 church burning and advocated bringing church burning into the states. The UK and Ireland are largely abandoning their Christian roots for a secular humanist attitude. As they do, the abortion industry's campaign against life is allowed to metastasize, especially in Ireland which recently abandoned its laws that protected the sanctity of unborn life. Radical leftism also contributes to the marginalization of Christian voices in the west, and much of the western church is deserting its convictions to conform with the pattern of leftist culture, or is bogged down in neutrality, new age practices, and the prosperity gospel.

Other Places: Here are some brief accounts of recent developments on Christian persecution in various other regions and nations. In Saudi Arabia religious freedoms are still under threat, Christian tourists risk being arrested and detained for having bibles, Christians have little trust in Saudi Government to loosen religious restrictions, and Christians are systemically and communally persecuted. North Korea systemically persecutes and stifles Christians in barbaric ways, and continues to hide its crimes against humanity from the eyes of the world. In Cameroon the radical Boko Haram group violently targets Christians, multiple bible translators were recently killed, and multiple priests were recently kidnapped. Boko Haram attacks are increasing in scale and frequency. In Sri Lanka in 2019, on Easter Sunday there were multiple bombings killing at least 290 people. These series of bombings were Islamic suicide terror attacks. Other countries where it is hard to be a Christian include Somalia, Libya, Vietnam, Eritrea, Sudan,[38] Yemen, Central African Republic, Burkina Faso, Columbia, Mali, Ethiopia, Angola, Russia, and Rwanda.

You may have noticed a running theme with the above information. Much of it has happened in just a few months. These types of events are ongoing, developing rapidly day by day. Much more will likely unfold by the time this book is published. In fact, Christian persecution abroad as well as the rapidly deteriorating political climate are both likely to continue to intensify at a rate which will render this book outdated and tame compared to what the future holds. The voice of these suffering people is not reaching the ears of the western world. This is partly because our ears are closed, and partly because their voices are intentionally drowned out by constant media noise about the American ideology war. It is important for us, Christians and non-Christians alike, to question the narratives that are being peddled to us daily and to investigate the more important truths that are unfolding all around us.

One may ask why I've included such an exhaustive chapter in a book about big *American* problems. I believe that providing a small glimpse in time concerning the world's worsening relationship with religion in general and Christianity in particular illustrates that the stranglehold of persecution is tightening everywhere, and the western world is also feeling it tighten. We exist in the wake of decades of anti-religious education and the emergence of the quasi-religion of secular humanism, the naturalistic framework for ethics and morality which has all but overthrown the Judeo-Christian worldview in the modern cultural climate. In addition to an ongoing media affront to Christianity, the general distaste of Christianity to the modern mouth and the growing popularity of socialism, western culture appears to be following suit. Most western hostility is ideological at this point, rather than circumstantial or state-sanctioned, but the latter two forms of persecution are beginning to rear their ugly heads following the coronavirus pandemic and the rise of radical leftism. Space prohibits the elaboration of this point, but much of this book has been dedicated to showing the why's and how's of America's most recent anti-Christian crusade. I will simply say that anyone who doesn't believe it's happening at all, or isn't seeing any of the signs, or is ignoring all the signs, may be in partial or total agreement with a system of religious discrimination and the growing threat to religious freedoms here in the western world. If that's you, and you're in the church, you should be having a major red flag go off.

Many will deny that Christian persecution is actually happening worldwide. Many will downplay it. Many will decry the various evils of Christianity. Much of the reason for this is because these happenings are ignored by the western world. The reality is that since Jesus walked the earth approximately seventy million Christians have been martyred for putting their trust in Him. The majority of this number was killed in the 20th century.

There have been and still are massive amounts of Christians killed all around the world. We don't know for certain what the true number is. We want to know this. The fact that we can't find a reliable number is alarming in itself, and telling. It's impossible to know exactly how many were killed in Mao's China and Stalin's Russia. Likely the number is much higher than what is estimated in these instances. Even if the lowest number is 12,000,000 Christian lives lost under a single communist regime, this doubles the number of Jews killed during the holocaust. This is not to downplay the horror and wickedness of the holocaust, but to put the number of Christians killed in perspective. Estimates show that 100,000 Christians are killed for their faith every year. 45,000,000 Christians were killed in the 20th century.

All around the world there is a stranglehold on Christians.

People are promoting anti-Christian narratives and propaganda, painting Christianity as an evil system. But the simple fact is that these numbers make it seem as though Christians are and have been one of *the most persecuted people on the planet*, with most Christian martyrdom happening under Islamic and Communist regimes. Here are some more staggering statistics on Christian persecution:

- 1,600,000 killed in the Ottoman Empire in the 1820s.
- 120,000 Greek Christians massacred in Smyrna in one day.
- 600,000 Sudanese Christians murdered by Islamic government in 1963.
- 1,200,000 Underground church Christians and Catholics perished under the Soviet Regime in 1925.
- 200,000 Ukrainian Christians were killed in 1927.
- 100,000 Lithuanian Christians were killed by the Nazis, then Soviets, from 1940-1980.
- 450,000 Yugoslav and Serbian Orthodox and others killed by Nazis and Soviets up to 1990.
- 125,000 Lutheran Confessing Church, Catholics, and others were killed by humanist Nazis during WWII.
- 200,000 Christians were executed during the Korean War by North Korean Communists (1950-2000).
- 500,000 Christians died in the 1994 Rwandan genocide.
- 300,000 Christians were killed in Colombia's La Violancia civil war from 1948-1958.
- At least 1 million Christians were killed in Nazi Germany.
- At least 15 million perished in Russia.
- 200,000 Christians and foreigners were killed in the Chinese Boxer Rebellion.

- Another 700,000 were killed in Communist China between 1950 and 1980.
- 100,000 Catholics were killed in Mexico in the early 20th century.
- 300,000 Christians are believed to have been killed under Idi Amin in Uganda between 1971 and 1979.

This is nothing more than a global religious genocide. People are becoming more impatient and frustrated with Christians. I was recently speaking with a man who vehemently hates evangelicals and justified the church burning in Canada. He spoke of the intolerance and bigotry of Christians, but was unable to see his own discriminating speech against an entire religious group. Many of my friends, family and acquaintances hold the same sentiment. People use isolated instances of Christian misbehavior to make blanket claims against all Christians. People truly hate Christianity. It is a fair question in this climate to ask when this objective and measurable hatred will translate into violence against Christians in the west. The devil is using widespread and spiritual darkness and blindness to turn the world against the church. Something evil is working behind the scenes.

We should be praying as Christians for these suffering people who are being terrorized in Afghanistan, imprisoned in North Korea, who are threatened by communism in China and evil governments in Iran and Armenia, who are being attacked by ISIS in Syria and Iraq, who are being driven from their homes and villages in India and Myanmar, who are being targeted for murder in Nigeria, and who are being slandered, mocked derided, and hated in Canada and America. At the very least, we should open our eyes as a church and send aid to our suffering brothers and sisters. The day we stop seeing these big Christian problems abroad as big American problems is the day we lose our soul, our identity and our sanity.

You're Truth, My Truth

When Jesus Christ was on trial before Pontius Pilate, Pilate asked Jesus if He was indeed a king. "Jesus answered, 'You are right in saying I am a king. In fact, for this reason I was born, and for this I came into the world, to testify to the truth. Everyone on the side of truth listens to me.' 'What is truth?' Pilate asked" (John 18:36-37). Pilot went on to obey his own truth, which included the growing social threat of a riot in his province as well as the threat that an uprising posed to his political clout. He reluctantly handed Jesus over to be flogged and crucified.

Jesus and His followers valued divine truth. Pilate's response to Him was timeless. Pilate and Jesus indeed were from two different worlds and held two different worldviews. Jesus' refusal to participate in the system of the world landed Him on death row in front of the Roman governor. Jesus' worldview was examined by an ambassador for the kingdom of this world. The salvation that Jesus brought into the world was viewed as unrecognizable to the world. "The truth that sets us free cannot ever be aptly defined," proclaims the world.

The worldly attitude of shifting truth carries as a theme throughout the scriptures. It was no less present at the beginning, nor is it now. The *nachash* questioned Eve about the definition of truth. It questioned God's truth, and when Eve corrected it, it tempted Eve to elevate her own truth, which was influenced by desire, above the truth of God and the authority of His command. It was the fall of man from this definition of God's truth that brought Christ before Pilate thousands of years later to have His truth scrutinized in similar fashion.

Pilate was a man of great power and prominence. He was considered a wise man of his age, able to judge immense matters. It was his world that was actually put on display before Christ and all who read the Gospel accounts from then on. Pilate's knowledge of the truth stemmed from his knowledge of good and evil. It seems that this was how he was temporarily able to be appointed as a worldly judge over God Himself. The knowledge that was inherited by man after the fall is also the curse of being arbiters of what is true and false, ourselves being deceived, and what is good and what is evil, even as our hearts innately trend toward the latter. When Jesus submitted to our curse for our own sakes, He also had to face the most prominent judgement system of his day, a system which had also emerged from the curse. Just as the serpent judged the truth of God at the beginning, so did Pilate, a representative of the dragon, at the end. So does mankind today. Putting ourselves in the judgement seat over God is a foolish place to be.

The Bible tells us that in our sin we also become corrupt judges of our neighbors and ourselves. After all, everything is out of balance in sin. God's truth is undermined in those who are alienated from Him. His truth is rejected as man's is elevated. It is this false scale that keeps the world in its bondage to decay. Pilate understood the secular rule of law, that the truth one has is greater than all others, especially the more powerful one becomes. Those who follow the prevailing system of the knowledge of good and evil may claim that there is a truth outside themselves that is higher than themselves, but it is only an arbitrary, unprovable claim. They really believe in a system that elevates them to the status of being their own gods. This results also in being their own judges and the judges of others. If there is one thing that God wants to set us free from, it's our own truth.

Transitioning to culture today, we can see the elevation

of self echo all around us. It is the individual who holds the true status of truth for him or herself, and it is the objective standard that is rejected, whether it be decent laws put forth by society or God's standard itself. This becomes nothing less than a collision of worlds that comes under scrutiny by the observer. This collision permeates the spiritual, cultural and political spheres, and it manifests as unpleasant arguments at the dinner table or riots in the streets. It results either in persuasion, alienation, or an agreement to disagree. Let's take a closer look at these three unavoidable occurrences.

Persuasion is the end goal for both parties: as people scrutinize each other's views, they also seek to convert one another, to win the war of the worldviews. If persuasion is unachievable, the result is either alienation or a neutral peace treaty, a "white flag waved." Alienation happens when one would rather protect their own position than allow for any change in perceptual ground to be covered—they are protecting their world from destabilizing and will sacrifice relationships to do so. The two minds must no longer meet in the middle. They must part ways in hostility or coldness. The agreement to disagree is the white flag waved. When one remains adherent to their own truth in the face of a conflicting reality, they often say "I agree to disagree." What they really mean is "you have your truth, I have mine," or even "what is truth?" It is usually the losing party that waves this white flag. "Their own truth" will deny reality itself instead of letting go of a convenient, popular or longstanding falsity. In Eve's eyes, the temporary pleasure and wisdom of the fruit was the momentary higher truth than God's warning about it and His command not to eat of it. She was persuaded by the serpent, along with Adam, and mankind was alienated from God.

Persuasion is a difficult goal when the difference in perspectives can be found in everything under the sun, and even the stuff behind it. From the laws of nature to the sanctity of life, common ground is quickly being claimed by one side or the other. When we cannot agree on the definitions of nature, life, or whether the earth is flat or round, it is more than likely that we will have disagreements on this or that political policy or candidate.

The issue is that there is always a side that is more powerful and a side that is less powerful in its truthfulness. The question "what is truth?" is really an assertion of superiority of the weaker but more popular opinion over the humble dominance of reality. Since people don't have much of a problem obeying their own truth, reacting in certain ways to the world from a mode of self-preservation and various ambitions, they are prone to elevate those things above whatever's contradictory or inconvenient, even if it's based in reality. In the world's eyes and in Pilate's, Pilate had the only real, visible power over Christ because his power was sanctioned both by the state and the religious mob outside his court. Even the religious elite persuaded Pilot to crucify their king with the words, "we have no king but Caesar."

We all know now that Pilot's power, although it was the most visible power to the naked eye, was virtually nonexistent: "Jesus Answered, 'You would have no power over me if it were not given to you from above'" (John 19:11).

Jesus' truth is much higher and more important than the relevance of this or that political issue. He spoke of the truth of the power relationship between God and man, which was inverted by man at the fall and is therefore difficult (if not impossible) for any man or woman to grasp. But often times the minor disagreements that result in a desire to persuade one another are symptomatic of the root systems of spirituality that gave rise to this initial power struggle. In other words, it is symptomatic of the fruit we reach for. This is why, when persuasion is the end goal, there is always a point and a counterpoint. One stands on the side of truth and one is only built on a prevailing vision of the world, structured on a powerful, persuasive belief. Often times the latter is more visible to the naked eye and advertises itself to the world as the more powerful truth. The eternally losing worldview often appears to be temporarily winning. It can be persuasive in that respect.

Alienation is usually what both sides are afraid of, and until one side or the other recognizes the inevitability of persuasion or alienation there will always be a white flag waved to some degree. Alienation, of course, is the least pleasant of the three outcomes of discussion, but often times is the most necessary. Often division is unavoidable if one is to maintain their stance. It is unfortunate to lose the respect of friends or loved ones for standing one's ground on an unpopular position that seems invisible to the world. But if the end goal is always persuasion and never division, the persuasion can sometimes come about in a way that is not genuine. Either the truth gets muddled with the lie or vice-versa. Alienation is not always unavoidable, and that is not always a bad thing.

The white flag of "your truth, my truth" is only putting a stop to the argument. In a religious conversation, this is in essence saying, "Stick to your scripture and keep your opinion away from my ears!" It is a sign of recognizing the weakness and untruthfulness of one's own position while also being afraid to sacrifice that position, because it either happens to be on the side of the cultural majority or feels really good. It is the proverbial period at the end of the sentence. There cannot be anymore said afterward without entering the territory of either persuasion or alienation. Both may need to happen. However, the statement, "your truth, my truth," unwittingly recognizes the existence of an objective and subjective position.

The reason that the subjective position is more often on the "your truth, my truth" side is because it is an objective truth that humanity in its entirety is not entirely objective. We are always destined to mix reality with our own way of perceiving it. The majority of people are following their own law, with the view that many paths will lead up the same mountain, regardless of how many signs they see on the way up which warn them that the path they're on will lead to the edge of a cliff.

∽

I have regrettably painted these results of argumentation in a negative light—and there are, as history has shown, many negative results in all three; persuasion can be disingenuous and lead to boasting, alienation can be needless and lead to war, and the white flag is often a sign of cowardice which leads to a boring conversation about nothing. But there are positive outcomes of all three of these positions. While persuasion as an end goal in itself can often result in a disingenuous outcome or deception, if persuasion is an organic outworking of honest conversation rooted in mutual love, respect, and open-mindedness, its fruit can be liberating and long lasting for both parties. This is because the objective truth which is by its nature reconstructive, in an honest skirmish, wins over subjective truth which by its nature can only deconstruct everything that contradicts it. If persuasion happens the other way around the end result is usually fragmentation, as persuasion for the sake of elevating one's personal truth was the only aim of the desire to persuade.

Alienation can be a good thing for a number of reasons; it can be an introduction to genuine persuasion, it can be a clear sign of two diverging paths, and it can be God awakening us to the toxicity of certain relationships. None of these seem like positive things at first. In fact, all three are what the subjective world warns us against: "don't say anything to anyone that might come between you." However, recognizing that at times alienation (when the world hates us) is unavoidable, is a good step towards overcoming the fear of man. I do not claim to be less guilty of being afraid of the opinions of others than anyone else. I also do not want to lead people into the attitude of despising the opinions of others just for the sake of pride. I simply want to acknowledge that at times alienation is unavoidable.

The white flag is also not always a bad thing, unless it is waved by the one who is on the side of objective truth. Otherwise, the white flag can be a sign that the argument has been won. The words "your truth, my truth" are simply an unconscious concession that right now "my truth" can find no weakness in "your truth" to attack, and therefore "my truth" will surrender to "your truth," as long as "my truth" can hold onto its life. But there is no such thing as "my truth, your truth." There is only *the truth*. The question, "what is truth," is a question that stands in every age.

It would be cruel and imperialistic for the front lines of the victorious army to gun down the surrendering truth in cold blood. Instead, the victor ought to take the surrendering truth prisoner, feed it, and give it water, and in so doing heap burning coals on its head. Both sides win. The surrendered truth gets to keep its life as it is shown kindness. The victorious truth is allowed to advance. If the tables turn to where the subjective truth is on the side of the victor, and it is the one on the side of the objective truth who surrenders, a peaceful outcome is less likely. The subjective truth must eradicate all objectivity if it is going to survive.

These principles manifest in many different tears of

importance. The lowest tear can be what to have for breakfast, and the highest can be whether or not there is a God and who that God is. I may say that we should have a box of donuts for breakfast. You may say that that is unhealthy and suggest a better option. While I may convince you by appealing to your taste buds, if you are persuaded it will be a negative outcome for both of our waistlines.

The nature of disagreement is timeless and infinite in scale. It was there at the beginning, it is here today. It trickles down from spiritual things to culture and politics, and even into the mundane. Jesus Himself was not unconcerned with the mundane. He used the simple allegory of food to tell of the most important and complex realities in the universe. He and His Father created our bodies to run on food. Food is what propels us forward physically through the challenges of our day. Likewise Jesus Himself is the food that our spirits need to survive the perils of sin and the world. We should not consider the basest forms of argument as nothing in themselves, but as symptoms or metaphors for deeper spiritual issues. Unfortunately, it will be impossible to never cross paths with the prevailing worldview. Even two breakfasts can come into conflict. Can we really expect to live out the gospel realistically and never cross paths with the prevailing worldview in culture or politics? This is why privatization is a myth.

One of the largest problems that faces us here is that, rather than the source of disagreement always being two competing worldviews, the dissention often comes from one infighting conflict arising from within the same perspective. An example is the false Christian gospel which wars against the real one. False gospels have been alive since the first century and are no less alive today. These are subjective claims to an objective truth, making themselves out to be the truth, when really they are just a "secret knowledge," a pseudo truth, and another version of "do as thou will" in the Christian vernacular.

In this "truth," the truth of the gospel has been repackaged to fit an individual's desires, and because this repackaging is done in like manner with the prevailing worldview, it is often times more appealing to the world from the outside looking in. It offers fulfillment in the flesh under the semblance of salvation. As the church gets more and more "with the times," the true gospel becomes less and less at the forefront of the sociopolitical battle. A little yeast spreads quickly through the whole loaf, but Jesus is still the bread of life.

As a church it is easy to become a victim of this "secret knowledge" if we remain unaware of its presence or consider it as unthreatening. Often times we compromise. Spiritual compromise is like the man who wants to eat donuts having a healthy breakfast with his friend only so he may devour a box of donuts secretly in his room.

~

In short, the world hates the church because it hated its founder first. Forcing Christians apart and constantly slandering them in the media is evidence that this attitude is nothing new. Today, persecution is widespread, and it crosses spiritual, cultural, and political boundaries. It is much worse around the world. Often times the contradicting views of morality and truth manifest in the latter two arenas. When our truth comes into conflict with the truth of the world, the war of the worldviews intensifies. Many on both sides seek common ground or grey areas where they can compromise. In these instances we have pastors who pander to the left or secular folk who acknowledge the benefits of religion in society. However, it has never been clearer that one ideology is destructive and one is not. Anyone covering any ground away from that destruction is headed in the right direction. But anyone who stands in the middle of the street will be hit by cars from both directions.

The good thing about the big American problem which is at its tipping point, is that many are coming to the conclusion that it is not a big American problem at all. The problems that face us in this age are ancient, although they pretend to be new problems. The mind of sinful man is still death and the mind of the Spirit is still life and peace. The seeds from old dead trees of past generations seem to sprout anew in generations to follow. The biggest problem that we are facing in our day and age is the abandonment of God. God is sovereign and holds in His hand the fabric of truth, order, and reality. As soon as we disregard Him, the fabric of our society separates from the fabric of truth, order and reality. We begin living out a chaotic myth indeed. This pattern is simply a new seed from ancient times.

In the Book of the prophet Daniel, king Nebuchadnezzar was rich in his own truth—where he was his own god, and the kingdom he'd given himself was the greatest on the earth. As he grew in power and stature, God blessed him with dreams and visions of the future, although these dreams and visions were not always a blessing to him directly, but a prophecy to be beheld by future generations. In one instance, Nebuchadnezzar dreamt of a tree, large and beautiful, touching the sky, and visible throughout all the earth. The tree was a refuge for the birds of the air and the beasts of the field, and fed many with its fruit. Eventually, the tree was cut down.

When Nebuchadnezzar summoned Daniel to interpret the dream, Daniel grew concerned. The dream was about the king. Twelve months later, king Nebuchadnezzar gave glory to himself as he stood on the rooftop of his palace and gloated over the kingdom of Babylon. God took his sanity from him and made him crawl on his hands and knees for seven years, until Nebuchadnezzar acknowledged that power does not come from men but from heaven.

Babylon is not quite a nation that we would expect God to give power to, in fact it waged war on Jerusalem and sent the Israelites into exile. But Babylon was a tool that God was using to teach Jerusalem a lesson that had been generations in the making, just as the removal of the king's sanity was a lesson for him. God's in charge, no matter what year, no matter what nation, no matter what man or woman.

Today Americans stand on the rooftops of our palaces and gloat over the lives we've made for ourselves. God has stolen our sanity from us. He had every right to do so. The story of America was written by God. It was its myth that was written by man. As Christians we have a responsibility to expose myths like these to the world, or continue to watch the myth undermine the truth. We are the only ones who are able to rightly interpret the dream for the king. Otherwise our story is just another dream to be forgotten, another enigma to be deciphered by the wisdom of the philosophers of this age, another vision to be interpreted by the whims of the world.

Chapter 6
Interpretations from the Intellectuals

Willfulness and Consequences

In the time of Daniel and king Nebuchadnezzar, the wise men of the age were put under great pressure to deliver accurate interpretations to the king. The king forced them to seek out impossible information and explain the mystery behind it, they would be executed if they were not up to the task. Fortunately for them, Daniel was up to it. With God's help, he interpreted the dream that told of the stories and times to come.

The apostle Paul was likewise adamant about the difference between the wisdom that is from God and the wisdom of the world, and that one makes foolish the other; "Where is the wise man? Where is the Scholar? Where is the philosopher of this age? Has not God made foolish the wisdom of the world?" (1 Corinthians 1:20). Because the wisdom of God ran so contrary to the wisdom of the world, those with the wisdom of God were often persecuted or put to death for telling the truth. Those with the wisdom of the world were quick to blame the prophets and the Christians for the evils of the world.

Today the intelligentsia is quick to place blame on everyone but itself. Only unlike Nebuchadnezzar's wise men, the new wise men are unlikely to face any substantial consequences when their interpretations are found out to be wrong or damaging to the real world.

In modern thought, the favor of the king has turned from those who give accurate interpretations to those who deliver false ones. It is no longer the liars who are put on trial but those who confront the lies with information, facts, and interpretations that interfere with the liars' own advancement. The more the lie is proven to be false, the more it is promoted as the truth. Often times even in the midst of hard evidence and proof of the failures of false visions and prophecies, the false prophets are still praised as having the wisdom of the gods, while flesh and blood people are left to clean up after the messes made by old ideas, even as we fearfully await the outcomes of new ones.

As mankind advanced into the new stages of enlightenment, from the inquisitions to the technological age, everything from microbes to men was delivered from the hand of God and given over to the hand of philosophy. Humanity began building the intellectual tower anew to reach toward the heavens at a quickened pace. The Judeo-Christian worldview was invited to help build when it was conducive, but denied input when it looked closer at the tower's architecture and warned the people of the various structural faults.

Heresy gave way to secularism as one century gave way to another. Eventually religion went from being respected for its contributive wisdom to being abhorred for its simplicity and ignorance. The knowledge of good and evil took total control over the mind of man, and the new universe split off from the old one. It was out with the old and in with the new. The nature of society and the nature of humanity changed due to the ambitions of the intelligentsia. Man was no longer created in God's image, but created in the image of nothing in particular, a result of randomness acting upon more randomness, another thoughtless thought experiment for the thoughtful to interpret whatever way they wished.

Man was no longer a creature created in God's own image, but a somewhat more fortunate blob of protoplasm and atoms to be molded and shaped and analyzed as the intelligentsia saw fit. Societies themselves were simply clusters of fortunate meat bags hovering around each other and bonking into one another here and there. They needed to be arranged and told what to do as such. Schools taught children "the real truth" about human existence. By the time they graduated high school they were random accidents of cosmic evolution in a mindless, godless universe, somehow emerging in an unlikely pocket of order in an otherwise chaotic reality. The restructuring of society began based on the new foundation of survival of the fittest. The intellectually fittest were the naturalists and those doomed to perish were the super-naturalists. The God of the universe became the "God of the gaps," who only could fill the few places of mystery left in the mind of an imbecile. Christianity was paralyzed.

The church in many respects blended its beliefs with those of the world and bowed its knee to the rising new age. The father of lies knocked Genesis 1:1 into Genesis 1:2 and the rest of the verses fell behind like dominoes in the minds of believers. The erasure of man and ultimate meaning led to a greater chasm between paradigms than ever before. Question after question filled the mind of the skeptic, one little seed of doubt grew into a tree that touched the top of the sky.

A conundrum of what exactly to believe and what not to still comes between Christians as they wonder just how much trust ought to be placed in the intelligentsia and how much ought to be placed in the God of scripture. America for many represents a believer in the midst of a faith crisis, not knowing whether to turn to the god of man's interpretation or the "God of the gaps." Although history has shown us a clear picture of what the future will look like when nations turn away from God completely, we still seem to think that we know best—there is a new interpretation that is soon to be unearthed that will save the world and restructure society in the proper way. It is the freedom of mankind that ultimately gets in the way of its truer version of freedom, the utopian mansion envisioned by the intellectual class. Hard work, economic and social liberty, and most of all Christianity are blocking the path of the philosopher kings. The imbecile knows not what is best for him. When he tries to interpret his own life in a way that is contrary to the vision of the astrologers, magicians, enchanters and diviners, we will cut his mind up into little pieces and leave him as a fragmented example to the rest of society.

The more the church allows the advancing vision of the interpretations of man into its sanctuary, the more fragmented the church will become. We cannot allow any more ground to be taken, and we must regain the ground that has been taken thus far. We must trade the myth of the Darwinian goo-man for the truth of the man created in God's image or we will create a self-fulfilling prophecy; we will become bags of meaningless protoplasm floating around in an indifferent universe, waiting helplessly for the slightly more enlightened bags of protoplasm to come and guide us through the void. As a church united we simply must reject the interpretations of the intellectual class just as Christ and the prophets before Him did. The interpretations of the intellectual class already rejected us a long time ago. In order to bring meaning back into the world, we must first bring meaning back into the world.

Interpreting Society, Culture, and Religion

In many ways the societies, cultures, and branches of religion we see around us today are shaped by the enlightened ones. Urbanization and city building has always been a result of prominent visions of the people, as well as conquest and the disintegration of past societies. Generally kingdoms and superpowers have been the result of a dominating religion, culture, or society which have themselves been influenced by thought leaders and people of power, who are often one and the same. This is not entirely unnatural, as the tendency to create and live within hierarchies is natural to people. What is more unnatural is when those who think they know best move into power with the intent either to flatten every hierarchy and restructure them to fit in with their own notions of the world. This has long been the objective of the intellectual class, to place interpretations on societies, cultures, and religions in order to diagnose them in the abstract, and then restructure them to fall in line with the prominent view of the way things ought to be. Real people are always much easier to understand in the abstract, as well as their places in society, their cultural viewpoints, and their religious beliefs.

The desire of the interpreters to flatten or restructure hierarchies has manifested in different ways from age to age. The first recorded push towards urbanization in the plains of Shinar with the city of Babel was driven by ideas of thought leaders who said "Come, let us build." They interpreted their society as flawed and sought to transcend it. For a time Israel was without a king, following the law of their God. When the people saw other nations with kings they became jealous. Their society interpreted their lack of a king as a shortcoming, and they demanded a king to be appointed so they could become more like other nations. Of course if you give them an inch, they will take a mile. After this, the nation experienced trial after trial as they fell into a pattern of not only emulating the politics of other nations, but worshipping the same gods as other nations, leading to their downfall. Greece was the first democracy and had many thought leaders that interpreted and restructured their society into moral oblivion. The kingdom of Rome was an example of one society with a more enlightened political perspective forcing itself upon other nations, often through conquest and dictatorship. There have been many nations to follow in this pattern. America may be seen as one. The negative results of philosopher kings are not restricted to the emergent age, but the developing age stands as another stark example of the path to *Sheol* being paved with good intentions.

The atrocities of the 20th century were often real world results of blindly following the philosophies of the interpreters of society, culture and religion. Stalin, Lenin, Pol Pot, Mao and other murderous tyrants followed the religion of Karl Marx, whose ideas to this day have likely had the most negative real world impact of any thought leader. Marx saw himself as the true manifestation of the enlightened age and saw the suffering of society as a result of unfair hierarchies, oddly reminiscent of the way in which he viewed his own personal circumstances. His interpretation of actual flesh and blood people, their cultures, their religions, and the real world implementation of that interpretation resulted in global mass atrocities. This interpretation still infects our world. Adolf Hitler seized the opportunity to interpret and restructure society to fit his Darwinian, pantheistic worldview.[39] There is no doubt that Darwin's philosophy, whether intended or not, also had grave consequences to real flesh and blood people when that philosophy proclaimed that life itself was essentially a meaningless power struggle between the more and less fit.

Interpreting society, culture, and religion through the lens of survival of the fittest inevitably resulted in the desire to destroy the unfit societies, cultures, and religions.

The mixture of Darwin and Marx was an alluring but deadly concoction. The ideas of these philosophers blended well in conflict theory and they were not restricted to Nazi Germany or communist regimes. Unstoppable in their ferocity, they made their way into the western world as well.

Many intellectuals in the democratic nations during the twentieth century likewise bowed their knee to atheistic nihilism, Marxism, and moral relativity in the 20th century. They also saw society, culture, and religion as needing to be interpreted and restructured to fit a prevailing vision. This vision fills the hearts and minds of many Americans today. They see the hierarchies that have arisen due to the economic, societal, and cultural growth of our nation—much of which is the result of society developing in a predominantly free market republic—as unfair on many different levels. In the eyes of many with the prevailing vision, including many in the church, America is irredeemably racist, sexist, classist, and homophobic. To the new intellectual class of the 20th-21st centuries, the US constitution and government are inevitably corrupt, outdated, and must be restructured to fit the prevailing vision. Without dismissing the reality of these evils in the hearts and minds of many *individuals* in our society and the certainty of corruption that will always be present when people are given power over other people, we must acknowledge the presence of the advancing vision that is only a new reproduction of ancient ideas brought forth by a dynasty of interpreters and philosopher kings, who thought of flesh and blood people and their values as blank slates and vague abstractions who needed to be remade.

Unfortunately for the interpreters, the magicians, the astrologers, the diviners, and the wise men of this age, the facts often do not always fit their prevailing vision—nor do the people and the societies, cultures and religions that they are a part of exist in the world that the philosophers have dreamt up for them. Faulty interpretations and bad ideas have their consequences on culture and societies, despite the general lack of consequences for the people who espouse them. These consequences grow with the power of persuasion and presence of confusion behind those interpretations and ideas; the more true they seem and the harder they are to understand, the more likely they are to infiltrate various levels of culture and society, and stick around for a long time. The intelligentsia have not necessarily succeeded in following the truth to its logical outworking, but in creating a new religion, often without calling it a religion. This non-religious religion, like other religions, also transcends downstream matters of culture and politics. This is why political and cultural dissentions from the non-religious religion so often are dismissed as "missing the larger point," just as denying certain Christian precepts based solely on materialistic objections would mean one is "missing the larger point" of the spiritual dimension surrounding the Christian religion.

The non-religious religion of the interpretation class is bounded by its total lack of boundaries. It is restricted by always seeking to do away with any restrictions. Its perpetual desire to transgress human limitations is its most limiting factor. The focus on a nihilistic utopia is more than an inconsistency or a fallacy, it is an oxymoron. History has shown us the utopian death camps and nihilistic gulags of the non-religious search for heaven on earth through political assimilation. This is because, contrary to the hopes of the prevailing vision, being our own gods and earning our own way into heaven only creates hell. Perhaps God confused the languages of the citizens of Babel because he knew that the tower they were building to heaven would eventually collapse in on itself and crush everyone inside. Then it would only be a tower of corpses.

The prevailing vision has run alongside reality since reality began. This is why both the prevailing vision and reality as God intended it are always at odds with one another. This is also why we cannot always understand one another, as if our languages have been confused, whether we are passing the salt or the sugar. It is all too often that two different universes sit across the table from one another. Whether we understand the word we use to be "salt" or "sugar" depends on the reservoir which is upstream of our language. We can end up with salt in our coffee or sugar on our steak.

Interpreting Race and Gender

The diversity found in the United States can be interpreted in one of two ways. Either the different ethnic and religious groups that make up the country, as well as their diverse skills and characteristics, can be understood and celebrated as what makes them unique among other groups. Or the economic or social differences that emerge between groups—whether ethnic or religious minorities or majorities—is always caused by implicit discrimination and inescapable genetic qualities pertaining to race, gender, or ethnicity that are inherent within individuals, groups and the societies they constitute, rather than a range of other factors. The second interpretation is favored more than the first by many 21st century intellectuals and is based on the same pattern of genetic determinism which fueled the racism of the progressive party in the 20th century.

In the early 20th century, notions of determining one's value based on skin color were favorable to further the progressive cause, leading to the very same discrimination the progressives claim to be fighting today. They are actually upholding new types of discrimination by instigating racial animosity and other animosities. When discrimination fell in line with the goals of the elite class, it was advertised and accepted wholesale, but when it was seen as politically advantageous to denounce specific types of discrimination and look for them in every nook and cranny, instances of discrimination became high in demand for the survival of the vision. The narrative of mass systemic discrimination could only be upheld by creating a newer type of discrimination, one that was more palatable in the modern era.

The modern discrimination is not necessarily based on race, gender, ethnicity, or other factors alone like past instances of discrimination, but on a fusion of many different group identities and dynamics being at odds with other group identities and dynamics. This new discrimination stems from cultural Marxism and conflict theory. The class that is most systemically discriminated against by the state are political dissidents, regardless of race or gender. It's simply those who reject the left's disturbing agenda.

In January 2021, Congresswoman Alexandra Ocasio Cortez suggested that political dissidents (whom she calls "conspiracy theorists" and "white supremacists") be sent to government funded reeducation programs. The Biden administration and the Democratic Party have targeted the free speech of dissidents multiple times through their collaboration with and oversight of tech monopolies and social media platforms. They have also forced an entire population to wear masks, and are promoting forced vaccinations for Covid-19, as well as a society where vaccination cards are required in order to go about daily life. Their media platforms slander political opposition on a daily basis, effectively producing an atmosphere of mass hysteria against dissidents among their audience. One of the ways they were able to create this new type of discrimination was by leveraging older types of discrimination like sexism and racism to their advantage.

After all, minorities aren't exempt from the modern discrimination of the Democratic Party. They are still expected to fall into line with the plans of the left, and if they disagree, they are derogatorily named "Uncle Toms." This means that if you are black, and you vote for someone the left doesn't like, you have become docile and obedient to an evil, racist system descending from slavery. The "Uncle Tom" has betrayed his cultural heritage and has condoned the evils of slavery by voting against the Democrats. In reality, the modern Democratic Party is the direct descendent of the slaveholding legacy. The left routinely claims that black republicans are puppets who are being used by the Republican Party only to showcase that they have black support, rather than free thinking people who have come to their own political conclusions.

Likewise, if a woman thinks for herself and votes against the Democrats, she is labelled a "Karen"—a name meant to suggest a typically white, blonde housewife who is unquestioningly subservient to the male-dominated-patriarchy, and usually racist. Such vague and sweeping stereotypes fit the textbook definition of discrimination and are pedaled wholesale by the party in power and the media they control.

It goes without saying that there are still instances of non-partisan discrimination based on gender, race, and other factors in American society today. However, using isolated instances of discrimination to make sweeping accusations of entire people groups in society is inexcusable. Yet this strategy is necessary for a new age form of discrimination against those who oppose the elite class to take root and quickly develop. From there, solutions such as eugenics and segregation do not seem too distanced, especially when considering that bigoted eugenics is already alive and well in the abortion industry's targeting of women and minorities. Also, a newer form of segregation seems to be approaching based on the left's modern day intersectionality propaganda. The left is trying to get away with creating a new master race, one dependent not on gender or skin color, but on an unquestioning obedience to its belief system.

The advancement of theories of different levels of victimhood and oppression, as well as their corresponding problem-solution harmony, are dependent on a bigoted and narrow minded value based system pertaining to things like race, gender, sexual preference, religion, lack of religion, political affiliation, or a mixture of them all. This doctrine has saturated various institutions of American culture for decades in order to restructure American society, so that social power can be administered to obedient party members who consistently uphold the most orthodox form of the advancing theories. Heretics can respectively be stripped of their power, influence and social status.

The doctrines of identity politics and political correctness often can neither be proven nor disproven. They are therefore vague, malleable, and longstanding. Such a formula is necessary to silence or shame those who dissent from that formula. The formula, like the former progressive philosophy of racism (now pinned on the church) brought about things like eugenics and segregation and relied heavily on highlighting inequalities between people groups. This focus helped create a vague utopian goal of a perfect order which has yet to be fully achieved, and likely never will be. Again, there was a "problem" for which the elite saw themselves as the only "solution."

The teachings of Jesus fly in the face of this reductionist narrative. But today the church is unanimously blamed for all yesterday's evils. Meanwhile, the left focuses again on the pattern of genetic determinism to guide the world into fulfilling its prophecies and interpretations. Intrinsic human inequality based on race is simply a necessary contingency for their proposed solution.

The Christian message is largely to thank for uprooting slavery from the world. The Christian idea of inherent human value between all people of all races and genders needed to be silenced once again in order to propagate identity politics. Real Christians recognized that genetic determinism was a dangerous myth brought forth by progressives and that racism and sexism[1] was a gross sin, then were labeled as the original perpetrators of all the world's evil by the original offenders of discrimination.

Christians who trend left routinely fall for this system of identity politics, as well as confess sins that they never committed. Not only this, many Christians today blame themselves in particular for abstract crimes that they have been accused of by the left, and blame the church in general for the many sins of the world. The theories of the left concerning race, gender, and discrimination have become an essential part of doctrine for many liberal and politically neutral churches. Those who stand accused by the left are also sometimes in danger of being labeled as apostate by church leaders if they refuse to adhere to the left's version of history and its vision of the future.

---

[1] Many make the claim that Christians are misogynist. However, Christians believe that women ought to be upheld with dignity and respect, and that they should not be used for their bodies. Mainstream secular society, however, seems to promote a "hook up culture," where using women (and men) for sex, then moving on to the next woman, is commonplace. It appears that Christians value the sanctity and dignity of women more than our post-secular culture, which has become obsessed with meaningless sex, even as it blames Christianity for inventing the patriarchy.

Interpreting War and Peace

War has long been an issue on which one can stand either on the side of good or the side of evil, in the eyes of the intellectuals. Much like the issues of race and gender, the definitive stance on war has shifted for the intellectuals depending on the time period.

In the early 20th century, war was viewed by intellectuals and politicians as a heroic cause. President Theodore Roosevelt saw war as a just measure, and foreign wars like the Spanish-American war seemed to mesh well with the president's image as an adventurer. In this war, the United States could pose as the just liberator of an oppressed people, while conveniently establishing itself as a colonial power by acquiring new lands in the Caribbean and Pacific. Of course this fact sparked controversy as to why the US was posing as anti-imperialist against the colonial interests of Spain, while simultaneously expanding its own global power. However, during this time US expansionist policies were in vogue among the American public.

America entered World War One under progressive president Woodrow Wilson. Up to the point of the sinking of the RMS Lusitania off the coast of Ireland, America desired to remain neutral in the war. The sinking of the Lusitania was found to be controversial as it was both highly tragic and highly irresponsible for politicians to allow American civilians to sail in a hostile maritime warzone, especially when the Lusitania was later found to be hauling ammunition. The facts regarding the sinking of the Lusitania, although highly controversial, were filtered into a propaganda campaign to convince the American public that entering war was necessary. Despite America's attempts to avoid the bloodiest war so far in history, she was lured in by what seemed from afar to be a just cause, but upon closer examination turned out to be a ploy to paint a tragic moment of political irresponsibility as a moment for America to display its heroism. A just cause to enter into war was created. The cost of life and limb from all nations involved in the First World War was incomprehensible. The intelligentsia and politicians who ran the nations scrambled to make themselves look like symbols of justice and bravery in an abstract world, while twenty million flesh and blood people forfeited their lives as a result.

After the Great War was ended, its ravages were seen for what they were and an entire continent was torn to shreds. The intelligentsia resorted once more to making themselves look as though they stood on the side of justice and truth. Intellectuals in democratic nations that once praised the heroism and adventure of war, now condemned all war as a needless evil. Those who advised military strength as a deterrent to aggressors were seen as warmongers and imperialists. As the Nazi Regime rose to power under Adolf Hitler, the intelligentsia in democratic nations did not admit the objective threat they posed. France's attitude after the devastation of WWI became vehemently anti-war and anti-military to their detriment. The British intelligentsia also condemned the evils of war in the wake of WWI. In the eyes of the public, war was seen as a needless abomination, no matter the circumstances. These nations weakened militarily in the midst of a growing threat, largely as a result of the virtue signaling of ideologues.

Many may not realize how closely the allied forces came to defeat because of the military weakening and the weakening of public morale in democratic nations between the first and second world wars. As the axis powers increased military power, they also recognized the weakening of the surrounding nations. Adolf Hitler may not have been so bold in his campaign if he didn't perceive the turmoil in nations like

France and Great Britain. France's passivism during Hitler's campaign allowed the Nazis to take greater military risks, investing in the hope that the nations it intended to conquer would be so bent against war that they'd virtually give up without a fight. He was right about France. Britain almost fell into this trap as well. The British intelligentsia suggested appeasement to Hitler in order to avoid further conflict.

It is sobering to think that WWII was almost lost. It may be more sobering to think that it may not have happened or would have been much less costly if democratic nations were not so busy manipulating public opinion on the matter. Selflessly promoting pacifism and denouncing all forms of military deterrence only benefitted the enemy in this particular circumstance. Japan attacked the United States because it recognized weakness and division in the American mindset. Those who continued to promote the virtuosity of their ideas were unable to recognize the potential real-world effects of those ideas, as long as they were seen as symbols of justice and honor for the time being. While western intellectuals were busy pacifying the public, Hitler was prepping his nation's attitude for conquest.

Since WWII the biggest threat to the free world still stands at the ready to seize any moment and conquer, to attack at any sign of weakness. The war against communism via the Korean, Vietnamese, and Cold War has long been condemned by the same anti-war intellectual sentiment. The ideologues viciously denounced America's involvement in these wars as needless and evil. America was frequently seen as the colonialist oppressor, recklessly seeking to conquer the downtrodden communists. As usual, the intelligentsia stood and still stands on the opposite side of reality in matters of the dangers of Marxism, Communism, and Socialism.

During the Vietnam War the media and intelligentsia,

using the news, Hollywood, and the academe, filtered information to shape the image of US soldiers as rapists, murderers of children, and drug attics. The media frequently highlighted examples of American and ARVN war crimes and gave platforms to anti-war Veterans (whose stories were often later falsified), while suppressing examples of Vietcong war crimes against south Vietnam citizens, which were much more frequent and barbaric. The Vietcong's victory over the US and conquest of South Vietnam was likely as much a result of the intelligentsia's anti-war movement in the US, as it was a result of North Vietnam's innovative use of guerilla warfare. Vietcong military leaders said so. The hearts and minds of the American public were quickly shaped by the intelligentsia to be against the war effort in Vietnam, otherwise we would have likely had victory in freeing Vietnam, at least partially, from communist oppression.

In the 1960's and in subsequent decades the communist movement largely manifested in western countries in many different forms. In America, Marxist thought leaders like Herbert Marcuse and Saul Alinski sought to bring the communist revolution into America. They recognized that the revolution which was "prophesied" by Marx likely would not come as a result of military conquest, but as a result of conceptual conquest. Today the intelligentsia and politicians of the left are shaped, influenced, and/or completely controlled by this sentiment which has been given free range under the first amendment to metastasize throughout the last half century. It infects every level of our culture. Every election cycle in America seems no longer to be a race between two candidates but a race between socialism and the American system. We can be sure that Marxism will find new ways to take root in the hearts and minds of the public in the years to come. We can also be sure that the intelligentsia's moral warfare of false interpretations against society will result not only in a weakening of our nation's moral and cultural fabric, but in a recognition of this weakness in the eyes of our enemies.

The misinterpretation of war and peace actually risks prolonged war and internal division. Ideologues and the media tirelessly misrepresent the facts of the real world and reform them to cultivate their vision of the world—one in which they remain on the side of the truth and justice no matter what, and everyone who disagrees with them remains on the side of the demons.

～

In the summer of 2021, the Biden administration withdrew troops out of Afghanistan after a two decade war against terrorism. Joe Biden rejected the advice given to him by military advisors and experts on the ground and moved forward with his plan.

The American sentiment was largely in support of withdrawal. However, the withdrawal was poorly planned and executed. American presence in Afghanistan was removed unconditionally, without forcing the Taliban to adhere to certain conditions. The Afghan Army was poorly trained and poorly resourced, and relied on some element of American military support in order to protect Afghanistan from the total takeover of the Taliban. But as soon as America withdrew, the vacuum was filled. The clumsy Afghan Army gave up without a fight, and Afghanistan was immediately controlled by the Taliban and left to their mercies and the mercies of other terror organizations.

President Joe Biden was on vacation during the military disaster he created. He left his vacation to make a ten minute speech, in which he blamed everyone but himself, claimed that the situation in Kabul would be nothing like the fall of Saigon (it turned out to be virtually identical the very next day), and then left without answering any questions, returning to Camp David to eat ice cream and play more golf.

In the few days following this speech, Afghans clung to the bottom of an American plane as it took off from the Kabul airport and fell to their deaths on the tarmac, a helicopter landed on top of the US Embassy to evacuate American personnel, the Taliban gained immediate control of Kabul and began going door to door to interrogate, beat and execute women and Christians, and ISIS bombed Kabul, killing over one hundred Afghans and thirteen American soldiers and wounding many more.

The media and the Biden administration claimed that the withdrawal had to happen, creating a strawman out of their critics by saying that those who disagree with the disaster only disagree because they want war to continue. No one did. The Biden administration acted foolishly and abused its power, giving the Taliban and other terror organizations an entire country, a base of operations, and billions of dollars' worth of military technology. They also handed the Taliban a list of Americans and Afghan allies in the area to "let out of the country," but likely sealed their death warrants by giving away their identities. Meanwhile the mainstream media continued to lie and twist the facts in order to protect the Biden administration from any criticism, hoping that we'd immediately forget one of the most disastrous and irresponsible foreign policy blunders in recent US history, and focus once again on the real threat—political nonconformists!

Sam Wittke

The Men, the Myths, the Legends

When I studied English at the University of Utah, I took an interest in theory. I quickly learned the allure of the ideas of certain philosophers and I was impressed by the level of their intelligence. As I learned the ideas with a desire to grow in knowledge, a side effect happened that I was unaware of. I was becoming alienated and prideful. I felt as though humanity had conned me in some way, and that I had a superior knowledge because of my insights. I also really respected my theory professor who masterfully worked through the ideas of progressive philosophers and tied their ideas in with popular culture. We became friends and would often chat for hours after class.

Among the many names we studied in his classroom were Gramsci, Marx and Althusser. I remember reading the biography of the Marxist scholar Louis Althusser and learning that he murdered his wife in his old age and that he couldn't stand trial because he was insane. As I read this, a fleeting thought went through my mind: why are we reading the philosophies of a murderer and a madman? I quickly shoved that thought aside and continued with my studies. I thought the writing to be so intellectual and impressive that the personal character of the writer didn't matter that much to me at the time. Now I still look back on that fleeting question, wishing I'd asked it in class. And now, I'm more convinced than ever that it is crucial to weigh people's ideas with who they are, especially if you are confused about their ideas, whether they are good or bad.

Philosophers like Marx, Nietzsche, and Foucault among others all struggled in their personal lives. They had bouts with insanity and prideful delusions of being gods or supermen. Karl Marx was quite simply a spoiled man-child who thought

264

that the world owed him everything. He was mad at the past, present and future—and held contempt for every inkling of authority from his parents to the Almighty. He had as much of a hard time holding a job as he did bathing. His slothfulness left him with little, barely able to feed his children. He frequently demanded his parents give him more money. This attitude caused him to resent everything in the world and to promote a philosophy of total destruction and hatred, and his lack of personal hygiene left him covered in painful sores which likely added to his misery and to the level of disdain in his writing.

Seeing Marxism as a theory concocted by a spoiled man-child who didn't receive his allowance helps us not to be quite as intimidated by the large words that organize it. The level of intelligence of the author becomes considerably less important when weighed against his moral character and the historical mutilation that his concepts thrust upon the world.

Nietzsche was another man behind a lot of words that still hold a lot of sway over people. But the man behind the big impressive words is not quite as big and impressive as the words in front of the man. Nietzsche, like Althusser, went mad in his old age. Writing letters about imagined tormentors, he was diagnosed by doctors with such psychologic disorders as manic depressive illness and periodic psychosis. He spent so much time denying God and any basis for reason that he lost his grip on the preeminence of reality. It may be a good idea to avoid the abyss of nihilism, Nietzsche already checked it out for us and it wasn't that enticing.

Foucault was another deconstructionist of all things relatively normal. His distaste for civilization and distrust of any cultural institution, which obviously included God first and foremost, led him to acute depression and attempted suicide.

It goes without saying that many more interpreters of the

Sam Wittke

times than this have come and gone, leaving destructive ideas in their wake, as well as a legacy of self-pity and nihilism, while conveniently not having to face any repercussions when they are found out to be lying, or their philosophies have negative real world impacts. In fact, their lionization among the public is almost always certain. When you believe in nothing but your own interpretation and consider yourself to be your own god, nothing will come to you except death and people will no doubt be harmed by the negative power of your ideas.

It is hard to picture such a dark and void place as nothingness, especially when one is living in total darkness and pretending to be the true light for the world. In the modern paradigm, it is not a stretch to go from happy go lucky college student to a bed of suicide if the conclusion of the matter of life is a total absence of meaning.

I would venture to say that the big American problem starts here—with perspective. Simple questions like who are we, where do we come from, and where are we going, no longer need to be asked in order to get along in this life. Even if they were needed, they would be impossible to answer without invoking fairytales or abstractions. It is better to focus on feeling good for the little bit of time we have and curse anyone or anything that tells us otherwise.

The cultural and political outworking of these spiritual issues have been clearly illustrated in the history books. Culturally, nihilism makes for unhappy communities where no one can agree on much at all and where all things good are just random blips of the cosmic evolution of the human herd. There is no objective basis for morality, and this translates to laws that contradict human nature, the conscience, and our common senses. Everything that is and is to be done can be judged subjectively. This leaves our societies, and much worse, our hearts wanting. Downstream from culture is politics.

Cultures that leave behind God and reason ultimately build governments and laws that do the same and that promote self-worship and idolatry—in another word, destruction.

America finds herself in the midst of a personal crisis. She is debating suicide because she has been indoctrinated by the will of the world. She was raised by Christian parents, but still has to make her own decision either for or against God. But she is legally not able to will it on her own. She can only be led by the people that lead her. The culture and government of America more and more strikingly represent this stark choice of paths. She cannot stay where she is now, she must move forward either in remembrance or denial of the teachings from her youth.

The Marxist thought leaders ingeniously realized that the culture revolution needed to emerge internally. The counter revolutionists ought to adopt the same guerilla tactics.

The age of secularism, Marxism, nihilism and many other "isms" has a firm hold on our culture and society's understanding of reality. The people who have led the world in these ideas have shown that these ideas didn't even work in their personal lives. They continue to plague the world and sear its conscience. Together they make an alternative religion that masks itself as antireligious, and is quickly growing as the most popular belief system on the planet.

Jesus told His disciples that He is the truth, the way, and the life—secular nihilism tells its disciples that the truth is relative, there is no way to find the way, and there is no life apart from the herd. It is no wonder that our worldviews in America are at such odds with one another. Every disagreement with the modern paradigm is now deemed a "micro-aggression," a nuclear assault on the mind. When the truth confronts the lie, the lie is in danger of perishing. This begs the question: if the person's worldview comes from nothing, and ultimately is trying to return to nothing, as the big bang, evolution and the reproduction of the mode of production presupposes, what territory exactly is the person trying to protect from this neurological nuke?

The sum of this chapter on the interpretation class is this: ideas often have irreversible consequences for better or worse. The consequences of bad ideas often don't stop those ideas or ideas like them from being retold in the future. It is often the aim of the intelligentsia to absolve themselves of all personal responsibility. Their philosophies grant them perpetual protection and zero accountability. The chain reaction of ideas happened throughout history. It made history happen. Today is the period at the end of that sentence.

Today is the last day in history as far as you and I are concerned. The present is the endgame. We have seen a constant book of words and ideas written by the hand of mankind, and we have seen an alternative book written by the hand that made mankind. Every man, woman and child will follow one book or the other. One book ends with the words "the end." The other ends with the words "Yes, I am coming soon" (Revelation 22:20), where the end is actually a new beginning. The first end claims to know both the beginning and the end, and those two things happen to be nothing, thus we know nothing. The second knows that we know nothing about the beginning or the end besides what was told to us by the Father who brought them about, granting us everything. The first ends in prideful destruction of the soul and mind. The second ends in humble ascension to the Father, the gift of the Spirit of life and peace. The first cannot wait for answers, the second can and must wait—there is no other option: "There is a way that seems right to a man, but in the end it leads to death" (Proverbs 14:12).

Watching the ancestry of ideas and people ought to make

us weary of the patterns of this world. Watching these things ought to in fact take our eyes off of this world as we've found there are no real answers there. If the answer that we are searching for transcends reality, He can only be the maker of that reality. We can exit reality by dying or realize reality by joining the Father through Christ. The ones who thought they could become gods over reality were soon turned into victims of mindlessness, like Nebuchadnezzar. The one who submitted only to the reality of the Father lives forever, even though Christ was temporarily slain by this world's reality.

Magicians and Soothsayers

It is common in the modern church to align with what's popular and less demanding. The culture grants temporary asylum to churchgoers who agree to ignore or implement its agenda. Many in the church are also unaware of this because of spiritual numbness. This numbness is a result of implementing not only ideologies, but alien teachings and practices of other religions such as pantheism and the occult into church worship. Many Christians today are having their love for Jesus outweighed by a love for new-age spirituality, which includes transcendental meditation, pantheism, yoga, magic, ufology, and countless other branches of the new age movement.

Transcendental meditation has long been trying to implement itself into the body of believers, beginning centuries ago with certain gnostic practices. This form of meditation invites the practitioner to relax and allow any thoughts, good or bad, angelic or demonic, to enter into them—inviting the practitioner to "channel" different "energies" (spirits or demonic entities). In such an encounter, the practitioner often becomes convinced that they have had an encounter with the

Holy Spirit. In reality they have made themselves a doorway for satanic thoughts and messages to come into themselves, into the world, and into the church.

Pantheism is the belief that God is synonymous with the universe, rather than existing outside the universe as the creator of the universe. When pantheism is consistent, it ends up resulting in the god-like-ness of everything and everyone, which becomes redundant. For example, if all human beings are by nature god, and everything else in nature is god—a rock, a piece of wood, a chair, a telephone—who's to say that a human being has any more or less value than a snail or a pinecone. This warped view of god also makes God nothing more than an impersonal force or energy, and a vague abstraction. Therefore, when a person has an encounter with "god" or "the universe" or "Christ consciousness" through meditation or yoga, they are probably actually experiencing something spiritual, that may *feel* extremely peaceful and relaxed, but in reality is only a counterfeit spirit, a demon manifesting as an entity of light, or their own imagination. As Christians become more immersed in the new age, they become less aware of God's Holy nature, His immutable characteristics, and His separation from the things of this world, and ultimately are more prone to spiritual confusion, open to whatever is able to make them feel good in the moment. In essence, "worshipping God" through various new age, pantheistic or gnostic techniques results rather in a worship that is more similar to the ancient worship of the Canaanite, Egyptian, and Babylonian demons that the chosen people were so often deceived by.

Yoga, like meditation, is also popular among evangelical Christians. Many Christians believe that it is only a series of stretches and exercises, but experienced yogis have concluded that it is impossible to separate this practice from its spiritual foundation—Hinduism. Yoga includes, among other things, the worship of the sun, oversexualized poses, the awakening of a serpent spirit (kundalini) and summoning it to control one's mind (opening the third eye), spiritual relativity (the dilution of religions all to the same level of righteousness or truthfulness), the worship of counterfeit gods (Brahman, Krishna, Kundalini, and a multiplicity of others), and an elevation of personal truth over objective truth, which results in a certain level of nonchalance regarding scripture and God's immutable Word. Yoga is mass-advertised to Christians and is thought to be spiritually neutral, in reality it has a religious agenda to desensitize the Christian.

Magic and the occult are an undeniable foundation of the new age, and many Christians are impressed by things that would be considered magic or occult if examined in depth. Our culture has whitewashed witchcraft, and succeeded in training children from childhood upward to admire witches and warlocks, desiring the power to cast spells. Films like Harry Potter, Dr. Strange, and many Disney movies successfully make witchcraft and wizardry look like just another innocent, healthy, and fun practice at an early age, when the reality has always been that it comes from sorcery, a practice which scripture condemns multiple times and is demonic in nature. Sorcery offers supernatural power to the practitioner without the need to obey or consult God. Because of its pervasiveness in our culture, sorcery and witchcraft is growing at an incredible rate. Anton Lavey, the founder of the church of Satan, used witchcraft and atheism to build the religion of Satanism. Today devil worship is highly organized against the things of God, using the power of the enemy to strengthen demonic principalities and powers over people, neighborhoods, and societies. In some ways it is more organized and aware of its mission than our church is. Lavey also openly criticized the new age movement for building itself up from the principles of

Satanism without acknowledging Satanism as its foundation—in other words, the new age is plagiarized Satanism. But since Satan is a plagiarist in the first place, I'm not sure he would disapprove if the method works out for his benefit in the end.

Ufology is the interest, obsession, or even worship of alien beings. Countless cultures throughout generations have seen things in the sky, and wondered what they were. Ufology has interested many Christians, but when considering what extra-terrestrial life would mean for the Christian worldview is often too much for Christians to bear. Ufology leads people to believe, based on the theory of evolution which downplays the incredible complexity of life and biological information systems, that life is nothing special, and is likely scattered exponentially throughout the galaxy and universe. Therefore, there are likely many different technologically advanced lifeforms who have mastered interstellar travel and made it here to earth. This interstellar commuting runs into physical problems of its own. Interestingly, these aliens have visited people in something akin to nightmares and sleep paralysis. They often bring a message of evolution and are repeatedly driven out in the name of Jesus. This is classic demonic behavior, and the understanding that demons are able to masquerade in different forms helps us to understand what these "space aliens" may actually be, to the degree that they are a real phenomenon. Even secular ufology advocates and thinkers have admitted that these are much more likely *interdimensional* beings than interstellar beings, based on their abilities to defy the laws of physics. This has massive theological implications, and one could see how it would confuse a Christian and throw them off track from the truth.

It should be noted that I would not have included the above paragraph, or this entire section, if these ideas weren't so pervasive and at the forefront of our thoughts in culture.

In 2020-21 the UFO phenomenon has broken in the national news multiple times, and the government has repeatedly suggested that they are sitting on copious amounts of evidence and data, and know exactly what this phenomenon is.

Soothsaying has pervaded the church largely as a result of the implementation of new age beliefs and practices, which remind us of Gnosticism in the early church. Many claim to have a secret knowledge about the things of God, a personal revelation of His will or nature that contradicts scripture, and the ability to hear directly from God on a whim. The word of faith movement is a result of these various heresies, wherein sound doctrine becomes diluted to suit what people's itching ears want to hear at any given time. Many in the church offer "a word from God" to their brothers and sisters, which is really just a word from their own imagination. This word is more often an affirmation, or an encouragement that seems more similar to the law of attraction than anything based in biblical reality. I'm not saying that no one should affirm or encourage, but suggesting that there may be danger in going around proclaiming that one is "speaking messages from the Lord." Especially if these "prophets" are living in or affirming lifestyles and practices that clearly run contrary to God's commands, and seem to cover any and all spiritual ground besides the elementary teachings of the gospel. False prophecy was taken so seriously in the Old Testament that it merited the death penalty. This is not to say that God is only moving in systematic and stale ways, but when churchgoers immerse themselves in alien teachings and practices, and then bring those teachings and practices into the church while claiming the status of prophets and soothsayers, Christians ought to be on their guard.

New age spirituality has largely affected the church and disguised itself as an angel of light. It only offers false promises.

Rather than meditating on the Word, many Christians have begun meditating on meaningless mantras or nothing at all, opening themselves up to outside entities. These encounters can lead to a vague pantheistic view of God as an impersonal force, or a warm fuzzy feeling that people are convinced is the Holy Spirit. Practices such as yoga are advertised as being spiritually neutral but in reality have an agenda that runs contrary to Christ's exclusivity. Some Christians even indulge in magic and the occult, thinking that they are protected as Christians from Satan's power and schemes. Although this is true to a degree, imagine how God feels when we trade our relationship with Him for a temporary conversation with an Ouija board. The advent of ufology corroborates ungodly philosophies such as relativism, nihilism, social Darwinism, and feelings of insignificance, and to the degree that there is a real phenomenon behind it, it is likely interdimensional rather than interstellar—in other words, angelic or demonic. Many in the new age have worked tirelessly to integrate their empty religion into Christianity in the name of having a secret knowledge, and have duped the church to a large degree. It is up to the church to reject old false teachings in new packages and to put its focus back on Christ.

Saving the World One Bad Idea at a Time

The world tells us that environmentalism is more compatible with the secular worldview. In the modern climate, the secular approach seems to appreciate environmentalism more than Christians do. Christians are more known for plundering the earth in name of God, for subjugating the earth according to His commands.

By now we may realize that such a stereotype is simply

playing into the overarching caricature that is consistently drawn of Christians in a post-secular culture, creating yet another false dichotomy, where the irreligious world takes care of the environment and Christians don't care. We simply want to get rich in the name of Christian capitalism. Marxist criticism and theory are what largely paved the way for advanced eco-critical theory, just like the other genres of criticism that emerged throughout the decades (feminism, gender, queer, race, economic, eco). All intensified in different waves. Each successive wave became more radicalized. This section will examine where the height of the eco-criticism intellectual movement has brought us presently, some of the problems earth faces, and some of the solutions proposed.

Eco theory started, like the others, with common sense notions concerning humanity's increasingly negative impact on the world around us. Writers like Edward Abbey were part of the first wave, with provocative ideas and precepts most people can get on board with. But the ever-evolving theory, like others, soon became too confusing, too postmodern, and too radical.

Edward Abbey's writing reflects the natural beauty of places such as Arches National Park in Utah and the red sandstone desert of the southwest—his focus in *Desert Solitaire*. Another work of his, *The Monkey Wrench Gang* retold instances of environmental sabotage of construction sites and oil rigs which he and his friends saw as a source for environmental destruction. Abbey was a very good writer and a talented poet, an eco-critical thinker with firm convictions concerning the environment. And even if we may disagree with some things he wrote and did now, some of his fears have been realized in the generations that followed him.

I grew up visiting Arches National Park every year with my parents. It holds a deep place in my heart. In ways I feel a connection with Abbey's work, even though we're generations removed. Sometimes when I visit, I think to myself, "Abbey would be rolling in his grave right now."

As a ranger in Arches, Abbey cared about the natural landscape being preserved, and not polluted by frequent travelers and tourists. One story of his relates an encounter with workers coming in to survey a new road into the park. His job was to stay in the remote wilderness of Arches during the 1950s. At that time there was not a lot of traffic in and out of arches, but even what there was Abbey believed was too much. Abbey thought the natural environment of Arches was not meant to be exploited for human pleasure, and the exploitation would lead to the desecration of the desert landscape and threaten the creatures and ecosystems therein. So after the workers surveyed the road, he ended up pulling an all-nighter to undo all the work they did, pulling out all the survey sticks and hiding them in order to sabotage the government crusade to plunder Arches and turn it into an amusement park.

Today, if we are being honest, we can see that his deep seated concerns (at the very least regarding Arches) were warranted—Arches is packed with people, and has become as much, if not more of a tourist attraction than a wilderness preservation site. For reasons like these, we should be aware of where eco-theory is grounded in the truth and where it deviates from the truth. We shouldn't dismiss the real concerns behind the theory.

Throughout the different waves of eco-criticism, the theory became increasingly radicalized and eager to place blame on Christianity. Ecocriticism is alluring, and like the other branch-theories, it's full of dazzling ideas that flaunt the intellect of the various writers. Seeing the world through an eco-critical lens, however, is like seeing it through the various other lenses of branch-theories which often contain big words, small ideas, and wrong conclusions. I recall one eco-critical essay about Christianity being the main problem of why we are in the catastrophic predicament that we are in. There's undeniably a little bit of truth in the accusation. But the Biblical lens explains just as well why we are where we are, and an equal amount of blame can be pinned on those outside religion. When man sinned and fell, creation simply was corrupted. Romans chapter eight tells that the creation was subjected to frustration, likely from the beginning. The Bible is full of world decay—famines, sicknesses, illnesses, droughts, floods, catastrophism, etc. This is either resulting from human sinfulness or human carelessness and wastefulness, which themselves are likely linked to human sinfulness.

Today where I live in Utah there is less water than there used to be. There are more people than there used to be too. The Great Salt Lake is diminishing because it's not filling up with water from the mountains like it used to, largely because the Salt Lake Valley over the last few years has been transformed from a desert landscape with little to no trees to a city with high amounts of vegetation as a result of skyrocketing population and urbanization. We have been in a substantial drought for well over a decade, largely because of millions of people, corporations, parks, and golf courses watering multiple acre lawns with an already sparse water supply. To say that humans have no effect on their environment (even right outside my bedroom window here in Utah) and the resources and animals therein, would be incredibly naïve and unfair.

In Utah much of the water people get comes from the Wasatch Mountains. Ever since Salt Lake City was established in the mid to late 19th century this has been the case. There are foreseen problems of the amount of water in our mountains not meeting the increasing requirements of the people who use it. It is likely that people will do well to rethink how to use, reuse, and preserve water in the midst of a rapidly increasing population rate.

It is apparent that even on local levels, environmental alarmism should not be disregarded, but just like every other issue, it ought to be weighed with careful consideration and discernment. It should be talked about and taken seriously through the Christian perspective, so that we better know how to be stewards of the earth. But how are we to address essays and attitudes that place an unfair amount of blame on Christianity for not caring about the environment? What is the Christian response to such an accusation? The best response is found in the notion of stewardship, especially when we acknowledge that the accusation comes from the postmodern ridicule of Christianity, as with the various other forms of theory and criticism. We know that God is real, and therefore ought to have good answers for how we address these issues, especially as we see landscapes changing and threats intensifying, largely due to luxurious human living.

Humans change the landscape around them, and have since civilization first began. To deny such a fact outright is foolish, and to think it to be a modern aberration is equally foolish. Admitting something is happening is important. The recognition that we do effect the world around us can be a bridge builder between Christian and secular thought, right and left. But we should keep the issues in perspective with the sanctity of human life and value. Things have changed in the past and will change in the future, and when allegiance to an intensifying ideology that resents humanity is integrated in the way people see the eco-injustices affecting past, present and future, finding common ground and solutions to the various problems we face becomes more problematic.

Eco-critics recognize the constant threat that humanity has posed to the world around it since very early on. They don't see just us in the here and now as being the sole problem, even if they do see modernity as being the highest manifestation of the problem. They saw that the first problems emerged at the beginning of civilization, moving through the agricultural, pastoral, and industrial epochs, among others. Mankind changed the landscape for exploitative means right when culture first manipulated nature. Some argue that wherever humanity moved, there it devastated ecosystems, wiped out entire populations of species, and transformed all the landscapes it set foot on, dating back tens of thousands of years. Therefore eco-critics see nature and culture as always distinctly being at odds with one another, while at the same time being doomed to forever be united with one another.

Culture's ravaging of nature is seen as an evil. For this reason it is tricky to make any ground on the issue when language itself, as a part of culture, can never adequately define the distinction between culture and nature. Language must always honor nature and condemn culture, to the best of its ability. Instead of adjusting either one or the other to create a solution, it condemns both with political correctness. Nature and wilderness become words that are seen as not quite proper to describe the beauty of natural reality. Again, there is truth in this sentiment. God's creation cannot be fully comprehended by us. Too much harm has been done, and so there's a slippage in humanity's ability to speak of what it sees but does not know. There is also an element of this sentiment which has been hijacked by politically correct and partisan thought police.

Political correctness makes speaking about ecology and environment an activity for which one is often flagged for either saying something wrong, minimizing the issue, or not taking problems or solutions seriously enough. It also politicizes and corrupts the beautiful conception that our words can never perfectly describe the awe of creation. Herein lie the beginning of the problems with the eco-critical movement's simultaneous radicalism, stagnation, and false solutions—in other words, where it deviates from the truth.

Such a philosophy, where no common ground can be covered, logically leads to a collective and simultaneous depression, pride, despair, animosity, and a looming deep resentment of humanity. Seeing humanity as the biggest threat to the world (as it very well might be), seeing people and their business as futile (as they very well might be), constantly raising one's level of awareness of the environment being affected by us, judging others for consuming too much, and seeing oneself as an altruistic defender of the world are the conclusions that the highest levels of eco theory lead to—even to the extreme of thinking of collective suicide as a species as the only realistic way out. This is a red flag for Christians, where death is the conclusion. A deep unifying "problem" has emerged for which an impossible and presumably immoral "solution" needs to be found. Such sentiment is growing more popular among governments and the public.

The thought that humanity needs to decrease via population control leaves many who remember what population control has meant historically without warm and fuzzy feelings. But such an unrealistic and dangerous solution is where the highest elite eco-critical theory has led. Apparently to appease the modern truth tellers, we need to die, or at the very least cut off our own legs and arms so that we can't tread on the grass or dig any more holes in mother earth.

The *Planet Earth* series hints at such anti-human thinking, but shows the cogs turning not only within some vague, abstract theoretical level, but at the sociopolitical level. World leaders and eco-intellectuals are heading a push toward eco-globalization with movements like the Green New Deal. A notion of a common enemy for which humanity can unite against has been presented. The common enemy seems to be humanity itself. More ideologues, celebrities, common folk and world leaders are hopping on board with what seems to be a series of counterintuitive measures to rebuild the infrastructure of the entire world. This begs the question, if one is trying to preserve resources, how is plundering the world to build it once over going to be an effective measure? The focus, as has even been admitted by some of the fiercest advocates of the Green New Deal, is not as much on restructuring human society in a more environmental way as it's on restructuring the world economy into a socialist utopia.

Meanwhile, people in power pretend to be passionate about the various problems, but see them more as an opportunity to insulate and increase their voting base, to capitalize, and to gain more power over people through another global unifying movement, even as they often go about daily life in a much less ecological way than the masses they preach to.

If you, the layman, criticize the popular interpretation of the "problem" or the "solution" proposed in the least, you are considered marked. Even if one doesn't oppose protecting wilderness, but voices concern about the push toward globalization and eugenics, one is considered to be an eco-heretic. World leaders forcing the masses to conform for the common good has never ended well. Population control can only be implemented through various restrictions to people's rights—sterilization, abortion, and eugenics come to mind. But the thought leaders of our time are already starting slow with this type of language. It's naïve to think such evils in the name of the "common good" are only behind us, or that we have grown and surpassed our ability as human beings to make grave mistakes when fueled by a godless ideology. Population control sounds great to the crowds, on the surface, as a one-size-fits-all measure, but there is only one way to do it effectively, and that is to force it onto societies, to infringe on people's rights, and ultimately to kill people.

There are an abundance of ideas for the greater good. What they often lead to is danger. Controlling populations through "reproductive health" measures should set off more red flags for Christians. What does this connote if not birth control and abortion? Moreover, how is it possible to push abortion farther than it's already been pushed in America? If that is not enough, then what? What about people who are a drain on society? Those who "waste" massive resources in their disabilities and old age? Those who are "useless eaters?" My mother is highly disabled and can't work. When it comes down to the wire, is she considered less valuable? What is to stop the intellectuals, the people in power, and the masses they influence to start thinking of entire societies through a problem-solution dichotomy, in which a state of ecological emergency has presented us with the need to look at people, nations and societies as a hospital would look at patients in a triage situation?

Progressive ideas of the last century are reemerging in cleverer, newer packages in the new age, assorting people once again by an achievement based value. This value depends on an allegiance to "the cause." The progressives of the not too distant past found eugenics, forced sterilization, and euthanasia to be viable measures to overcome the various "problems" for which a "solution" was needed.

Population control is the collective mode of self-preservation. Backing it is not altruistic, but helps many see themselves as salvific figures who are "on the side of science." Unfortunately, many in the masses who began with admirable intentions concerning ecological thinking have been swept up into the more sinister aspects of the ideology without knowing it. Finding the solution in population control and divvying people up based on arbitrary notions of value fits the definition of the evil that preceded our generation, which makes sense as this solution still stems from similar ethical frameworks such as social Darwinism, atheism, racial determinism, Marxism, and even pantheism. Every person has value, despite some being unable to do the things capable people can.

Population control and reproductive control have immense problems. The motifs that introduced the palatability of eugenics and euthanasia to the masses in the 20th century seem to be reemerging in the present age. Such perversity requires a certain level of moral nonchalance, as well as relative values and truth claims. In our increasingly pluralistic society, it's becoming less tolerable to tell someone flat out that they're wrong, let alone point to similarities between today's ideas and yesterday's, which led to genocide. This intolerance increases exponentially when telling someone their wrong about radical ecological solutions automatically means one stands in opposition to science and the world. "The science" is synonymous with the leftist worldview. The more radical ecological ideas have evolved throughout the last few decades to bring us to where are now, reconsidering policies that have already ended in failure and madness.

It's clear, intellectuals today are simply echoing intellectuals yesterday. One may say the echo has become even louder, calling for an even more radicalized form of population control—mass suicide! This is not an unwarranted assumption. For suicide was the height of the advanced eco-critical philosophy, which saw humanity as the metastasizing cancer of the world. Even President Biden's nominee to head the Bureau of Land Management stated, "We must breed fewer consuming humans," and "if there were fewer of us, we would have less impact." Admittedly, she is not suggesting forced measures yet, but the rhetoric is certainly alarming.

Christians need to recognize that there are problems, but bring these problems back under God, the creator of the world. We need to look at the Bible for guidance. God often brought punishment to nations *by using* environmental catastrophe. Do we really think augmenting abortion and other forms of evil is going to please Him? Looking at sin and human corruption as a part of our environmental situation is not unrealistic. Beforehand, in Eden, there was a clear harmony. Everything was distorted after the fall. The harmony between culture and nature was perverted by us. The secular lens recognizes this in part, that from the beginning mankind learned how to use tools and manipulate his environment. From the beginning we were doomed to descend into greed, envy, violence, and selfish ambition. Isn't global pathos true at the most basic, instinctual level? We're mortal. So is the world. Recognizing the world's mortality, and Christians' existence as its salt seems wise. Falling for the population control ploy and the "build the world once over in order to save it" gambit, especially as Christians, does not seem wise. Pride, greed, and other sins are largely responsible for the problems we see before us, not human existence itself. These are still symptoms of the corruptible humans who propose to have the only "solutions." We should be suspicious of their motivations and even more suspicious of their end goals.

There is a huge stake of interest for many who promote the most radical aspects of eco-theory. There is an economic interest, a virtuosity, and an opportunity to champion the latest ideas. As Christians we need to preserve the earth and to appreciate God's creation. It would do us well to also remember that there are some things the land cannot bear up underneath, besides plastic straws.

⮬

What is the Christian perspective on the matter? It emerges from the simple fact that we live in God's creation. The only way to live a life of reconciliation with creation is to submit ourselves to the creator. Otherwise we're only blindly groping along the walls of creation and finding the solution in senseless things like population control or eugenics. From a Christian perspective we need to own up to the mistakes made and the existing problems. But if the Christian worldview is true, the creator is going to instill in us an innate love and appreciation for His creation, as well as a bitter hatred for the evil that plagues it.

Another problem with the total secular environmental lens emerges from social Darwinism. Operating from such a worldview, 20th century human beings found their highest propensity to kill, steal and destroy. This all came from the misunderstanding and false sense of value that seeing ourselves as nothing more than bacteria growing on a rock in space results in. From the same worldview, environmental catastrophism leads us to a sense of urgency (I dare not say a false sense of urgency) which stems from a faulty motivation and a relativistic reality. This brings us to the wrong conclusion. It all comes down to a simple question of human value. Under social Darwinism, there is no objective way to ascribe more or less value to a chicken or a human being. Many advanced-wave eco-thinkers understood this. In *The Ecological Thought,* Timothy Morton tells of the "strange strangers"—creepy crawlies such as spiders—having equal value to human beings. Again, there is no way to argue against this objectively under social Darwinism and pantheism, even though we know that's not true, no matter how deep one is in atheism. If presented with the choice to kill a spider or a human, any atheist will choose the spider.

Christians do have an objective way to make sense of

different level of values for different creatures. Humans are more valuable than kittens. Kittens are more valuable than ants. We know this innately, but intellectuals have successfully philosophized us into a moral and intellectual oblivion that any child recognizes is absurd. When there are no higher or lower truths, but only a substrata of relativity, trimming up the hedges of humanity doesn't seem so icky. The relativity of postmodernism is one of the fueling motivators for the eco movement. This is cause for concern among Christians, not because we want to destroy the earth, but because of a radicalized philosophy and a push toward globalization fueled by that philosophy, under the guise of being environmentally conscientious.

There is also a problem with the way in which people who see problems everywhere but within themselves also see themselves as the only solutions to those exterior problems. Understanding the presuppositions, motivations and self-perceived-virtuosity that propel much of the eco movement is paramount. Right now, its conceptual peak merits the destruction of either all or most of humanity along with its fundamental institutions in order to preserve our planet's longevity. Of course, most thought leaders who've concluded this won't say "humanity must die" quite so bluntly, but a massive amount of celebrities, philosophers, activists, and politicians have inadvertently backed population control, and taken their privileged position all the way to the bank. Most of these people average a much higher net worth than you and me. They've attained this net worth, and multiple homes, largely by criticizing your very existence. The outcry against wasteful humans and their capitalistic tendencies comes from some of the highest beneficiaries of that same system. Here are some examples of what I mean:

- President Joe Biden and Vice President Kamala Harris want to restrict your right to fill up your gas tank at an affordable rate and use plastic straws, even while they run heat and electricity to their multiple million dollar homes.

- Activist Greta Thunberg, an eighteen year old, wants to end "fossil capitalism." I wonder, would she mind distributing some of the million dollar bankroll she's made off of her activism in order to fund electric cars for people who are in humbler economic circumstances than her once her dream has come true and "fossil capitalism" has ended?

- When multi-millionaire socialist politicians such as Bernie Sanders and Alexandria Ocasio Cortez suggest we should tax the rich, distribute income, become a socialist country, and cease using fossil fuels, do they intend to personally deliver your dinner after you're no longer allowed to cook with a gas stove or drive to the grocery store? We can be sure that they'll continue to have full bellies and bank accounts long after their plans have negatively impacted your most basic livelihood.

- Basketball star LeBron James is very adamant that you drive less, ride more bikes, and use less water. Meanwhile, he owns four homes and *at least* fifteen cars. One of his homes is worth over 20 million dollars. Another is worth over 30 million dollars. His words have expressed very negative emotions towards the various evils of the free market, but his $500,000,000 net worth seems to speak much louder than his anti-capitalistic words.

- Top environmental activists and naturalists including Malaika Vaz, Jane Goodall, Greta Thunberg, James

Hansen, Paul Hawken, Lennox Yearwood Jr, Katharine Hayhoe, Rachel Carson, David Attenborough, Jamie Margolin, George Washington Carver, and Aldo Leopold have all become millionaires from their environmental campaigns (some have crossed the ten and even one hundred million dollar threshold). There are many more that benefit from the capitalist system they blame for our ecological predicament.

There is someone in my life who is very close to me, who has deep seated environmental convictions. Although I don't agree with all of her conclusions, although I know that some of her heroes may be listed above, and although she may not like what I've written in this section, I respect her values and ideas much more than any of the above people. The reason is straightforward, *she practices what she preaches.* She is not world famous for her views. She owns a modest home, she rides her bike as much as she can, she works hard to create awareness at a local level, she helps people in poorer circumstances, and she works at a farm that treats its animals very humanely. I'll take her more seriously than these heroes of the left, even if I take what she says with a grain of salt.

I've cared about the environment for a long time. I haven't been perfect, but I try my best to be conscientious and not to be wasteful. Nowadays that's not enough. You must care about the environment *and* be a member of the elite class in order to be truly environmental. In fact, you can own less and leave a much smaller ecological and economic footprint than so many world famous activists, philosophers, politicians, and celebrities, and still be considered an anti-scientific, anti-environmental megalomaniac if you don't subscribe to their underlying ideology on the matters of *how exactly to be stewards.*

Christians have an understanding that is realistic,

beginning with the obviousness of mortality. It is our job as humans to care for the world and to recognize God's sovereignty over the world. Things are getting bad and will get worse, and we recognize why this is happening. Eco-catastrophe doesn't contradict the biblical worldview. World decay is tragic, but God's plan is to bring restoration. Such an understanding ought to enrich the conversation with those who disagree, but some will not tolerate one iota of dissent from their reductionist problem-solution and oppressor-oppressed dichotomies.

Christ leads us into all truth. He likely wants us to see these issues through the lens of the Spirit, wherein we can help find real, less insane solutions. To exclude Christians and blame them for all the evil under the sun as far as environmentalism is concerned is a grave misunderstanding. 20th century regimes were atheistic. I seem to recall that they all but destroyed an entire continent, causing terrible damage on the planet. In fact, it was probably the worst thing that has ever happened in recorded history. But because Christianity gets muddled in with capitalism, the magicians, astrologers, diviners, wise men, and soothsayers of our age say that "Christian capitalism" is the entity to blame first and foremost for the forest fires that their own conceptual predecessors lit. Christians need to take a comprehensive look at how we are to address the multifaceted problems without dismissing our own issues, while bringing the problems as one problem *under God*, in hope—a hope in the narrow way of Christ, not the wide road of the social Darwinian worldview.

Jesus knew the hope of following his father. "The path of righteousness is like the morning sun, shining ever brighter till the full light of day" (Proverbs 4:18). Jesus said that walking in the day we will not stumble, but walking in the night we are prone to stumble, even when we think we are providing a great light for the world. If that utopian light is really just more darkness, how great is that darkness?

Chapter 7

Conclusion

Interpretations of the Unpopular

There has never been a more important time to know where we stand and what we believe. The American problems are secondary to the spiritual ones, the ones relating to the kingdom of Christ. The world boldly proclaims the pitfalls of the unpopular interpretation of things, but the unpopular interpretation happens to be the true one. It has stood the test of the times, and still stands stubbornly and glaringly in the face of evil. Suppressing the truth for fear of being laughed at, sounding ignorant, or diverging from popular opinion is destroying the church. In other words, Christians' cultural and political involvement in the issues that face this world and threaten it are not what is destroying the church, as so many claim. Their perceived neutrality is.

As Christians we must not let secularism reinterpret the Bible and the world for us. The Bible is still the key for interpreting the world as it was inspired by the One who created the world. The One who created the world still has His people in the world to this day. What ought He to make of our complacency, our blindness to the things that are happening all around us? The neutral person can be so focused on pleasing the world and camouflaging with it, that he becomes invisible and unthreatening to it. We must realize that every era in every nation has its big problems. These problems will seem small to anyone who ignores their reality and the nature of their devastation.

Neutrality invites conflict, it doesn't quell it. Many today stand neutral on many different issues; the validity of scripture, the nature of God, the divinity of Christ, the reality of sin, and the problems of the world that have trickled into the cultural and political sphere. Taking a firm stance on issues like socialism and abortion is not an ungodly thing to do, even if this manifests itself in an administrative statement like a vote, or a conversation among the elders of the church, or even (God forbid) a sermon.

Some preachers would say that this partisan involvement is ungodly, and is ruining the church. However, the vote is spiritual when the ballot is cast with the sanctity of human life, the reality of private property, or the increasing presence of authoritarianism in mind. In fact voting is one of the few weapons we have left to stand against the emergence of post-post-modernity and the further destruction of all God's boundaries. But progressive Christianity tells us it is a sin to stand firm in the midst of these issues, to not give up any ground, even as they are applauded by the entities that frequently label Christians as evil. If we listen to their advice, we become complacent in the advancement of the new-age religion, whose biggest enemy is Christianity wherever it arises, wherein we can become passive information consumers, standing at the ready to be swayed by the wind.

When did we begin to think we are no longer in great spiritual peril? When did we come to shake hands with the enemy of our hearts? Why did we give up so much ground already? This is war, and every day is a battle. This book is meant to be a call to arms for the soldiers of Christ and common sense. I do not suggest acting with the same military and interpretive tactics as our ideological enemies. As our enemies stand tall and stand out on the battlefield they will be easily identified. If we stay low and hide in the grass we will not be seen. Our enemies may have more firepower, but they do not have more fire. It is time for the truth to revolt against the lie and love to revolt against hate. Revolution must rise up against revolution with spiritual guerilla warfare. This revolution must be through the truth and love of Christ, and these are rarely complacent or agreeable.

The Christians who were martyred by tyrannical governments were not afraid to take a stand, although their legs would be tortured for standing. They were not afraid to speak out, though their tongues would be cut out for uttering words against the rulers of the time. Their interpretations caused them great anguish unlike the philosophers of this age, who call the world something other than what it is and are richly rewarded. The men and women of God were not afraid to stand on the front lines as ground was being taken from beneath their feet. Their bodies were given over to the flames, but their legacy lives on as fire in our hearts. Should the church of nowadays forget their suffering and imagine a utopian world of futility? Should we prophesy our own visions and wrest the Word to our own destruction, labeling the fertile soil of our nation as a myth?

When one can smell the scent of the beast, he knows the beast is nearby even though he cannot see it. Today the scent of tyranny fills our noses, but we pinch our noses and close our eyes, pressing forward in hopes to somehow stumble upon the "American dream." This is a bigger American problem than what we fear to be the biggest ones.

Tyranny cannot be permitted to repeat its mistakes, it

must find new and improved ways to manifest—it is like the serpent in its craftiness. The same lie is used, but it takes on a different shape to beguile each generation. This is the nature of temptation as it ranges from person to person. The temptation tells us yes and no where we say no and yes, until our yes becomes no and our no becomes yes. Temptation tomorrow may not feel like today's temptation, and today's temptation may not feel like yesterday's, unless yesterday worked well in achieving its goal. Today our temptation is to forsake our humanity for a vague notion of divinity, to trade Christ's divinity for man's interpretation of humanity. It is a dangerous game to give this darkness any more ground.

The new secular revolution is not a show of military power, but of thought. It knows that the best time to strike is when the enemy is weak and unsure of himself. This is why sound doctrine is under attack. Original sin is no longer original. Sin is only a myth to be increasingly debunked by evolutionary interpretations as nothing more than our innate animalism. Apparently the only thing greater than our beastliness is our inherent divinity. In the new-age we are all as gods. We bow to others in recognition of their divinity, and they ours. The modern man reaches toward the heavens, not for help, but as a challenge; not with open arms, but with a fist. There is no more desire to tend the garden, but to uproot it in hope to plant a better one. Mankind can only plant the seed and water it, it is God who makes it grow. Indeed, all we can do at that point is watch.

Secularism is making its way into the church, and the church is making its way into secularism. We often no longer look at the Word of God as authoritative, but the interpretations of man. We blend our paradigm with the world in hope to win the world over. The world has the same intent. We must hold fast to the Word given to us by God, especially when the waves of the world get higher and more threatening. A man cannot appease a storm, he can only ride it out. This wave of darkness will pass away even if it outlasts the world, and casting our convictions into the wave will neither strengthen our convictions nor stop the wave.

Let God Fill the American Gap

"The God of the gaps" is what the secular world sees when they look at the Christian God. Interestingly, every other religion demands the respect of the new age, and the countless false gods in the world today cannot be criticized in the slightest. But the God of the gaps can be criticized without restraint and without end. The God of the gaps, to critics, is a figment of our imagination that can be put in the place of any vacuous area of discomfort or uncertainty. The God of the gaps is not real to the world today, except where His ideas can be used fragmentarily for one's own benefit or personal philosophy. The slanderous name this world has given to the God of this universe is actually more accurate than they intended. He is the God of the gaps, but not the gaps of wishful thinking and fantasy.

There is a gap between reality and humanity's ability to understand it. God fills this gap. Two hundred years ago not much was known about the vastness of the heavens, or the intricacy of cellular life. Atheists and naturalists saw this as an opportunity to fill that gap of human knowledge with vast amounts of theory and speculation. As more about the universe was discovered throughout the centuries it became less and less likely that the world had happened by accident. Similarly, as more about the complexities of cellular life were discovered since the Darwinian revolution, the less his theories lived up to the biochemical challenges that faced it, among others. As human knowledge in these areas grow, the burden of proof is on those who believe in a purposeless existence to fill the gaps that they claim exist. Saying that God creates both the cell and the universe is not simply a nonsense explanation to fill the gaps of what we do not know about those things, but the logical conclusion that the growing base of knowledge that we have about those things leads us to.

God is the God of another gap—the gap of the human heart. The human heart, like clockwork, always strives to meet certain standards, and always falls below those standards at one point or another. There is a natural human law that is present in the conscience, and it is undeniable that objective standards of morality exist—otherwise no man's standard of morality would be higher or lower than another's, which is absurd. Though many may deny this fact, each person in his or her own heart makes judgments based on these objective standards and is able to identify good and evil. Of course, at times these scales become false as the conscience is seared to no longer be able to recognize the difference between good and evil. This law of human nature which transcends individual moral standards and laws of society indicates that there is a designer of human nature. The fact that we fall short of the law of human nature, illustrates that there is another gap that can either be filled by God or by something else.

The third gap we will talk about here is the gap of harmony between people. If there is one thing that can be known about societies, cultures, and nations, it's that they cannot get along. Our world has always been plagued by injustices like greed and war. The illusive idea of world peace still eludes us to this day. The main difference between the secular, new age view on human relations and the Christian view is the way in which we see the reason for this prolonged divide between people.

The former individual views this divide as a symptom of the society being the source of this problem, the latter individual sees this divide as a symptom of the issues that arise out of the individual himself. The former recognizes the fallibility of all others from a place of their own perceived superiority, and the latter recognizes first and foremost the shortcomings of his own heart as a source for great evil. In other words, we can either see the world as a place of great evil without recognizing it in ourselves, or recognize that the problem begins at the individual level and spreads outward. The latter view indicates the correct and common sense way to observe this gap and it indicates the existence and necessity of the only God who can fill it.

Let us look at the big American problems for a moment in light of these three gaps: the gap of human reason, the gap of individual morality, and the gap of relationships between people. After observing this, perhaps we can both diagnose the issue and prescribe something for it that might fill these three voids.

Human reason and ingenuity seem limitless in what they're able to achieve, and always have as we have seen with the tower of Babel. Today we live in an age of endless information. We can pull up virtually anything, good or bad, on our phones or IPads in a matter of seconds. The wonders of technology have advanced in incredible and terrifying ways in the past century—and the largest advancements are likely yet to come. We've also trained our youth in the ways of the world, teaching them to link these milestones of human achievement to the rise of the secular age. Teachers and professors train children to view the advancements of the world in general and America in particular through the lens of secularism. This indoctrination begins at an early age, encouraging kids to leave God behind and travel into new territories of achievement. In

America, the free market and free speech environment grows these technological advancements, and invites alternative worldviews to thrive and overthrow our psyche.

As individual morality became less objective and more subjective with the growth of alternative worldviews, the loudest voices of America proclaimed the good news of "your truth, my truth." At every milestone of technological achievement or achievement in knowledge, America gave words of affirmation to its own increasingly malleable bounds. More and more stones of myth were being overturned. Finally our nation was given the ability, through superior reasoning and morality, to be our own gods and to do only as we will. The integration of secularism, postmodernism, and pluralism into the American culture—as well as the eventual marginalization of those who dissented—went hand in hand with the disintegration of our moral fabric and the nullification of our spiritual identity. When each man's spiritual truth became equal to another's, the truth itself was diluted.

The rejection of objective morality and the elevation of self-law guaranteed the national decline in its relational identity. From America's founding each citizen has been entitled with the freedom to choose between two things, God and self. The first choice would have been the recognition of our own identity as a fallible culture, the second would have been the usurpation of real laws by our own fleeting decrees, resulting in an amorphous national identity which resulted primarily from usurping the reality God had made. When America chose self-law over the law which was intended during its foundation, it chose an increasing atmosphere of division, which granted various temporary pleasures. As long as we followed ourselves and rejected God, we would be doomed to tear each other apart from the inside out, whether or not we believe that to be true.

It would be difficult to reject these premises in light of the increasing division in our spiritual, cultural and political spheres. We are building the new temple so furiously that we are forgetting what we are building and why we are building it. We have mythologized the original foundation and its intended architecture. Meanwhile our language is becoming increasingly confused. These American problems are indeed too big for us to fix without outside help. Constitutionally, America still offers freedom of choice. Even if it no longer did, God would still offer it to us freely, regardless of whether or not the human laws were to punish us for the choices we make. The natural law of man states that when he trusts only in himself and worships himself, he falls into alienation, madness and wickedness. He forgets God and others to find himself, losing himself in the process. It has been the aim of this project to show that this law and the punishment which comes from rejecting our creator extend from people to the nations they command. (Matthew 16:25).

Afterword

To the Progressive Church

For the first three years of my Christian walk I was on the left. God was still with me in incredible ways. I sensed His presence every day. He did not need me to change my political views in order to come to Him. My political views shifted on a number of issues before they shifted entirely. I still do not consider myself "on the right." I use the word "conservative" to describe my political views, but I do not agree with everything conservatives and republicans say or do. I am pro second amendment, but I don't think I could ever shoot another human being as a Christian, even in self-defense. I am pro-life, obviously, but the pro-life position has its own monsters in the closet that it needs to deal with. For example, if a woman takes the morning after pill, should she be charged with first degree homicide or given a five hundred dollar fine? Though I've stated this question painfully bluntly, this is the most difficult challenge for consistent pro-lifers to address. It presents an array of questions about how we address abortion as a crime if and when it becomes a crime. Leaving this question out of my book to simply win the argument is not being entirely truthful.

Some people I greatly respect are on the left, including some Christians. I strongly disagree with their political views, and I do think that there are times when we all need correction. This correction may translate to why we should or should not support a certain ideology, politician, or political agenda. Though this book seems like an outright assault on the progressive ideology, it does not mean I hate anyone who carries with them these beliefs, even if I hate some of the beliefs. I know people involved with antifa who absolutely hate my guts for being an outspoken Christian conservative. Of course, this hurts, and sometimes in my flesh it angers me. But in my spirit, I cannot wish ill-will on them. This would contradict Christ. But I cannot address their beliefs in a wishy washy, complacent way, just like in the above paragraph I cannot address the biggest pro-life dilemma I see without just saying it. I still stand by every harsh word I said about the pro-choice position and the abortion industry.

My political opinion shifted when I learned more about abortion, when I watched riots erupt across the United States, when I started learning about the extent of media-manipulation, when I came to understand the level of power one side of the government grabbed following the pandemic, and when I witnessed people I love become influenced by cultural Marxism.

The church that I attend is actually not "on the right." I don't think it's on the left either. It could technically be classified as neutral. There are definitely people on both sides of the political aisle in my church. I love that. There are people I disagree with very strongly. I may know much more about the dangers of cultural Marxism than they do. They may know much more than me about other social injustices. But does this mean that we don't have the same spirit of God living in us? Whoever is born of God is born of God, period. But we *should be of one mind and one spirit.*

One thing I can almost always find common ground on with people is that the basic left-right dichotomy of American politics is too constraining and is one of the contributing factors for the ongoing and widening social divide. I've talked at length about why I think this is, and that I believe there is an inescapable quality in the political spectrum that corresponds to the spiritual spectrum, but maybe there is truth in the resurfacing notion that we need to find a new form of politics entirely—the old one has led us to nothing less than a cold civil war. There are aspects of the political spectrum that will never go away no matter when or where we live. Some were present in first century Judea. These are the aspects that parallel human nature.

All this being said, it has been my privilege and my duty to sound the warning bell on what I think the biggest American problems are. Maybe I sounded the bell too loudly and without enough grace. Perhaps I sounded it too softly and without enough zeal. But I've sounded it nonetheless, and I fear I must stand by the sound of the bell long after it rings. After all, this warning continues to ring in my heart, either gently in the background of my everyday life or forcefully at the forefront of my thoughts and actions.

"The Best Guess: Asking Life's Big Questions
in an Age of Unlimited Answers"

"Check out Sam Wittke's other book about theology and apologetics, *The Best Guess*. *The Best Guess* examines over 25 different subjects that people struggle with when considering Christianity in a fun, thoughtful and engaging way. Visit **samwittke.com** to learn more and to get *The Best Guess*." Please add image of cover of The Best Guess if possible.

Works Cited

1   Editors, H. (2009, November 16). *Francisco Pizarro traps Incan emperor Atahualpa*. Retrieved from History.com: https://www.history.com/this-day-in-history/pizarro-traps-incan-emperor-atahualpa

2   McKellar, K. (2021, July 8). *Why did Black Lives Matter Utah call people who fly the American flag racists?* Retrieved from Deseret.com: https://www.deseret.com/utah/2021/7/8/22568053/why-did-black-lives-matter-utah-call-people-who-fly-the-american-flag-racists-facebook-july-4

3   Lock, S. (2021, October 21). *theguardian.com*. Retrieved from Rightwing US pundit Candace Owens compares Australian government to the Taliban, calling it a 'tyrannical police state': https://www.theguardian.com/world/2021/oct/22/rightwing-us-pundit-candace-owens-compares-australian-government-to-the-taliban-calling-it-a-tyrannical-police-state-

4   Marx, K. (1837). Marx Engels Collected Works Vol 1. In K. Marx, *Book of verse* (pp. pg 683-685). International Publishers.

5   Marx, K. (1837). Marx Engels Collected Works Vol 1. International Publishers.

6   Denis Mack Smith, *Mussolini: A Biography*, 1983

7   O'Brien, C. (2021, July 8). *NY Times blasted for defending 'pornography literacy' for first graders: 'These people are sick'*. Retrieved from foxnews.com: https://www.foxnews.com/media/ny-times-blasted-for-defending-pornography-literacy-for-first-graders-these-people-are-sick

8   Musto, J. (2021, November 10). *Vermont first state to require access to condoms in all secondary schools: reports*. Retrieved from foxnews.com:

https://www.foxnews.com/health/vermont-first-state-require-access-condoms-secondary-schools

9   Barakat, M. (2021, September 24). *School System Pulls 2 Books With Graphic Sex From Libraries*. Retrieved from usnews. com: https://www.usnews.com/news/us/articles/2021-09-24/ school-system-pulls-2-books-with-graphic-sex-from-libraries

10   *Rohingya Christians Face a Double Threat: Myanmar Military & Rohingya Neighbors*. (2021, August 27). Retrieved from persecution.org: https://www.persecution.org/2021/08/30/ rohingya-christians-face-double-threat-myanmar-military-rohingya-neighbors/

11   *Majority of Christians in Myanmar Live in Conflict Zones after the Coup*. (2021, September 3). Retrieved from https://www. persecution.org/: https://www.persecution.org/2021/09/03/ christians-in-myanmar-live-in-conflict-zones/

12   *Two Families Beaten Unconscious for Converting to Christianity*. (2021, October 5). Retrieved from https://www.persecution.org/: https://www.persecution.org/2021/10/05/two-families-beaten-unconsciousness-converting-christianity/

13   *Leaders in India's Karnataka State Plan to Introduce Anti-Conversion Law*. (2021, September 25). Retrieved from persecution.org: https:// www.persecution.org/2021/09/25/leaders-indias-karnataka-state-plan-introduce-anti-conversion-law/

14   *Five Christians in India's Uttar Pradesh State Arrested On False Forced Conversion Charges*. (2021, September 26). Retrieved from persecution.org/: https://www.persecution.org/2021/09/26/ five-christians-indias-uttar-pradesh-state-arrested-false-forced-conversion-charges/

15   *Church Forced Underground by New Crackdown in Central India*. (2021, September 27). Retrieved from persecution.org: https:// www.persecution.org/2021/09/27/church-forced-underground-central-india/

16   *Radical Hindu Nationalists Burn Four Christian Homes in India*. (2021, September 28). Retrieved from persecution.org: https:// www.persecution.org/2021/09/28/radical-hindu-nationalists-burn-four-christian-homes-in-india/

17 *Six Christians in India's Karnataka State Falsely Accused of Crimes as Government Calls for Anti-Conversion Law.* (2021, September 30). Retrieved from persecution.org: https://www.persecution.org/2021/09/30/six-christians-indias-karnataka-state-falsely-accused-crimes-government-calls-anti-conversion-law/

18 *Christian Attacked with Acid in India Dies After 46 Days in Hospital.* (2021, 10 01). Retrieved from persecution.org: https://www.persecution.org/2021/10/01/christian-attacked-acid-india-dies-46-days-hospital/

19 *Christian Wedding Ceremony Ambushed in India.* (2021, 10 2). Retrieved from persecution.org: https://www.persecution.org/2021/10/02/christian-wedding-ceremony-ambushed-india/

20

21 *ICC Publishes a Report on Criminal Sharia Law in Nigeria.* (2021, September 18). Retrieved from persecution.org: https://www.persecution.org/2021/09/18/icc-publishes-report-criminal-sharia-law-nigeria/

22 *50 Killed During Incessant Attacks on Nigerian Christian Community.* (2021, 9 23). Retrieved from persecution.org: https://www.persecution.org/2021/09/23/50-killed-incessant-attacks-nigerian-christian-community/

23 *Man Given Gun to "Go and Kill Christians" in Nigeria.* (2021, September 25). Retrieved from persecution.org: https://www.persecution.org/2021/09/25/man-given-gun-go-kill-christians/

24 *At Least 30 Killed During Overnight Massacre in Nigeria.* (2021, September 28). Retrieved from persecution.org: https://www.persecution.org/2021/09/28/least-30-killed-overnight-massacre-nigeria/

25 *Gunmen Attack Church in Nigeria, Kill Worshipper.* (2021, September 30). Retrieved from persecution.org: https://www.persecution.org/2021/09/30/gunmen-attack-church-nigeria-kill-worshipper/

26 *Mob Kills Christian Leader in Nigeria, Burns Down Church and Christian School.* (2021, September 9). Retrieved from persecution.org: https://www.persecution.org/2021/09/29/mob-kills-christian-leader-nigeria-burns-church-christian-school/

27 *3,462 Christians Killed in Nigeria in 200 days, 3000 Abducted, 300 Churches Attacked*. (2021, July 21). Retrieved from persecution. org: https://www.persecution.org/2021/07/21/3462-christians-killed-nigeria-200-days-3000-abducted-300-churches-attacked/

28 *US Condemns Growing Persecution in China*. (2021, May 28). Retrieved from persecution.org: https://www.persecution. org/2021/05/28/us-condemns-growing-persecution-china/

29 *China Tightens Border Control with Myanmar to Prevent "Religious Infiltration"*. (2021, July 10). Retrieved from persecution.org: https://www.persecution.org/2021/07/10/china-tightens-border-control-myanmar-prevent-religious-infiltration/

30 *China's Latest Ban of Christian Content on Social Media*. (2021, July 13). Retrieved from persecution.org: https://www.persecution. org/2021/07/13/chinas-latest-ban-christian-content-social-media/

31 *China Threatens Christian Parents with Their Children's Education*. (2021, July 29). Retrieved from persecution.org: https://www. persecution.org/2021/07/29/china-threatens-christian-parents-childrens-education/

32 *New Pakistani Anti-Conversion Bill Again in Question*. (2021, September 13). Retrieved from persecution.org: https://www. persecution.org/2021/09/21/new-pakistani-anti-conversion-bill-question/

33 *Pakistan Refuses to Accept Refugees from Afghanistan*. (2021, September 21). Retrieved from persecution.org: https://www.persecution. org/2021/09/21/pakistan-refuses-accept-refugees-afghanistan/

34 *Pakistan Refuses to Accept Refugees from Afghanistan*. (2021, September 21). Retrieved from persecution.org: https://www.persecution. org/2021/09/21/pakistan-refuses-accept-refugees-afghanistan/

35 *Custody of a 14-Year-Old Christian in Pakistan Awarded to Her Abductor by High Court*. (2021, September 29). Retrieved from persecution.org: https://www.persecution.org/2021/09/29/custody-14-year-old-christian-pakistan-awarded-abductor-high-court/

36 *Updated Report: The Voiceless Victims of Pakistan's Blasphemy Laws*. (2021, September 24). Retrieved from persecution.org: https:// www.persecution.org/2021/10/06/voiceless-victims-pakistan-blasphemy-laws-september-2021/

37 *The Silent Screams of Pakistan's Most Vulnerable.* (2021, September 30). Retrieved from persecution.org: https://www.persecution.org/2021/09/30/silent-screams-pakistans-vulnerable/

38 Jasek, P. (2020). *Imprisoned with ISIS: Faith in the Face of Evil.* Washington, DC: Voice of the Martyrs.

39 Keith, Sir Arthur, *Evolution and Ethics* (New York, NY: G. P. Putnam's Sons, 1947), 230

Printed in the United States
by Baker & Taylor Publisher Services